Taking Indian Lands

Taking Indian Lands

The Cherokee (Jerome) Commission
1889–1893

William T. Hagan

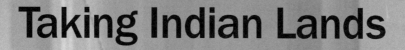

University of Oklahoma Press
Norman

Other books by William T. Hagan

The Sac and Fox Indians (Norman, 1958 and 1980)
American Indians (Chicago, 1961; rev. eds. 1979 and 1993)
Indian Police and Judges (New Haven, 1966; Lincoln, 1980)
United States-Comanche Relations (New Haven, 1976; Norman, 1990)
The Indian Rights Association (Tucson, 1985)
Quanah Parker, Comanche Chief (Norman, 1993)
Theodore Roosevelt and Six Friends of the Indian (Norman, 1997)

Publication of this book is made possible through the generosity of Edith Kinney Gaylord.

Library of Congress Cataloging-in-Publication Data

Hagan, William Thomas.
  Taking Indian lands : the Cherokee (Jerome) Commission, 1889–1893 / William T. Hagan.
    p. cm.
  Includes bibliographical references and index.
  ISBN 0-8061-3513-1 (alk. paper)
    1. Indian land transfers—Indian Territory.   2. United States. Cherokee Commission.   3. Indians of North America—Government relations.   I. Title.

E78.I5 H34 2003
976.6'04—dc 21   2002074038

The paper in this book meets the guidelines for permanence and durability of the Committee on Production Guidelines for Book Longevity of the Council on Library Resources, Inc. ∞

Contents

Illustrations

Preface

IN THE PERIOD 1889–93 THE CHEROKEE COMMISSION purchased fifteen million acres of land from Oklahoma tribes. Almost all of this land became available to settlers by 1900, making possible the appearance of the State of Oklahoma. To the Indians the loss of the land was devastating. Their practice of holding large areas in common had been the foundation of a distinctive and satisfying way of life. Not only would they lose the land that had shaped them, they would also be scattered among an unfriendly white population that would, very quickly, badly outnumber them.

This tragedy for the Indians of Oklahoma, which was the concluding phase of their long struggle to withstand the remorseless advance of the white population, was not peculiar to Oklahoma tribes. Elsewhere in the American West a dozen or more commissions were acquiring land from Indians on terms similar to those imposed on the Oklahoma tribes. What made the Cherokee Commission unique were the number of tribes with which it dealt and the duration of the commission. While other commissions focused on one or a few tribes and completed their assignments in a matter of weeks or at most a few months, the Cherokee Commission dealt with nearly twenty tribes and had a life of fifty-two months.

The journals of the commission's deliberations total almost two thousand pages. They provide an unparalleled record of a single commission's efforts to coerce the tribes into allotment in severalty and the sale of their remaining acreage, the so-called "surplus land." The Cherokees were a special case, as they had been exempted from allotment by the 1887 Dawes Severalty Act. They did, however, hold the Cherokee Outlet, a block of more than six million acres between the 96th and 100th meridians that the commission was directed to purchase.

The commission's journals also provide abundant testimony to the hopes and fears, the fundamental beliefs of the Indians involved, as well as to their strategies for opposing the designs of the United States. Their attachment to the land and their recognition that their way of life would be drastically altered are poignantly expressed by Indian spokesmen, but in vain—the picture of a powerful nation imposing its will on its wards is not a pretty one.

As was inevitable given the scope of this book, I am indebted to a host of people. Foremost among them is Berlin B. Chapman, an indefatigable researcher who uncovered the basic documents and wrote a series of articles on the subject. I have also benefited from treatments of the Cherokee Commission in relevant tribal studies by such scholars as Donald J. Berthrong, Martha Royce Blaine, and A. M. Gibson.

Staffs of several institutions have been most helpful, and I must single out some individuals for special commendation. These are John Lovett of the Western History Collections of the University of Oklahoma, Robert Kvasnicka and Mary Francis Morrow of the National Archives, William Welge and Chester Cowen of the Oklahoma Historical Society, Ann L. Hoyt and Kelly Swartz of the Public Libraries of Saginaw, LeRoy Barnett of the Michigan Historical Center, Caroline Autry of the Indiana Historical Society, Alan F. January of the Indiana State Archives, and Andrea F. Cantrell of the University of Arkansas Libraries. The staff of the University of Oklahoma's Bizzell Library, and especially the personnel of the Government Documents division, have been most cooperative. Jacki Thompson Rand initially served as my research assistant and later made her own contribution to the history of the Cherokee Commission with an able Master's thesis. Finally, I wish to express my deep appreciation to Doni J. Fox for her effective rendering of the maps; to Sarah Nestor, who did her usual efficient job of editing a manuscript of mine that badly needed it; and to my wife, Charlotte N. Hagan, who displayed her usual forbearance and loving support.

Taking Indian Lands

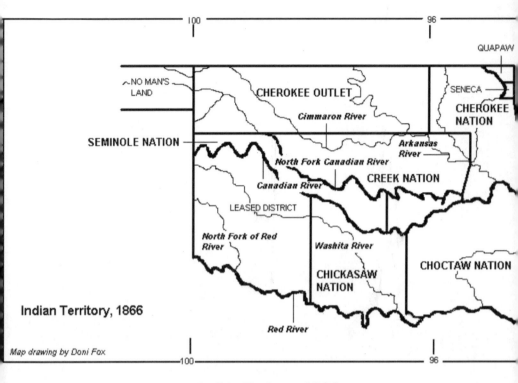

Indian Territory, 1866

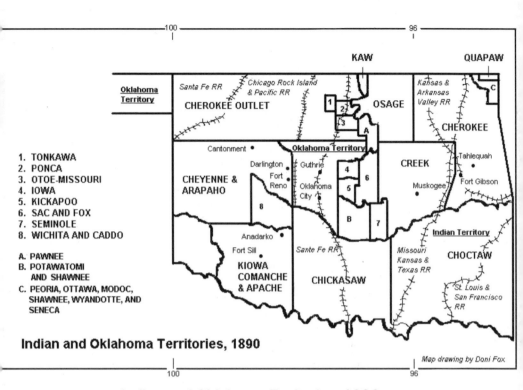

1. TONKAWA
2. PONCA
3. OTOE-MISSOURI
4. IOWA
5. KICKAPOO
6. SAC AND FOX
7. SEMINOLE
8. WICHITA AND CADDO

A. PAWNEE
B. POTAWATOMI
   AND SHAWNEE
C. PEORIA, OTTAWA, MODOC,
   SHAWNEE, WYANDOTTE, AND
   SENECA

Indian and Oklahoma Territories, 1890

Map drawing by Doni Fox

Indian and Oklahoma Territories, 1890

1

The Origins of the Cherokee Commission

IT IS OFTEN OBSERVED THAT FROM THE PASSAGE OF THE Dawes Severalty Act in 1887 to the reversal of that policy by the Wheeler-Howard Indian Reorganization Act of 1934, the Native American land base shrank from roughly 138,000,000 acres to 52,000,000.[1] Much of this loss is attributable to commissions such as the Cherokee, of which there were over a dozen. Although the authorizations for these bodies did not necessarily mention allotment in severalty, the amount of land that tribes would be asked to sell to the United States was usually the "surplus" remaining after tribal members had been allotted homesteads. Their agreements generally called for both allotment and the sale of any remaining tribal land to the United States.

Allotment in severalty was hardly a new idea in the 1880s. Secretary of War Henry Knox, the first to occupy that office and assume the responsibilities for Indian affairs that it included, had been truly concerned with the treatment of Native Americans and their ultimate "civilization." "Were it possible to introduce among the Indians a love for exclusive property," he advised President Washington in 1789, "it would be a happy commencement to the business."[2] By the 1850s the government had decided not to wait any longer for the tribal peoples to develop an appreciation for private property, on their own, and it began to impose treaties containing provisions for allotment.

In the post–Civil War era the white population almost unanimously endorsed severalty for Indians. It was a policy lauded with equal fervor by humanitarians and by those citizens lusting after Indian land. The humanitarians sincerely believed that holding land in common was a serious handicap to full development of Indian potential. That, they believed, would require a system that stressed individual achievement in a competitive environment. And hundreds of thousands of white home seekers and their representatives in Congress were excited about the prospect of allotment of reservations, making millions of acres available to settlers. Greed and humanitarianism rarely coalesced so beautifully in support of a policy. This was a synergy that would produce results.

In the 1850s American Indian policy had also incorporated the concept of concentrating midwestern and plains tribes in northern and southern enclaves, the latter to include Oklahoma and Kansas. In 1854, however, Kansas became a federal territory, accessible to white settlers and with the potential for statehood. When it did become a state in 1861, Kansans had their own congressional delegation to urge that reservations in their state be reduced in size and number and that their Indian populations be shifted south to Indian Territory, as Oklahoma was beginning to be called.

Indian Territory had never been recognized as an official territory with a recognized route to statehood. Rather, it had evolved as a result of the policy launched by Congress with the 1830 Removal Act to relieve the *cis*-Mississippi states of their Indian populations. The most notorious of these removals was the Cherokees' Trail of Tears. But four other southern tribes, the Creeks, Seminoles, Choctaws, and Chickasaws, also underwent the ordeal of removal to Indian Territory. In the 1870s these tribes would begin to be identified as the Five Civilized Tribes, to distinguish them from neighboring peoples that some still classified as "savage." In uneasy proximity, these five tribes occupied the territory south of Kansas, north of Texas, and west of Arkansas as far as 100° longitude—what today is the beginning of the Oklahoma Panhandle.

Two decades after their removal, the tribes began to feel the first pressure to make room for other Indians. In 1855 the United States persuaded the Choctaws and Chickasaws to lease their land in Indian Territory west of 96° longitude for $800,000, the area to be used as reservations for the Wichitas and several other small tribes. In time the Leased District, as it was dubbed, would also house Kiowas, Comanches, and Apaches on one reservation and Cheyennes and Arapahos on another to the north of them.

The participation in the Civil War of the Five Civilized Tribes, all of whom allied to some degree with the Confederacy, would help rationalize U.S. demands that they cede more land. As early as November 1862 Senator S. C. Pomeroy of Kansas proposed that tribes resident in Kansas be removed to Indian Territory. To justify this he used what was already an old argument—removal would spare the Indians the corruption that seemed to result inevitably from their contact with frontier settlements. Pomeroy also cited the recent Sioux outbreak in Minnesota that had resulted in the deaths of several hundred settlers, observing, "we have the same combustible material in my own State, some misguided hand may apply the torch of destruction here."[3]

Commissioner of Indian Affairs William P. Dole responded favorably to Pomeroy's suggestion, but the inability of Union troops to hold Indian Territory ruled out any action until after the war. Dole, however, did support the idea in his 1864 annual report, declaring that the population density of Indian Territory was less than one per square mile and "vastly in excess of [Indian] wants." He advocated requiring the Five Civilized Tribes to make room for other friendly tribes. This would contribute, said Dole, to "the convenience and comfort of the citizens of Kansas and Nebraska, and, above all, the welfare . . . of the Indians."[4] It is unlikely that many Native Americans would have supported that statement, but the stage was being set for the postwar treaties.

Indian Territory was devastated by the war, particularly the homelands of the Creeks, Seminoles, and Cherokees, as they had been deeply divided in their wartime loyalties. In addition the Cherokees were still torn by factionalism stemming from their differences over removal in the 1830s, when Cherokees had killed Cherokees, and the wounds had yet to heal completely. In the postwar negotiations federal authorities had to insist that the loyal faction of the tribe moderate the punishment it was inflicting on the defeated Confederate Cherokees. For its part the United States punished the innocent with the guilty. Ironically, the Choctaws and Chickasaws who had been most united in support of the Confederacy suffered the least onerous reconstruction terms. There were advantages in being relatively united, even if you were on the losing side.

The United States held the first postwar conference with the Five Civilized Tribes in September 1865 at Fort Smith, Arkansas. Federal officials began by informing the tribes that by allying with the Confederacy they had broken their treaties and "forfeited all *rights* under them, and must be considered as at the mercy of the government."[5] What that meant the Indians discovered the next year in Washington, when they were forced to accept the reconstruction treaties. The Choctaws and Chickasaws had to sell the Leased District to the United States for three hundred thousand dollars,[6] and the

Creeks had to cede the entire western half of their national territory, 3,250,560 acres, for less than one million dollars.[7]

The Seminoles, the smallest of the five tribes and the least capable of resisting federal pressure, suffered the most. They had to sell all of their national domain, over 2,000,000 acres, while being permitted to buy only 200,000 acres of the Creek cession from the United States. The transaction was even more reprehensible in that while the Seminoles had received only fifteen cents per acre for their cession to the United States, they had to pay fifty cents per acre for the former Creek land, for which the government had paid only thirty cents.[8] Being a ward of the United States could be expensive.

The Cherokee negotiations also cost them dearly and, since they affected the later bargaining with the Cherokee Commission, must be looked at in greater detail. Article 15 of the Cherokee treaty provided that: "The United States may settle any civilized Indians, friendly with the Cherokees and adjacent tribes, within the Cherokee country, on unoccupied lands east of 96°, on such terms as may be agreed upon by any such tribe and the Cherokees."[9] Article 16 provided something similiar for the Cherokee country west of 96° longitude.

The distinction between east and west of 96° was important. The United States never challenged the Cherokees' title to the eastern area, although it did come to question their claim to the over six million acres west of 96° known as the Cherokee Outlet or Strip. "Cherokee Strip," however, was more accurately applied to a tract on the southern boundary of Kansas, two and one-half miles wide and extending from the eastern boundary of the Cherokee Nation to the western end of the Outlet. The United States bought this strip by the 1866 reconstruction treaty negotiated in Washington.

Between 1866 and 1889 the United States located several tribes on the Outlet as permitted by Article 16: the Osage, Kaw, Tonkawa, Ponca, Otoe-Missouri, and Pawnee Tribes. West of them, all the way to the end of the Outlet at 100° longitude, the land was unoccupied. It had very little attraction for the Cherokees, who could still find farm sites in the eastern portion of their nation and were not inclined to abandon their family and clan ties to pioneer in the Outlet. Indeed, the Cherokees were interested in selling the Outlet to the United States—until cattlemen began leasing pasture there.[10]

The Cherokees had attempted, with very little success, to levy a tax on Texas cattle crossing the Outlet en route to shipping points in Kansas. Their first efforts to collect pasture rent from cattlemen did not come until 1879, and three years later they were producing only about forty-one thousand dollars a year. Owners of about one-half of the cattle on the Outlet were evading payment, many of them Kansans who drifted herds south to feed on Cherokee grass. The Indians requested army assistance in expelling those who failed to pay, forcing authorities to determine whether they even had the right to rent their pasture. Meanwhile, a few ranchers began to fence areas in the Outlet, creating still another issue.[11]

Before these matters could be resolved, other problems arose. The ranchers building fence were using posts cut from Outlet timber, an increasingly scarce resource that was already depleted by Kansas intruders. Early in 1883 the Interior Department ordered the ranchers to remove their fences or the army would confiscate them. Although the order was later modified, it did shock the ranchers into combining in self-defense, resulting in the formation of the Cherokee Strip Livestock Association in March 1883.

The association was not an unwelcome development for the Cherokee officials. Eager to maximize their revenue from the Outlet, they found the new group a vehicle for simplifying the taxing problem by permitting them to deal with a single entity, and one with an incentive to cooperate. Nation officials prepared a five-year lease, which was signed by representatives of the cattlemen in July. The deal provided for semiannual payments of fifty thousand dollars, less than two cents per acre but more than doubling the best income previously received. The nation and the association would have less than a decade to enjoy the mutually profitable arrangement.[12]

Even before the lease had been executed, settlers, speculators, and businessmen had begun eyeing the Outlet and the Unassigned Lands. The latter totaled about two million acres that the United States had purchased in 1866 from the Creeks and Seminoles for reservations not yet established. Ironically, it was a Cherokee, Colonel Elias C. Boudinot, who in February 1879 called the nation's attention to the Unassigned Lands as potential homesteads for American citizens. Within months, organizations of Boomers—agitators for the opening of Indian Territory—had appeared in Kansas and Texas. Thousands of Boomers were involved in activities that included efforts to evade authorities and plant colonies in the Unassigned Lands. Although they were unsuccessful in these forays, the Boomers attracted sympathetic attention in the national press and Congress.

As early as May 1879, Missouri Senator George G. Vest announced his intention to introduce a bill conferring statehood on Indian Territory.

Successive Congresses saw other bills brought forward that, by allotment of reservations or otherwise, would advance the Boomer cause. The most likely targets were the Outlet and the Unassigned Lands, the latter now being referred to as the Oklahoma District, or simply as Oklahoma. Senator Preston B. Plumb of Kansas was willing to take action without consulting the Indians. Senator Vest, however, insisted that the Creeks and Seminoles had residual rights that must first be extinguished, as the 1866 treaties with them had specified that the cessions would be employed to house only tribes friendly to the Creeks and Seminoles.

Ultimately, Senator Vest had his way. In March 1885 Congress authorized negotiations to quiet residual Seminole, Creek, and Cherokee claims to both the Outlet and Oklahoma.[13] The Boomers were delighted; little did they know that they faced another four years of waiting before they would get access to Oklahoma, and the Outlet would not be opened for yet another four years.

As the Boomer agitation continued, members prepared several bills that related in some way to the opening of Oklahoma and the Outlet. The area known as No Man's Land, the strip of public land that later would become the Oklahoma Panhandle, also became the subject of congressional debate. The Cherokees claimed title to No Man's Land but did not seriously press their case.

William M. Springer of Illinois, chairman of the House Committee on Territories, was principally responsible for bringing the long debate over Oklahoma to a head. The author of several bills for organizing an Oklahoma Territory, he introduced another in January 1888, this time limiting it to the area west of the Five Civilized Tribes. His bill attracted the support of Boomers who, in a meeting in Kansas City, damned the "chiefs, squawmen, and half-breeds" trying to block progress and protect their own privileged positions.[14]

The most active organization of eastern friends of the Indian, the Indian Rights Association, also supported the Springer Bill. Indeed, the association claimed credit for helping shape the final legislation and defended it in a six-page pamphlet. Its rationale for opening more Indian land to white settlement was the necessity of "the absorption of the Indians into the religious, political and social life of the American people. Only in this way," argued the association, "can they be preserved as individuals from ultimate destruction."[15] This was also a familiar refrain at Lake Mohonk conferences of eastern friends of the Indian.

The Cherokee Nation's position on the Oklahoma bill is most easily followed in the pages of the *Cherokee Advocate,* a weekly published by the nation whose editor proudly proclaimed it to be the "mouthpiece" of the government.[16] The weekly published the reports of the Cherokee delegates when Congress was in session and responded to attacks on the nation in such major newspapers as the *St. Louis Globe-Democrat* and *The Washington Post.* The *Advocate* spared no one, and that included Senator Henry L. Dawes of Massachusetts, forever linked with the 1887 law making allotment in severalty general policy. The paper chided Dawes for having concluded, "in his cool calculating manner . . . that the Massachusetts' idea of land and Government are the only proper ideas."[17] The *Advocate* also charged that the Springer Bill was "down right robbery" and sacrificed "every idea of honor on the part of the United States."[18] And when the *Globe-Democrat* endorsed the Springer Bill, the weekly ridiculed its description of the bill as opening Oklahoma "under fair and honest conditions."[19]

"Is it honest," queried the *Advocate,* "to take land from us and present it to men who are citizens of England, Ireland and Germany, six months ago, or by men crowded out by them, which amounts to the same thing?"[20] It also emphasized that the Springer Bill, as it emerged from the House, would cancel the Cherokee Strip Livestock Association's lease, which was the major source of income for the Cherokee Nation. To the *Globe-Democrat's* charge that the Cherokees had "utterly failed to develop a capacity for self-government, and that not one Cherokee in a hundred comprehended American political institutions," the *Advocate* fired back: "We have two National colleges, male and female. . . . Over 100 public schools. We have Cherokees among us, graduates from the best colleges in the United States, Harvard, Princeton, Andover, Dartmouth, Yale, Ann Arbor and tens of others of lesser fame. No man or woman who has ever been among the Cherokees goes home saying that we are not able to govern."[21]

The *Advocate* likewise kept the Cherokees aware of the efforts on their behalf made by their delegates in Washington. The Treaty of 1835 had provided that Congress could authorize the Cherokee Nation to send a delegate to Congress, although that body never took such action. Nevertheless, the Cherokees began sending delegates to lobby for them in Washington. In early 1889, when the Springer Bill was being debated vigorously, Dennis W. Bushyhead and C. Johnson Harris were the delegates. Both men were highly qualified. Bushyhead had recently completed two terms as principal chief; Harris was a prominent politician who would occupy that post on the death of Chief Joel B. Mayes in 1891.

Elected in 1887, Chief Mayes was only one-eighth Cherokee but had come over the Trail of Tears in 1837 as a child and thoroughly identified with his people. Educated in Cherokee schools, he taught briefly, then became a farmer and stockman. During the Civil War Mayes enlisted in the Confederate Indian brigade, rising to the rank of major. At the end of hostilities he lived first in north Texas and then among the Choctaws, not thinking it safe to return to the Cherokee Nation until 1867. In the next twenty years he prospered in the cattle trade and became active in politics, holding several offices. In 1887, while he was chief justice of the Cherokee Supreme Court, he won election as principal chief on the Downing Party ticket. When the incumbent National Party delayed acknowledging his victory, armed supporters installed Mayes in office.[22]

After that unpropitious beginning, Chief Mayes worked to restore unity and asserted firm control of the national government. Exercising his veto power, he forced the National Council to require the Cherokee Strip Livestock Association to increase its payments to two hundred thousand dollars a year, a 100 percent increase.[23] Mayes's ability to hang tough in negotiations would stand him in good stead in his dealings with federal officials. As early as 11 January 1888, the *Advocate* identified the tactic to which the Cherokees would be forced to resort—protracted delay while trying to mobilize support in Congress.[24]

A report on the Springer Bill issued by the House Committee on Territories early in 1888 demonstrated in its majority and minority opinions the range of opposition to and support of the Cherokees. The majority segment stressed the needs of the Boomers: "Thousands of people are now watching the action of Congress on this bill, hoping thereby to secure themselves homes."[25] The majority maintained that the Cherokees had much more land than they could possibly utilize and that since they lacked a clear title to the Outlet, their leases to the cattlemen were illegal. The majority also described the Outlet in very unflattering terms as "a vast region . . . now unoccupied by Indians . . . but which has been appropriated, in violation of law, to the exclusive use of cattle companies, and has become the refuge of criminals and desperadoes from all parts of the country."[26]

Two members of the committee, George T. Barnes of Georgia and William Elliot of South Carolina, filed the minority report. They argued that the Cherokee title was sound and quoted an opinion given by Henry M. Teller when he was serving as secretary of the Interior. "The land is theirs," said Teller, "and they have an undoubted right to use it in any way that a white man would."[27] Furthermore, Barnes and Elliott pointed out, Interior Department policy had been neither to approve nor to disapprove leasing. For Congress now to declare leases illegal in order to bring pressure to bear on the Cherokees, they held, was morally wrong: "National honor forbids a departure from treaty obligations to these dependent people."[28] Nevertheless, the House passed the Springer Bill, although it would fail in the Senate.

As the bill reached the upper house late in the session, time was a factor in its defeat. Debate, however, revealed the same conflicting interests that had been apparent in the House Committee on Territories. Three principal speakers to address the Oklahoma issue—George G. Vest of Missouri, Shelby M. Cullom of Illinois, and William M. Stewart of Nevada—were harshly critical of the Cherokees. Defending them were M. C. Butler of South Carolina and former Interior Department secretary Henry M. Teller of Denver. Party affiliation seems not to have been a factor, and Teller's support indicates that the West was not a bloc on this issue.

Opening the debate, Vest set the tone, sketching a conspiracy in which "a few cattle barons" (he later referred to them as "cattle kings") enjoyed a monopoly of the Outlet obtained by freely dispensing bribes and liquor to corrupt Cherokee legislators. Moreover, he declared, "I do not concede . . . that the Cherokee Indians in letter or in spirit own anything in this Cherokee Outlet at all." He deplored the advantages enjoyed by speculators and cattlemen, "whilst the white people . . . the men who sustain this Government, and upon whose energy and brain our civilization at last depends, are excluded."[29] Vest also warned of the "baleful shadow" of the Indian Territory looming over the future of the surrounding states. He condemned the territory as a "refuge for criminals, a Botany Bay with no law, a blank, unoccupied piece of territory, so far as civilization is concerned."[30]

Senator Stewart's attack on the Cherokees was even more extreme. The Coloradan said that the Outlet was only an "easement" granted to give the Cherokees access to buffalo country. When the herds disappeared, the Cherokees, according to Stewart, had "abandoned" the Outlet, which had reverted to the United States. In the interest of a speedy settlement, however, Stewart was willing to buy the area from the Cherokees. He depicted them as "the richest people in the United States," about half of whom were "white men who have gone in there and married squaws." The root of the problem, he maintained, was that, "We can not have a country in the heart of the United States . . . dedicated to monopoly." In his eyes it was simply "a contest between barbarism and civilization . . . between cattle barons and the people"—a nice populist touch.[31]

The Cherokees had their fervent supporters, although they were a distinct minority. The first to respond to the attacks was South Carolina's M. C. Butler, who—having lost a foot as a Confederate cavalryman—was no stranger to lost causes. He did not resort to empty rhetoric, preferring to cite legal authorities ranging from District Judge Isaac Charles Parker, the notorious "hanging judge," to justices of the Supreme Court. Senator Butler reminded his audience that the United States had recognized Cherokee title when it accepted that nation's transfer of portions of the Outlet to groups of Indians that the United States wished to locate there. Obviously, the federal authorities could not accept the validity of Cherokee title when it was to their interest and in other situations deny it.

Butler introduced a number of documents into evidence to sustain his position, including a letter from then Secretary of the Interior Henry Teller in which he stated that his department "has for years recognized the right of the Indians to receive compensation for the pasturage of stock on the reservation." Butler stated heatedly that he had never seen "so disgraceful, so flagrant, so shameless a lobby" as the speculators who roamed congressional halls peddling stock in town-site companies involving "the very land which they want to take from the Indians." Finally, he deplored the "reckless and disgraceful attempts" of the supporters of the Boomers "to thrust their legislation down the throat of Congress in defiance of right and justice."[32]

Meanwhile the Cherokees were active in their own behalf, engaging the services of two law firms and appearing with their attorneys before House and Senate committees. In February 1889 delegates Bushyhead and Harris concluded that the situation was so serious that Chief Mayes himself should join them in Washington. The chief, who was deeply concerned, had strong views on the proper tactics to employ. As the seller, he believed, the Cherokee Nation was entitled to set the price for the Outlet and should delay as long as possible, because the property could only accrue in value. His fundamental error was in assuming that justice would prevail and the price would be arrived at through bargaining, instead of the United States' dictating what it would pay.

On 11 February the Cherokees and two of their attorneys testified before the Senate Committee on Territories. One attorney argued that any provision in the Springer Bill incorporating Cherokee land in the proposed territory was "a most flagrant violation of the solemn guarantees of the treaties between the United States and the Cherokee Nation."[33] As was to be the case with other witnesses for the Indians, he received a hostile reception from Senator Stewart, while Senator Butler was supportive.

Chief Mayes covered some of the same ground as the attorney but made a request that would have reverberations. Stressing that the government had no right to dictate terms, he added: "We would simply ask you to send a committee down there and tell our people what you want."[34] What he was protesting was a provision in the bill specifying, without consulting the owner, a price of $1.25 an acre for the Outlet and a procedure for payment. The latter would have forced the Cherokees to wait for their money until settlers had taken homesteads and paid the government, a process that could run on for years. For the poorest land, it could be a very long time before the Cherokees saw any money.

In addition the bill provided that the Cherokees were to receive no pay for the two sections of land per township—1,280 acres—customarily set aside to support public schools. These clearly were not the terms on which the Indians would choose to sell, nor was Chief Mayes exhibiting a desire to sell on any terms. Nevertheless, those anxious to acquire the Outlet chose to infer from the chief's statement that he was ready to bargain.

Mayes told the committee that the Cherokees had received an offer of $18,000,000 for the roughly six million acres. This $3-per-acre offer was over twice what the United States was prepared to pay. The chief acknowledged that the Indians were well aware they could not sell the Outlet to a third party without the permission of the United States, but he wanted to make the point that $1.25 per acre badly undervalued the tract. When he was asked how the Cherokees would react to an effort by the United States to buy the land, the chief responded: "Well, it takes two to make a bargain. One man can not make a trade by himself." Senator Butler interjected, "Unless he does by force?" To which Mayes responded that his people could not resist the United States, but would if they had the power. The chief and other Cherokee spokesmen had made effective presentations; unfortunately for them, the majority of the committee was more responsive to the Boomers.[35]

The Cherokees also had to contend with the press. The Washington *Post* carried two editorials that sounded as if they had been written by Boomers. In the first, after the obligatory references to "cattle kings" and "cattle barons," the writer referred to the flood of settlers moving westward until they met the arid lands beyond the Rockies and were forced to retreat. Thousands of these disappointed home seekers, according to the editorial, were gathering on the borders of Indian Territory awaiting its opening. The writer warned that the House, "the popular branch of Congress," recognized their need and that the Senate must. If this did not occur, the editorial offered a possible scenario in which the settlers invaded the territory and were bloodily expelled by troops. That, the writer concluded, would be "disastrous to the political party . . . whose Executive may be responsible."[36]

Two days later the *Post* revisited the issue. Again, violence was predicted if the Boomers were not given access. Should that occur, the administration of President Benjamin Harrison, due to take office shortly, "will at the outset be baptized with blood." In such a situation, the editorial declared, "The *Post* is with the people," who "seek to build up this fertile country and supplant barbarism and lawlessness with civilization, law, tilled fields, and all the . . . blessings of thriving industry."[37]

Chief Mayes, delegates Bushyhead and Harris, and two delegates of the Chickasaw Nation responded with a letter to the *Post*, reprinted in the *Advocate*. They complained of "the appropriation of our property . . . and the crippling of our national revenues," a reference to the proposed cancellation of the grazing leases. "It will be a disgraceful day," the letter read, "when the United States, with all the prowess of its arms . . . shall be compelled to surrender" to the Boomers. They ended with a reference to the lobbyists attacked by Senator Butler: "We necessarily view with alarm the proposed legislation invading our rights, particularly when it is backed by railroads and town site companies . . . in the spoliation of our property."[38]

The Cherokee efforts contributed to a slowing of the Springer Bill's passage through Congress, a pace that guaranteed it could not become law in the second session of the 51st Congress. Once it became apparent late in the session that the regular procedure was too slow, an effort was made to get it through by attaching it to the Indian Service appropriation bill. When that also failed, Senator Butler proposed an amendment to the Indian Service bill authorizing the creation of a commission "to negotiate with the Cherokee Indians and with all other Indians owning or claiming lands west of the ninety-sixth degree of longitude in Indian Territory . . . upon the same terms [$1.25 per acre] as is provided in the agreement with the Creek Indians" of 19 January 1889.[39] Any agreements with the tribes that it would negotiate would require approval of both houses of Congress, unlike the treaty process that Congress had terminated in 1871 as it related to Indians. At least agreements that had the nominal approval of the tribes would be preferable to agreements done by Congress without consultation with the Indian owners. The bill became law 2 March 1889, giving President Harrison authority to create the Cherokee Commission.

The long struggle over the Springer Bill and comparable bills had revealed the forces working relentlessly to reduce the Indian land base. Now the focus would shift to the work of the Cherokee Commission, but first its members would have to be appointed and instructed.

2

Initial Contacts with the Cherokees, Iowas, Sac and Fox, and Kickapoos

GIVEN THE TIME THAT IT TOOK NEWLY INSTALLED President Harrison to appoint members of the Cherokee Commission, it would appear that it was not a top choice of the legion of office seekers in a party just returned to power. Three of the first four appointees declined to serve. Congress had specified that no more than two of the three commissioners could be of the same party; thus, one Democrat was assured of appointment. That was Harrison's easiest choice and the only one who would serve for the life of the commission. The lucky Democrat was Alfred M. Wilson of Fayetteville, Arkansas.

"Uncle Alf" to the *Advocate* and those who knew him best, Wilson was nominated by Representative Samuel W. Peel and Senator James K. Jones, both Arkansas Democrats. They had staked out a claim to the patronage when the enabling legislation was being shaped. Wilson did have a respectable public record, having served well as a federal attorney and a state judge. Moreover, he had a wide acquaintance among the Cherokees. Elias C. Boudinot, a prominent Cherokee attorney and entrepreneur, had studied law in Judge Wilson's office and wrote in behalf of his mentor, claiming to be "authorized to say in behalf of the Cherokees," that Wilson's appointment "would be eminently satisfactory to all the Cherokee people."[1] Judge Isaac Charles Parker, in whose court Wilson had appeared, also gave his endorsement: "He has the respect and confidence of the Cherokee Indians."[2] However questionable these statements may have been, Wilson got the seat.

Several of those considered for the Republican positions on the commission declined appointment. Among them was John D. Miles, a Quaker who had served as Cheyenne and Arapaho agent for twelve years. He preferred to remain associated with attorneys expecting to represent those tribes when they negotiated with the Cherokee Commission.

Lucius Fairchild was the first Republican to accept appointment. Unlike Wilson, who was in dire financial straits and badly needed the job, Fairchild was affluent. It would appear that his name was first advanced by a fellow ex-governor of Wisconsin whom Harrison had selected to be his secretary of Agriculture. Fairchild had the advantage of being well known in Republican circles as a vigorous campaigner for the party's presidential candidates and as a past National Commander of the Grand Army of the Republic, virtually an adjunct of the Republican Party. As head of the GAR, Fairchild had made his mark by a highly emotional attack on President Grover Cleveland for returning captured battle flags to the southern states. His own war record was impeccable, Fairchild having risen to the rank of brigadier general and lost his left arm at Gettysburg. Before being appointed, he had to fill out a form required of Republican office seekers, detailing his military service and any wounds suffered. Nor was this his first trip to the public trough; for ten years Fairchild had served in diplomatic posts in England, France, and Spain.[3]

In his final sales pitch to Fairchild, Secretary of the Interior John W. Noble expressed his pleasure at the prospect of Fairchild's acceptance and sketched the situation. Noble identified acquisition of the Cherokee Outlet as the commission's "chief purpose." He estimated that its work could be completed in a few months, but in any event "will not extend over any great length of time." Anxious to get Fairchild on board, the secretary appealed to his sense of duty: "The result of a favorable conclusion to the Commission's work would reach many thousands of our fellow citizens as well as being a blessing to the Indian tribes."[4] The Cherokee Commission was many things, but a blessing to the tribes it was not.

The other Republican seat on the commission went to another Civil War hero, John F. Hartranft of Pennsylvania. His claim to fame was that he had led his brigade in the assault that finally seized the notorious stone bridge at Antietam. Like Fairchild an ex-governor, Hartranft also had enjoyed his party's patronage, serving as postmaster of Philadelphia and then collector of its port. Not now in good health, he had declined the pensions commissionership and accepted a place on the Cherokee Commission only because it promised to be of short duration.

With its three members finally on board, only a secretary was needed for the commission. Its first would be Horace Speed. Of a prominent

Kentucky family and for a year associated with Benjamin Harrison's Indianapolis law firm, Speed was ambitious but as yet had little to show for it. He had applied for a seat on the commission, but his credentials were insufficient for that. His plan was to use his connection with the commission to facilitate his entry into Oklahoma politics. Competent and aggressive, Speed would play a role far beyond that of the usual secretary.

The commission would be under the direction of Interior secretary John W. Noble, another former Union general as well as an ex–federal attorney who had done very well in private practice. Noble was acquainted with Fairchild through their work in the GAR. Although the Indian Service would be in his jurisdiction, and The Washington *Post* described the Interior Department as the "most harassing, complex and complicated department under the Government,"[5] Noble entered office relatively ignorant of Native Americans. What he did think of them may have been colored by his participation in the Battle of Pea Ridge, in which Confederate Indians were charged with scalping Union dead.

Secretary Noble wasted no time in summoning the commissioners to Washington to receive instructions. Lucius Fairchild arrived in late June 1889 and was briefed by Noble and the commissioner of Indian affairs. From them he learned that no more important commission to buy Indian land had ever been established.[6] This was possibly an exaggeration, although the commission would open millions of acres to white settlement and in the process deprive tribes of a viable land base. Fairchild also got a very optimistic estimate of the time it would take to accomplish their mission. Once they were in Indian Territory, he was advised again that the negotiations could be completed in two or three months. That estimate was off by about four years.

The Cherokee Commission's organization meeting occurred 1 July. The president had appointed Fairchild chairman, and Secretary Noble specified the remuneration. The commissioners would be reimbursed for all transportation costs and receive $5 per diem for food and lodging. Each day they were in service they would be compensated at the rate of $10.[7] Noble also provided the commissioners with almost forty pages of instructions prepared by the commissioner of Indian affairs, most of it referring to the various titles under which the tribes held land. The commission was directed to first negotiate with the Cherokees for the Outlet, offering $1.25 an acre. Should they reject this offer, the commission was authorized to offer other terms "as may be just and equitable," although it would negotiate as if the $1.25 were carved in stone.[8]

Organized and instructed, the commission members dispersed to their homes with plans to meet at Tahlequah, the Cherokee capital, in late July. Meanwhile, Indian Territory was abuzz with rumors and speculation about the government's interest in acquiring more Indian land. The *Advocate* kept the Cherokees informed as to designs the United States had on their home-land and possible Indian defense strategies. Particular concern was expressed regarding the absence of any reference in the enabling legislation as to how and when the government would pay for the Outlet if the Cherokees agreed to sell. The *Advocate* envisioned a scenario in which the Outlet was "gobbled up by the government and the Cherokees would have the fun of waiting for their pay and of cooling their heels in the Capital corridors."[9] There was also considerable discussion of how the Cherokee government could legally dis-pose of land. This was no small matter in a nation that had seen citizens killed for signing treaties of cession that other Cherokees deemed unconsti-tutional.

Keeping its readers apprised of the real threat to their landed estate, the *Advocate* cited newspapers that espoused the Boomers' cause. "Unjust and false, though it is well to know what some prominent papers say," was the *Advocate*'s comment on one editorial in the *St. Louis Globe-Democrat*. The writer had referred to the impending opening of the Oklahoma District as "the beginning of the end of the Indian Territory." And, the editorial con-tinued: "It is idle to talk about the alleged solemn guarantees of treaties when such guarantees conflict with the obvious practical rights and interests of the white race." Moreover, the writer maintained that the Cherokees had no land title sufficiently sound "to arrest the course of civilization and prevent worthy white men from obtaining homes on American soil." The time had come, the writer argued, "to dismiss sentimental considerations" and force the Indians to accept a "fair price."[10] That would not be the last time the Cherokees would read or hear such threats.

Another *Globe-Democrat* allegation to which the *Advocate* felt compelled to respond was that Chief Mayes had indicated before a congressional com-mittee that the Cherokees wanted to sell the Outlet, simply because he had suggested that the government send people to Tahlequah to talk about it. The *Advocate*'s rejoinder was that the chief simply was insisting that Congress could not legislate the acquisition—that any sale must be negotiated, not dictated. To illustrate the point the Cherokee journal published a dialogue between "Big Man" and "Little Man" over Big Man's effort to buy half of Little Man's farm. It was obvious what the writer had in mind when he had Big Man say, "I'm big enough to take your land 'for nothing.'" However, he had the dialogue end on a somewhat positive note, with Big Man agreeing to help secure Little Man's right to the half of his farm that he was permitted to retain.[11]

It was recognized by many Cherokees that retaining that half of their national domain east of 96° longitude was probably the most that they could hope for. Among the other things to which they would like to commit the United States in return for its ability to purchase the Outlet was a pledge that it would live up to its promise in the 1866 Treaty to rid the Cherokee Nation of the thousands of intruders afflicting it. Some of these had entered legitimately as contract workers for Indian entrepreneurs, but had refused to leave when their contracts expired. Others were African Americans claiming to have been Cheokee slaves and thus entitled to land, or people presumably of Cherokee blood but not recognized by the nation. In the latter category the most obnoxious group was the Watts Association, which numbered in the thousands, each member claiming to have some degree of Cherokee blood.[12] Cherokee officials had been pleading for years for assistance in ridding the nation of these intruders, but U.S. officials had been more concerned with possible violations of the rights of the intruders. As the *Advocate* phrased it so well, "Unless the Cherokees can be secured in possession and use of their property the property will end in being worth nothing to them."[13]

The *Advocate* also kept its readers informed of the opening moves of the Cherokee Commission. Well before it reached Indian Territory, its first appointed member, Judge Wilson, secured the consent of Secretary Noble to approach the Cherokees. Wilson did so in a letter to Chief Mayes suggesting that he should call a special session of the national council in anticipation of negotiations.[14] That caused an uproar that led some to speculate that Wilson would be removed from the commission; indeed, he offered to resign.[15] The *Advocate* tried to calm the waters, speaking cordially of "Uncle Alf" and the "affectionate esteem" in which he was held by the Cherokees.[16]

Early in July, Secretary Noble officially informed Chief Mayes of the appointment of the commission and its impending visit to Tahlequah, expressing his wish that the Cherokee Nation prepare for the negotiations.

Mayes replied that he would "kindly and courteously receive said commission" and requested a copy of its instructions. Noble said that would be up to the commission, and it would be an issue in the early negotiations.[17]

Even before the arrival of the Cherokee Commission, it was apparent that the overwhelming majority of the Indians did not want to sell the Outlet. One of the very few to openly advocate sale was Elias C. Boudinot. To an audience attracted by a picnic, he argued that in the end they would have to surrender to United States' pressure, so why not take the initiative and negotiate the best terms possible? Boudinot thought that they might get as much as ten million dollars. He whetted their appetites by proposing that it be distributed per capita, giving every Cherokee a vision of a small windfall.[18]

Chief Mayes, however, had no interest in selling because he was busy trying to leverage a higher rent from the cattlemen with herds on the Outlet. He began to spread the word that an extension of the lease for ten years, at the terms he was proposing, would produce more revenue for the nation than outright sale to the United States at $1.25 per acre. That was certainly a very persuasive argument for the Cherokees not to sell the Outlet. The commission, however, was already enroute to Tahlequah to open the negotiations, expecting to close the deal in a few weeks.

The only commissioner to leave a record of his progress to the Cherokee capital was Lucius Fairchild. He wrote his wife frequently and instructed her to preserve his letters—a real boon to historians. His first letter was from Fayetteville, Arkansas, which he reached by train. He was accompanied by the commission's secretary, Horace Speed, and Judge Wilson joined them there. Fairchild's initial impressions of Arkansas were favorable, leading him to invest ten thousand dollars in land there.[19] The Yankee, however, detected the "usual southern want of thrift."[20] He also concluded from discussions with a few Cherokees in Fayetteville that negotiations might not be as successful as he had been led to believe in Washington.

Before proceeding on to Tahlequah, Fairchild, Wilson, and Speed detoured to Muskogee to meet leaders of the Creek Nation. They traveled in a mule-drawn army ambulance almost as well sprung as a stagecoach. The transport was supplied by the commandant of nearby Fort Gibson at the request of Secretary Noble, and he would continue to provide equipment and personnel to facilitate the commission's work.

The trip to Muskogee was the commissioners' first introduction to the rigors of such travel. They crossed a flooding, log- and brush-laden Arkansas

River on a "ramshackle ferry,"[21] an experience they would forego on the return trip by taking a train on a much more roundabout course. Once in Muskogee, they dined with Mrs. Narcissa Owen and her son, Colonel Robert L. Owen. The mother was a mixed-blood Cherokee who had married a white man who built railroads. Their one-sixteenth Cherokee son was born in Virginia and educated at Washington and Lee College. In 1879 he had moved to the Cherokee Nation to seek his fortune. When the commissioners met him Robert Owen was already well established, having recently resigned his position as Indian agent for the Five Civilized Tribes (Union Agency). Owen had also begun to exploit the advantages of tribal membership, seeking a lease to 250,000 acres in the Outlet and pursuing other opportunities open to an educated and enterprising citizen of the nation. He would later serve almost twenty years in the U.S. Senate and would be remembered for authoring the Glass-Owen Act, which created the Federal Reserve System.[22]

Once back in Fort Gibson, Fairchild and Wilson found Hartranft awaiting them. On 29 July they all boarded a mule-drawn ambulance for a twelve-mile ride to Tahlequah. Two miles west of the town they were met by a seven-man welcoming committee, and the party entered Tahlequah to find its population lining the street to greet them. Their lodgings were in the new female seminary that was being readied for its first classes that September. Fairchild was pleased with their reception, describing his quarters as equal to those anywhere. Then Chief Mayes made a formal call, and the commissioners could be excused for feeling that things were going well.

Lucius Fairchild was optimistic that the impending negotiations could be completed in about two weeks. That also initially colored his view of the Cherokees and their country. He described Chief Mayes as "a large, rather fat gentleman, looks strong intellectually and seems amiable." The Cherokee country, he told his wife, was "a very beautiful land. . . . many fine farms . . . all can gain a good livelihood. A most favored people I think." On the basis of the relatively few Cherokees he had seen, he concluded, erroneously, that the "white and nearly white element largely outnumber the bloods."[23]

Two days after their arrival, the commissioners had an opportunity to observe the Cherokee political system at work. An election for members of the Cherokee National Council was only two weeks off, and the Downing and National parties were having a joint political meeting in the Tahlequah town square. Featuring a barbecue dinner and several speakers, the meeting lasted from midmorning until early evening and attracted about a thousand people. Fairchild could not avoid observing that whatever other issues the parade of speakers differed on, regardless of party, all expressed their opposition to sale of the Outlet. He was told that the same consensus had been expressed at other campaign events. Fairchild now concluded that "it looks as if we are in a hole."[24] It would prove to be deep.

Nevertheless, Fairchild was flattering in his observations on the day's events. He found the speeches "very good and some of them very effective," no small praise from a political orator of his caliber. He reported no problems from alcohol and appeared pleasantly surprised at the "many bright, educated men" he had met, among them a number of college graduates. That must have impressed him, as he himself lacked a college education. He also learned, however, that two of the chief's cabinet did not speak English.[25]

Fairchild entertained his wife with a description of the barbecue dinner. Beef of five oxen and bread constituted the menu, and there were neither plates nor knives and forks. The commissioners sat at a table with Chief Mayes and dealt directly with their chunks of beef and bread. Fairchild described with amusement the antics of two small boys who swiped the chief's food when he was distracted. No drink of any kind was provided, but their host kindly took them and a few others—each clutching his meat and bread—to his executive offices, where they all drank water from one dipper.

At the end of the speech making the commissioners had a session with Chief Mayes, the second chief, and cabinet members. Fairchild contented himself with thanking the chief for the pleasant reception and hospitality, stressing the friendly feeling of the commissioners and the American people for the Cherokees. The chief responded in kind. The social conventions had all been observed, but now the bargaining would begin, and Fairchild, Wilson, and Hartranft had heard enough that day to erode their confidence.

On 2 August the commissioners made a formal offer by letter for the Outlet. General Hartranft, whose health was failing, then departed for home, promising to return in November when the new National Council convened. That left Fairchild and Judge Wilson to deal with Chief Mayes, who would prove to be a formidable opponent. Their offer was $1.25 per acre for "the entire acreage" west of 96° longitude, subtracting from that any money already paid for land the Cherokees had sold to friendly tribes under the provision in the 1866 treaty. The sale would nullify any residual claims the Cherokees might have to the land now in the hands of the friendly tribes.[26]

Ten days passed before the chief responded, and Fairchild observed to his wife that, "Our good nature is being tested somewhat."[27] When the chief did answer, he upset the commissioners. Mayes faulted the offer on several counts, characterizing it as "not only vague but misleading" and lacking "legal grounds" for some provisions. The chief then summarized the evidence for the Cherokees' having a fee-simple title to all their land, including the Outlet, citing specific treaty provisions. He questioned the offer including the land the Cherokees had already sold to the Poncas, Pawnees, Nez Perce, and Otoe-Missouris as "an invitation to unsettle the status of these tribes." Under any circumstance, Mayes insisted, the Cherokee Constitution specified that the nation's land was held in common. Therefore, a constitutional amendment would be needed to sell the Outlet, and that would take time, if it could be done at all. The chief's conclusion was a moving appeal for justice: "we confidently trust that the great and powerful government which has in so many ways, in so many places and at so many times given us pledge after pledge of protection and good faith, nor either by direct act or any indirection deprive us of our property rights. . . . the Cherokee people place their trust in the magnanimity and honor of the most August assembly on earth."[28]

It was a trust sadly misplaced, as the commissioners were already calculating how to force the Cherokees to sell. The most obvious way was to make the Outlet valueless to them by eliminating the pasture lease payments. From the viewpoint of the commissioners, a group of cattlemen, part of the Cherokee Strip Livestock Association, had made this a necessity. These cattlemen had discussed with Chief Mayes an adherence to the current lease at the rate of $200,000 a year for the final years of that contract. They offered much better terms for an extension, however. For the first five years they were willing to pay $400,000 a year and for the next five, $720,000 annually. This would provide the Cherokees a total of $6,600,000, a sum approaching what the United States was offering for outright purchase of the Outlet. Mayes publicly announced the offer on 29 July, adding: "I am assured today that this offer will be made at the next regular session of the National Council, if circumstances remain as they are."[29]

The commissioners took steps to close off this possibility, which could only fuel Cherokee opposition to the sale of the Outlet. At Fairchild's request

General Hartranft, on his return east, had written Secretary Noble, delicately referring to "the legal questions that may be raised as to the validity of the lease."[30] He suggested that Noble summon the commissioners to Washington to confer on the issue. The secretary had already prepared an alternative strategy—dealing first with smaller tribes incapable of resistance in order to give the Cherokees a feeling of growing white encirclement. Noble also directed Judge Wilson to capitalize on his wide acquaintance with Cherokees to try to prepare them to negotiate.[31] Noble even found time from his summer vacation in upstate New York to meet Fairchild and hear from him directly regarding the commission's trials and tribulations.

Meanwhile, the commissioners marked time awaiting the returns from the voting districts. Chief Mayes and other officials had dispersed to their homes to cast their ballots. Fairchild dispatched their secretary, Horace Speed, to the Creek Nation to learn conditions there. The chairman also gave leave to their recently employed stenographer, Alice M. Robertson.

Robertson was the daughter of missionaries to the Creeks and Cherokees and granddaughter of Samuel Austin Worcester, of *Worcester* v. *Georgia* fame. Born in 1854 in Indian Territory, she had served as a clerk in the Office of Indian Affairs in Washington, a secretary at Carlisle Indian Industrial School, a secretary for Union Agent Robert Owen, and a teacher in and founder of Indian schools in the Creek Nation. Robertson was also well known to the eastern friends of the Indian, and during a lull in the commission's affairs in October she spoke at their Lake Mohonk Conference. She brought a badly needed practical knowledge of Indian Territory to the Cherokee Commission, and, like Horace Speed, would play a role much beyond her job description. She did not participate, however, in the initial exchanges between the commissioners and Chief Mayes.

Until they reconvened in mid-October, Fairchild, Wilson, and Speed discussed by mail the tactics they should employ. Speed, who had begun a law practice in Guthrie and was anxious to see the opening of tribal lands east of that mushrooming town, urged visiting the Iowas, Potawatomis, and Sac and Fox. Getting a million acres from those tribes, he insisted, would have the effect of helping undercut Cherokee resistance to a cession. Speed was also writing letters to the *Kansas City Times* and the St. Louis *Globe-Democrat,* inspiring editorials in those papers based on his novel thesis that the Cherokee Nation had actually become extinct because it was in the hands of mixed bloods and intermarried whites, both frequently American citizens.[32]

Judge Wilson, for his part, was talking to newly elected Council members, trying to win converts to the idea of selling the Outlet. He was somewhat optimistic: "The influence of Chief Mayes and the cattle syndicate to the contrary notwithstanding."[33] Secretary Noble, however, was warning Fairchild that, for the present at least, he could not get the president to approve an order removing the cattle. Speed was particularly anxious to use this lever, as he believed that failure to acquire the Outlet would not only be bad for the territory but would also "almost ruin those who fail to open the land."[34] For one like Speed, with high hopes of an Oklahoma political career, failure was not an outcome he could afford.

The *Advocate* continued to keep its readers informed of the forces arrayed against them. It reprinted a story from the St. Louis *Globe-Democrat* regarding the views of Chairman Springer and others of the House Committee on Indian Affairs. They argued that the Cherokees had only an easement to the Outlet, not a title in fee simple, and that essentially the Cherokees had "abandoned" the Outlet by leasing it to the cattlemen. The *Advocate* acknowledged that "'fight' is out of the question" but expressed confidence that the Cherokees could win with "the weapons so justly prized in this enlightened country and age to secure peace by the discovery and pursuit of what is 'right.'"[35] The small tribes about to meet the Cherokee Commission would need all that and more.

Secretary Noble endorsed the tactic of approaching smaller tribes before the National Council met early in November. He believed that approach would be "a course of action that would weaken the position, which I deem very unreasonable, of the Cherokee Nation."[36] Hartranft notified Fairchild that his health would not permit him to visit these small tribes. He cushioned that news with word that he had just turned down appointment to be pensions commissioner but had recommended Fairchild for the post.[37] Hartranft was indeed in poor health and died several days later.

The commissioners left Guthrie on 15 October for what would be a ten-day camping trip, during which they would confer with the Iowas, the Sac and Fox, the Kickapoos, and the Potawatomis. The army supported the expedition by supplying three wagons and teams, a stove, a large tent, and five enlisted men to do the chores. An incidental benefit of having an armed escort was that they supplied plenty of game—quail, squirrels, wild turkeys, and grouse—to supplement their supplies. The commission hired a cook and a wagon to transport his outfit and Fairchild found the food more than adequate. Generally all went well until the last day, when they awakened to find that most of their horses had disappeared during the night. That meant that the commissioners had to leave all the wagons but one, which carried them on to Oklahoma City. Presumably the soldiers recovered the horses because—although the government was still quibbling nearly three years later about expense-account items such as sixteen dollars for cigars for the Indians and the rental of a wagon and hire of a driver—it did not seek reimbursement for strayed horses.[38]

The commissioners had never planned to do more than prepare tribes for later serious negotiations, and this they accomplished. They first visited the Iowas, only eighty-four people and in no way comparable to the over twenty thousand Cherokees, with their more than one hundred schools and a government modeled on the American one and led by educated men at ease in the halls of Congress. The Iowa experience with the United States was a paradigm of the fate of small Indian societies in the way of Euro-American expansion. Around 1700 they had their first encounter with French explorers in what is now Minnesota. Never a large group, the Iowas usually occupied scattered autonomous villages. They came under pressure from American settlers after the War of 1812 and in 1836 were forced to take up residence on a reservation in Nebraska. Less than half a century later, the United States coerced the Iowas into accepting allotments and selling the surplus of their reservation to whites. In the several years leading up to allotment, about half of the Iowas made clear their strong opposition to the process. Some of these departed in small bands for Indian Territory, where they hoped to find opportunities to continue the traditional Iowa life.[39]

The 84 Iowas whom the commission met in October 1889 had succeeded, in return for abandoning any claim to the Nebraska reservation, in being assigned a new reservation by presidential executive order. The reservation consisted of 226,000 acres carved from the area that the United States had acquired from the Creeks after the Civil War. There the Iowas were leading a marginal existence when the commissioners met them. Each band member had an income of $63 a year from earlier cessions to the United States and a lease to cattlemen of grazing rights on the present reservation.[40]

Fairchild, Wilson, and Speed reached the Iowas the afternoon of 18 October. They promptly conferred in council with the village leaders and continued the talks the following morning. The commissioners spent their time trying to persuade the Indians, who had fled Nebraska to avoid allotment in severalty, of the benefits—indeed, the inevitability—of abandoning their custom of holding property in common. Not surprisingly, the Iowas declared that they would prefer removal to another location to submitting to allotment, which they believed would destroy their deeply cherished lifestyle. The Iowas also recounted their history of abuse at the hands of Americans.

In their official report to Secretary Noble, the commissioners described the Iowas as living in "rude bark huts . . . unfit for human habitation," much "as did their savage fore-fathers." They pointed out, however, that about a third of the Indians had opened individual farms up to ten miles away in order "that the improvident villagers cannot visit them daily and abuse the hospitable Indian custom of feeding all comers."[41] Fairchild assured his wife that the Iowas, "a dirty lot they are," would come to terms on the next visit of the commission, or "the Govt. will compel them."[42]

After a journey of about thirty miles that entailed camping one night along the road, the commission reached the Sac and Fox. They numbered 519 and owned 476,000 acres that the United States had encouraged them to buy from the Creeks in 1867 as part of the post–Civil War concentration policy. The Sac and Fox had already suffered three removals, beginning with a defeat suffered at American hands in the Black Hawk War of 1832. That had resulted in their forced relocation first from Illinois to Iowa, then to Kansas, and finally to Indian Territory. Once they had contested with the Santee Sioux for supremacy of the upper Mississippi; now the 519 represented the largest Sac and Fox community, with smaller bands in Iowa and Nebraska.[43]

Most Indian Territory Sac and Fox depended on a combined annuity and leased-pasture annual income of $62 each, the produce from small garden plots, and the diminishing game resources of the area.[44] Their most prominent political leader was Moses Keokuk, son of Keokuk the Watchful Fox, the Sac chief who had opposed Black Hawk's resort to armed force to resist American expansion. Like his father, Moses Keokuk championed accommodation as the only feasible policy and was the principal spokesman for the Indians in council.

Once again Chairman Fairchild made the pitch that the Indians should accept allotment and sell their surplus land to the United States. He stressed that they could choose the best land and the government would pay $1.25 per acre for the surplus. Chief Keokuk asked several questions about the terms, but Fairchild found these Indians much more amenable and con-

TAKING INDIAN LANDS

cluded that the effort "may bear fruit."[45] Their reception from the Sac and Fox looked even better to Fairchild and Wilson after they met the Kickapoos.

The Mexican Kickapoos, as this band was known because of their two decades of residence in the Republic of Mexico, had a well-deserved reputation for independence and a willingness to fight for it. Originally from the same general area of the upper Mississippi Valley as the Sac and Fox, these Kickapoos had migrated to Mexico after being twice displaced by the Americans in forty years—from Illinois to Missouri and from there to Indian Territory. Unwilling to permanently ally themselves with either of the combatants in the Civil War, some of the Kickapoos had accepted Mexican offers to settle in that country. The motivation for the invitations reflected Kickapoo prowess. The Mexicans hoped that they would serve as a bulwark against Apache and Comanche raiders, but once in Mexico the Kickapoos found it more profitable to raid Texas settlements. They found a ready market for Texas cattle and horses in Mexican dealers and were so active in their raiding that Texans implored Washington to protect them.[46]

Not until 1873 did U.S. Cavalry under Colonel Ranald S. Mackenzie violate the Mexican boundary to storm Kickapoo villages. That, combined with pressure on Mexican officials and bribes distributed among band leaders, led to the reluctant agreement of three hundred Kickapoos, from a total of over seven hundred, to be moved back to Indian Territory. Thus they were on an executive-order reservation of 200,000 acres when approached by the Cherokee Commission. The Kickapoos were receiving no cash annuities or lease money and depended on garden plots, a little hunting, and government rations for a livelihood. They would not send their children to school and had brusquely rejected suggestions that they accept allotment. The Kickapoos did not warmly receive Lucius Fairchild and Judge Wilson.

Fairchild had crossed the plains as a forty-niner at age seventeen and had remained in California for six years. That experience helped shape the views on Indians that he expressed on meeting the Kickapoos. He found them "as dirty and filthy and picturesque as all Indians are." He judged them as no longer a threat: "because they were thoroughly thrashed they are peaceful—only they will steal small things." Nor was the chairman favorably impressed that the blind Kickapoo chief's first words on their meeting were a plea for tobacco.[47]

The council was brief. The commissioners delivered what were becoming standard speeches on the advantages of accepting allotments and selling the surplus land. There was a single response from a Kickapoo speaking for the chief, essentially a declaration that these Indians would not abandon village life and establish individual homesteads. The council ended that round of negotiations, as the Potawatomis failed to meet the commissioners when they moved on to Oklahoma City, presumably because of heavy rains. Fairchild had not been favorably impressed by the Iowas, Kickapoos, and Sac and Fox, "the same dirty filthy people I used to see in the Indian country when I was a boy on the plains and in California."[48]

On 25 October the commissioners departed for Tahlequah by rail. It was only 125 miles as the crow flies, but the commissioners were happy to take the much more circuitous route by train. Fairchild was finding the primitive roads a jarring and painful experience for a man with a sensitive stump of an arm. Going by way of Fort Worth at least got him into Texas for the first time, and he enjoyed seeing the southern part of Indian Territory. He predicted that the Choctaw and Chickasaw countries would become "a wonderfully fruitful land when the white men get in for cultivation."[49] And he found Muskogee, the Creek capital, attractive although housing was so scarce that he and Judge Wilson had to share a bed. The next day they continued on to Fort Gibson, where the army supplied them a four-mule ambulance for the last leg to Tahlequah.

Fairchild was pessimistic about pending negotiations with the Cherokees, "but it is barely possible they may show more horse-sense than I now give them credit for." Recognizing that as long as the Indians enjoyed lease revenues from the Outlet they had no incentive to sell it, he telegraphed Secretary Noble asking that the cattlemen be given a deadline of 15 May or 1 June to remove their herds. Meanwhile, Fairchild tried to get negotiations underway, beginning with a courtesy call on Chief Mayes. No business was brought up, and the chairman termed it "a pleasant chat."[50] From this point on, however, relations between the commissioners and the Cherokees steadily worsened.

Secretary Noble needed no prompting from Fairchild on the lease issue. He already had dispatched a long letter to the chairman in which he declared the leases "unlawful and illegal." Noble damned the Cherokee Strip Livestock Association for making "extravagant" offers to the Cherokees to counter the "not only fair, but munificent" United States' offer. Noble declared that "lessees should be compelled to leave said Outlet . . . *on or before the first of June next.*" He also dismissed the Cherokee title to the Outlet as "precarious, and liable to be defeated utterly" and referred to the authority of the government "to assert its right by superior title." Intending the letter to intimidate the Cherokees, Noble authorized Fairchild to communicate it to Chief Mayes and the National Council.[51] Fairchild did so and followed it up with a copy of an opinion by the assistant attorney general who was assigned to the Interior Department. As might have been expected, this official held that a Cherokee cession would not be a violation of their constitution.

Chief Mayes's response was quick and sharp. He stated that Secretary Noble had no authority to interfere with the Cherokee "sacred right" to grant grazing leases of their own land and that they would continue to do so until the secretary "shall see fit to dispossess the Cherokees . . . by force." As to the legal opinion that his people could constitutionally sell land, the chief responded tartly that his "conscience and sense of duty . . . will govern me and not the opinion of the Attorney General, not the act of Congress creating your Commission."[52]

Mayes extended his remarks and altered his tone in his annual message that appeared in the *Advocate*. There he expressed his "faith in that proud and honorable government . . . with such a noble and good man as Benjamin Harrison at its head, that she cannot stoop to such a low act as to rob a helpless and defenseless race of people." And he went on: "if the land is ever sold, it should be done by the people . . . without being coerced or bulldozed into sale, and at a price equal to its full value."[53] Little wonder that Fairchild confided to his wife: "The Cherokee Chief has openly declared war . . . but he will not win."[54]

Lucius Fairchild's temper was fraying. In public he attempted to present an affable front, but in his private correspondence he was harsh. Increasingly he suggested that Chief Mayes was in the pay of the cattlemen, "boodled" was his term. Nor did he confine his denunciations to the chief. His landlord was charging him a "monstrous" rent and was "a fair specimen of the class which is in control of Cherokee affairs. They are all d——d thieves." And he concluded, "I feel contaminated by the contact with the dishonest whelps who are in the lead of affairs here."[55]

In his annual report Secretary Noble was also critical, but in more restrained language. After lauding the opening of the Oklahoma District as producing in a few months "wonderful results of Christian American civilization"[56] and celebrating the admission of the Dakotas, Montana, and Washington to statehood, Noble turned to the Cherokee Commission and its effort to acquire the Outlet. "It would be a great boon to the country," said the secretary, "if this vast and fertile land could be redeemed from the use now made of it for merely herding cattle by persons to whom illegal leases have been made." This "corporation"—as he referred to it—was attempting, Noble maintained, "to thwart the national progress and to prejudice the minds of the Indians against a fair consideration of the offer of the United States." He insisted that the Indian policy of President Benjamin Harrison had "a strong desire and purpose to alleviate their condition and lead them into the higher plane of civilization." He warned that there were laws "making it a penal offense to alienate or *to attempt to alienate the confidence of any Indian or Indians* from the Government of the United States."[57] Harrison echoed this in his State of the Union message: "it can not be allowed that those who by sufferance occupy these lands shall interpose to defeat the wise and beneficent purposes of the Government."[58]

This administration had determined to acquire the Outlet, and it did not intend to tolerate opposition from its own citizens. Dr. Thomas A. Bland, editor of *Council Fire* and founder of the National Indian Defense Association, was an outspoken critic of the efforts to rush Indians into severalty. He showed up in Indian Territory early in November, and Fairchild reported to Secretary Noble that he was fomenting trouble for the government. Noble immediately responded that Bland had no authority to be in the territory; if he caused trouble, Fairchild should have the agent for the Five Civilized Tribes expel him. Given the refusal of the government to take action against the thousands of non-Cherokee intruders about whom Chief Mayes had been bitterly complaining, the secretary's willingness to move promptly against Dr. Bland gives a clue as to Noble's priorities.[59]

President Harrison had moved expeditiously to get a replacement for General Hartranft. He appointed Warren G. Sayre, a prominent Indiana Republican who had once earned then–Senator Benjamin Harrison's gratitude by trying to stop a Democratic gerrymander of the state's legislature that could have cost Harrison his Senate seat.[60] For several years before he ascended to the presidency, he and Sayre had corresponded about political matters, particularly patronage. Sayre was also well acquainted with the president's executive secretary, Eligah W. Halford, a former Indianapolis newspaper editor. Sayre frequently addressed his requests to Halford, confident that the secretary would bring them to the attention of the president. On a few occasions, Sayre presumed on his relationship with Harrison to discuss

Cherokee Commission matters. This was particularly true after the commissioners began to believe that people in Congress and the Interior Department were undercutting them.

The Democrat newspaper in Wabash, Indiana, on hearing of Sayre's appointment, described him as "only five feet tall, but he is the biggest Republican in Wabash." It informed its readers that Sayre's salary would be "$10 a day with perquisites that might run the emoluments up to $5,000 a year." Readers also learned that Miami Indians in the county, after learning of Sayre's appointment, made him an honorary chief with the name "Fat Man Without Whiskers."[61] Chairman Fairchild soon concluded that Horace Speed had accurately evaluated Sayre as an able man. Although he had not sought the position and had no experience with Indians, Sayre was bright and industrious and had a cheery disposition. The last quality was badly needed, as Fairchild was increasingly despondent about their chances of success and anxious to get back to his family in Wisconsin.

Negotiations of a sort did take place between a Cherokee committee and the commission, but it was quickly apparent that the Indians were only engaging in delaying tactics. The commissioners believed that the Cherokee leaders hoped to stall in the hopes of a better deal from Congress, where they had some friends such as Senator Henry Dawes who might be able to sweeten the government's offer. Fairchild and Secretary Noble differed only in Noble's assigning more blame to the cattlemen, while the chairman continued to assail Chief Mayes and the other Cherokee leaders.

On 26 November, after only ten days in Tahlequah, Warren Sayre, with the approval of Fairchild, wrote President Harrison to acquaint him with the problems they faced. He marked the letter "Personal" and asked that it not become a part of Interior Department records, "although I would be pleased to have the Secretary know what I write." Clearly he was bypassing official channels, taking advantage of his personal relationship with the president— something that Noble would probably resent. In the seven-page letter Sayre described the Cherokees with whom the commission was negotiating as either having only a trace of Indian blood or being white men with Indian wives. "The real Cherokees," he declared, "have long since been pushed over into the hills and hollows in eastern parts of the Territory and have no more real power than the most friendless Negro in Mississippi." Sayre observed that many Cherokee citizens wanted to accept the commission's offer and have the payment distributed per capita, instead of its being held in the

Cherokee national treasury and administered by "the Gang." "Cherokee greed and dishonesty and the self interest of the cattle syndicate stand in the Nation's path," he proclaimed. Therefore, the president should order the cattlemen off the Outlet, depriving the Cherokees of sufficient income to operate their government. The commissioners strongly opposed permitting the Indians to stall in the hope that Congress might offer them more. If necessary, however, Sayre and his colleagues proposed that Congress simply open the Outlet to settlement and determine later what to pay the Cherokees.[62]

About seven weeks elapsed between the organization of the new National Council in early November and its adjournment on 27 December. The commissioners tried both the carrot and the stick to achieve their objective. They first wrote expressing a willingness to abrogate the 15th article of the Treaty of 1866, which had opened the door to the location of tribes friendly to the Cherokees in the area east of 96° longitude. Then, in a letter to Chief Mayes in mid-December after the gloves were off, the commissioners asked ominously if the Cherokees had any objections to the government's shifting Indians from the Plains tribes' reservations east to the Cherokee homeland. To make it more explicit, the question was asked individually for thirteen groups of Indians, including the Kiowas and Comanches and the Cheyennes and Arapahos, all of whom the Cherokees on occasion still referred to as "savages."[63] This was a blatant effort to frighten Cherokee leaders into compliance with the government's demands.

It did not work. Chief Mayes responded the same day by publishing both letters in the *Advocate*. In addition, he denounced the scheme as "preposterous in the extreme, and contrary to treaty stipulations." He said that "any conception of this plan or policy . . . is oppression . . . and ought to be beneath the dignity of so brave and honorable a race or nation as the United States."[64] The commissioners then begged Noble to publish a proclamation ordering the cattlemen and their herds off the Outlet. The secretary was willing, but the order had to be issued by President Harrison, who sincerely believed in small government and, according to a biographer, made decisions "in a methodical, legalistic way."[65] He refused to be hurried into action, to the exasperation of the commissioners and Secretary Noble.

Fairchild and his colleagues continued to stew. They vented some of their frustration by making uncomplimentary remarks about the Cherokee legislators after observing sessions of both houses of the National Council.

Fairchild and Sayre were repelled by the informal dress of the legislators and the casual way that business was transacted. The president of the Senate was singled out for ridicule for being in his shirtsleeves with the collar of his dirty shirt unbuttoned, revealing his red underwear. Sayre was struck by the president's taking advantage of a break for interpreting to cut small pieces from a plug of tobacco, which he then massaged to prepare them for his pipe.[66] Meanwhile, day followed day and the commissioners fretted.

Until three days before Christmas they expected to be with their families for the holiday. The Council was still in session, however, and Fairchild feared that if they went home for Christmas, the Cherokees would claim that the commissioners had missed a chance to conclude an agreement. He reassured his wife that he would be able to have Christmas dinner at the Presbyterian mission, "but I'll never forgive this Council for not adjourning in time for us to reach home."[67]

Judge Wilson did make it, as his home was in Fayetteville; Fairchild and Sayre had the dubious pleasure of observing a Tahlequah Christmas. The chairman did find it different: "All night long [Christmas Eve] the fireworks and guns and pistols cracked and fizzled." Two men were shot, one mortally, and Christmas Day the shooting continued. Fairchild bitterly described the scene: "There goes another shooting scrape again. I see the people running and heard several shots—good riddance of bad rubbish if they *kill a lot* of each other."[68] Two days after Christmas the National Council adjourned, and Fairchild and Sayre notified Chief Mayes that they were withdrawing the offer made 31 July for the Outlet. Secretary Noble, who had authorized the withdrawal, also invited the commissioners to Washington in January to meet with a Cherokee delegation scheduled to arrive at that time.

After three months of implying to his wife that he would not remain with the commission to the bloody end, Fairchild finally announced to her that he would resign when he reached Madison. He did not feel that President Harrison, by his delay in issuing an eviction order to the ranchers in the Outlet, had given them "proper backing."[69] Moreover, he had found the rough roads very debilitating to someone in his physical condition. He had undertaken the assignment with the expectation that the Cherokees would quickly come to terms. Their continued stalling by demanding greater information on the offer, questioning the commission's authority, and refusing to enter into meaningful negotiations—all things the Cherokees had a perfect right to do—had put him in "a chronic state of 'dam it.'"[70] A day after informing his wife that he would resign and that it was increasingly probable that he would miss Christmas in Madison, an angry Fairchild described the Cherokee leaders to her as "the most corrupt and cowardly rascals I've ever met anywhere."[71]

Chief Mayes responded to the withdrawal of the commission's offer with a calm and well-reasoned rebuttal. He insisted that while efforts had been made to reply to the bid, the two houses of the National Council could not agree that they had the power to sell the nation's land. "When it comes to an Indian putting a price on his land," the chief said, "he is at a loss as he has never considered it a matter of speculation." Finally, Mayes invoked the idea of "Mother Earth," to the Indian "almost a literal expression," and reminded the commissioners that the Cherokees already had parted with over eighty-one million acres and were now being asked to sell half of the relatively little that remained.[72]

In its first six months the Cherokee Commission had obviously made little headway, but they had laid the groundwork for future negotiations. When it reconvened in Washington in January, the commission was without Lucius Fairchild. The day after he returned to Madison, he had written letters of resignation to President Harrison and Secretary Noble. To the president he complained of the "intense suffering" brought on by traveling the rough roads in the territory with a "*short* arm . . . very sore and tender" and his fear of permanent injury to his health.[73] Fairchild left it to the discretion of the president as to when to announce his resignation. It was six weeks before his fellow commissioners learned that he had bowed out, and in the meantime his absence was attributed to a severe case of influenza that had confined him to his bed.[74]

By the middle of January Sayre and Wilson, Speed, and the stenographer Alice Robertson were present for duty in Washington. Speed, with an eye out for his Oklahoma political future, was trying to help shape a territory bill, as well as to pressure the Cherokees into a cession. He busied himself testifying before congressional committees, lobbied members of Congress, and contacted Secretary Noble and Attorney General W. H. H. Miller. Speed even accompanied Noble to discuss with the president the question of an executive order to cancel the cattlemen's leases on the Outlet. And he at least claimed to have had an impact on the attorney general's opinion on the validity of those leases. Horace Speed was a man in a hurry, obtaining letters from Fairchild, Noble, and the attorney general that recommended him to Harrison as Oklahoma Territory's first governor. He confided to Fairchild that his real ambition was to be a federal judge in the future State of Oklahoma at a salary of five thousand dollars a year.[75] His reach exceeded his grasp, however; he had to content himself with an appointment as federal attorney in the new territory.

Alice Robertson was another staff overachiever. She may have been hired to be a stenographer, but she also lobbied members of Congress, testified before committees, and researched the record to buttress positions taken by the commission. Speed described her as "extremely effective," and Commissioner Sayre dubbed her "omnipresent and irrepressible."[76]

Their opposition was also busy. John L. Adair and Dennis W. Bushyhead, Cherokee delegates nominated by Chief Mayes and approved by the Cherokee Senate, were in Washington by January to lobby in behalf of national interests. Adair had served in the Confederate Indian brigade under General Stand Watie and after the war took refuge in Texas. In 1866 Adair begged his old commander for help in obtaining a span of mules, or even a single horse or mule, so that he might get a crop in to support his family.[77] When wartime passions ebbed, Adair returned to the Cherokee Nation and became active in politics, holding several positions in district and national governments.

By January 1890 both delegates were in Washington, ready to lobby in behalf of Cherokee national interests. As a two-term chief and a former delegate, Bushyhead was much better known, but he let Adair take the lead in reporting to the *Advocate*. The weekly letter helped keep Cherokees abreast of developments in Washington. Bills to open portions of Indian Territory to settlers were a major concern, and Adair was present when Horace Speed appeared before the House Committee on Territories. Adair thus heard him propose that "a lot of blanket Indians" be removed to the Cherokee land east of 96° longitude. His justification for that proposal was that the Cherokees had failed to oppose the removal that the commission had suggested in its letter of 16 December. Adair got the floor and corrected Speed, stating that the Cherokees had actually rejected the suggestion and Speed should have known that only "*civilized* and not blanket Indians" were acceptable as settlers in the Cherokee Nation under the Treaty of 1866.[78] In a subsequent report Adair acknowledged Speed's influence by referring to one bill to organize the territory, introduced by a New York congressman, as actually having been drafted by Speed.

What ideas Adair had held when he was appointed delegate we do not know, but after a month in Washington he began to argue for selling the Outlet at the highest price possible, which in a fit of optimism he estimated to be about $2.50 an acre. He also told his readers that he had learned the Cherokee Commission had been authorized to offer more than $1.25 an acre and might have done so had negotiations not reached an impasse so early.[79]

On 17 February 1890, President Harrison finally issued the proclamation that Secretary Noble and Lucius Fairchild had been urging. It banned further introduction of livestock into the Outlet and ordered all livestock off by 1 October. In vain Chief Mayes cited the patent by which the United States had transferred the area to the Cherokees, "a very beautiful document" with "the proud Eagle, the emblem of American liberty" and under it "the Indian and the white man shaking hands in friendship." More to the point, Mayes spoke of the devastating loss to the Cherokees of the $200,000 income from the leases, the single major source of income for the nation. He pled that Harrison "pause and consider before you take our property . . . which we have held and used so long undisturbed by this sacred title, a Patent from your Government."[80] His appeal was in vain. The president's only concern now was that if the cattle were ordered off abruptly, their owners would have to dump them on the market and would depress it dangerously.

Commission members were delighted that the president had finally acted, but this was balanced by vague charges circulating in Washington that the commission had performed poorly and might be terminated. Alarmed at the prospect of unemployment, Warren Sayre dropped a note to his friend in the White House. He informed Harrison that "the attempted negotiations were fashioned beyond recall before I joined . . . ," implying that he had not approved of Fairchild's handling of the assignment.[81] A month later, however, writing his chairman, Sayre expressed the hope that Fairchild would be reappointed, revealing a willingness to play both sides. He also assured Fairchild that the Cherokees were on their knees and ultimately would have to take what was offered. Nevertheless, Sayre believed that "the white Indians understand Congress much better than Congress understands the white Indians," so they might be able to do better in Washington.[82] That was his reaction to a conference he had held with Robert Owen, the mixed-blood

Cherokee and former head of the Union Agency for the Five Civilized Tribes, who was now serving as legal counsel to the Choctaws.

Charges that the Cherokee Commission had failed surfaced during the debate of territorial bills that touched on the Outlet issue. Colorado's Senator Teller was also highly critical of suggestions that the Cherokees must sell, and at whatever price the government set. He argued that Washington had no more right to take Cherokee property than it had to take his. And he expressed anger that every time a senator stood "for right, and for decency, and for justice" for the Cherokees he was accused of fronting for the cattlemen.[83]

Senator J. J. Ingalls of Kansas was even more impassioned in his defense of the Cherokees. He described how they had been removed from their "empire" in the East but promised security of their possessions in their new homeland "so long as grass should grow and water run and time endure." Ingalls spoke highly of Cherokee civilization, scorning the idea that "because we are 65,000,000 and they are 15,000 or 20,000 we have a right to take possession of their property because white men want it."[84] He scoffed at the argument of Secretary Noble and Senator Vest of Missouri that the Cherokees had no right to charge for the increased value of their land as the result of economic activity in surrounding areas. (Thorstein Veblen had not yet coined the term "unearned increment.")

After months of haggling in the halls of Congress, a bill organizing Oklahoma Territory finally reached the president; he signed it into law on 2 May 1890. The *Advocate*, with surprised relief, described it "as not so very objectionable after all."[85] It neither placed the Outlet in the jurisdiction of the new territory nor dictated terms upon which the Cherokees had to sell, both of which had been proposed during debate and committee hearings. It would be another two years before the Cherokee Nation and the United States could agree on the terms for a transfer of Outlet title. Meanwhile, efforts to persuade other tribes to sell land would occupy the energies of a reconstituted Cherokee Commission.

3

Agreements with the Iowas, Sac and Fox, Potawatomis, and Shawnees—Failure with the Kickapoos

THE OTHER MEMBERS OF THE CHEROKEE COMMISSION seemed genuinely disappointed at Lucius Fairchild's resignation, and the administration had some difficulty finding a replacement. The post was first offered to Charles Foster, a former congressman and governor of Ohio. When he declined, it was extended to Angus Cameron, an ex-Wisconsin senator. Cameron accepted and was sworn in, only to resign within three weeks because of family problems. Back in Wabash, Warren Sayre, who was fretting, complained to President Harrision's executive secretary: "Delay is dangerous to the best interests of the Govt."[1] But even as he wrote, the solution was being found.

With Senator James McMillan of Michigan acting as intermediary, the appointment was given to a former governor of Michigan, David H. Jerome, who headed a large hardware firm in Saginaw. Like Fairchild, he had participated in the California gold rush and had served, although briefly and not in combat, in the Civil War. Unfortunately, he would lack Fairchild's sense of history and make no effort to preserve his correspondence, nor would he communicate with Secretary Noble as frequently as had Fairchild.

In terms of experience, however, Jerome was unusually well qualified. Judge Wilson may have been familiar with the Cherokees because of his long residence near them and his practice of law in the Fort Smith federal court, which handled cases involving Cherokees, but Jerome had a much broader experience with Indians. For four years he had served on the Board of Indian Commissioners, which Congress, at the instigation of eastern friends of the Indian, had created to oversee Office of Indian Affairs expenditures. Its presidential appointees came from the ranks of Christian philanthropists who received no pay, only compensation for expenses while they were on government assignments.

By the time Jerome joined the board, it had expanded its surveillance to include most operations of the Indian Service. As a commissioner Jerome investigated conditions on several reservations. In 1876 he chaired the "Civil and Military Commission to Nez Percé Indians," which made recommendations on how to resolve the problems between them and the local settlers and permanently locate the Indians on a reservation. The commission's report, however, may actually have contributed to the war the next year that is principally remembered for the role of Chief Joseph. In 1878 Jerome served on another commission, this one to select new locations for Lakota Indians of the bands of Red Cloud and Sitting Bull. In 1879 he represented the government in preliminary negotiations with Uncompahgre Utes for the purchase of twelve million acres in Colorado.

Jerome also participated in the formulation of board positions on various facets of Indian policy, including allotment in severalty, of which he was a strong advocate. This is reflected in a report that he wrote after his negotiations with the Utes. He stated that these people faced problems common to other reservation Indians; they possessed more land than they could use and were plagued by intruders—miners, ranchers, and settlers. The solution he proposed was essentially the one he would be implementing as chair of the Cherokee Commission: "make a vigorous effort to concentrate them upon such tracts of land as are necessary for their use as citizens, and sell the unused territory . . . for the benefit of the Indian."[2] And, he might have added, for the benefit of non-Indians. Patently, Chief Mayes's efforts to prolong the Cherokee custom of holding land in common would inspire little sympathy from David Jerome.

As chairman of the Cherokee Commission, Jerome proved as confident and assertive as Lucius Fairchild. When Horace Speed resigned from the staff to accept appointment as federal attorney for Oklahoma Territory, Jerome successfully proposed C. L. King, another citizen of Guthrie, to succeed him. He also secured the dismissal—before he had even met her—of Alice Robertson, whom, as a woman, he regarded as "unfitted for the camp life we may have to resort to."[3] That was not his best decision. Given her lengthy association with Indians and demonstrated political skills, Robertson would have made Jerome's task easier. Furthermore, he must have seen women camping for months on end when, like Lucius Fairchild, he crossed the plains to try his luck in the goldfields.

From mid-May to mid-July the commission was in the field, negotiating with the Iowas, the Sac and Fox, the Citizen Potawatomis, the Absentee Shawnees, the Kickapoos, and the Cheyennes and Arapahos, in that order. Jerome and his colleagues departed Guthrie 16 May, courtesy of the army, which provided transportation, camping equipment, and an escort. They arrived at the Iowa reservation the following day and met with, among others, Chief William Tohee, the elderly, blind leader of the band.

The commissioners were with the Iowas for twelve days, conducting numerous conversations with the Indians and holding five formal councils, recorded in a journal, only thirty-six pages of which survive. The previous October, after their brief discussions with the Iowas, Lucius Fairchild had predicted that on their next visit the Indians would quickly come to terms. But Jerome, Sayre, and Wilson found themselves hard-pressed to convince the eighty-six Iowas of the wisdom of the government's policy.

At the first council, in a schoolhouse to which the Iowas refused to send their children, the commissioners laid out the government's proposal through an interpreter and the Indians responded in kind. In his opening statement David Jerome told the Indians that the president wanted to prepare them for changes that were imminent. Their practice of leasing land to cattlemen would end in October, he warned, and white men were "pressing very hard to get land on which to make homes."[4] Therefore, according to Jerome, before the president did anything to satisfy the whites he wanted to see the Iowas established on their own homesteads, which they could locate wherever they wished on the reservation. The land that remained would then be purchased by the government and made available to the whites.

Chief Tohee spoke first for the Iowas, followed by Hogarshe and others. The chief made clear that he and his people wanted to retain the entire reservation and proposed that the commission first negotiate with the tribes that had been in Indian Territory for a longer time. He also expressed concern about having enough land to provide allotments for their children yet to be born—a concern that the commissioners would hear from other tribes as well. Tohee then asked for an adjournment until they could consult Iowas who were still in Nebraska but were considering moving south to join them.

Chairman Jerome responded that there were two hundred white men seeking a home for every Indian to be allotted and that thousands of citizens were urging their government to act. He reminded the Iowas that the commission had met with them the previous October. Now was the time for serious negotiations rather than leaving the government to resolve the situation by "arbitrary action,"[5] an ominous reference to the power that the Dawes Act had given the president to impose allotment at his discretion.

Hogarshe then spoke at some length, asking that the Iowas be permitted to remain as they were and citing bad experiences that the Iowas, Kickapoos, and Potawatomis already had had with allotment on reservations in Kansas and Nebraska. They had quickly lost their homesteads, he lamented, "fooled it away," selling them at the first opportunity, and then "went around in fine clothes and fast horses and were proud and suddenly broke down and now go around begging." Hogarshe continued, "I wish the Great Father would take pity on the Indians because we are afraid we can not hold our own."[6] The interpreter's syntax was a little confused, but Hogarshe's message was clear—allotment cost Indians their land and left them impoverished.

Awicora, another Iowa speaker, brought up a favorite Indian theme, government delinquencies: "The great father owes us a great deal of money . . . they think we don't know anything about these debts but I am old enough and have heard them talk about them."[7] Judge Wilson ignored the complaint and disclaimed any personal financial interest in the proposal. He stressed the need for a cession, as "there are thousands and ten thousands of poor people who have not a foot of land and are pestering the government for a home."[8]

Other Indians voiced their concerns about providing land for children born after allotment and the need to consult with members of their tribe in Nebraska. Most speakers emphasized their reluctance to sell on any terms. Towards the end of the council Jerome did not attempt to react to each of the issues raised, confining himself to reassurances that "no power on earth except the Indian himself can get [his allotment] away from him," and that it was "the desire of the President . . . to make you better if he can instead of worse."[9]

Before closing the meeting to permit the Indians to talk the matter over among themselves, Jerome declared that the president was dealing more generously with the Indians than with the white man. He pointed out that in Oklahoma a white man and his family could obtain only a single 160-acre homestead, whereas every member of an Iowa family would be allotted land.

He did not address the fact that after allotment the tribe would be required to sell roughly 95 percent of their reservation at a price dictated by the United States.

In an attempt to put the Iowas in a more receptive mood after the council, men from Guthrie—with a stake in opening the reservation only twenty miles from what they hoped would become the capital of Oklahoma—hosted a barbecue. Indian dancing followed and continued intermittently during the negotiations. The commissioners described it as a "grotesque dance to the music of a bass drum accompanied by sleigh-bells." They also hazarded a guess that the Iowas were thus "invoking aid from on high to guide them in their negotiations."[10]

The *Advocate* speculated about the motives of the men from Guthrie who provided the feast, observing caustically: "we had supposed that the day for any species of bribery, in dealing with an uneducated people for the purchase of their property had passed away. . . . To elevate a people in the scale of civilization by first corrupting them, is paradoxical in the extreme. We hope to hear no more of this."[11]

When the council reconvened on 19 May, Jerome opened it with a reference to the feast and his expectation that the Iowas were returning to the negotiations "in a good frame of mind."[12] After he had repeated the argument that circumstances were forcing the Indians to alter their lifestyle along the lines proposed by the government, Warren Sayre rose to specify the size of the tract each Indian would receive—eighty acres—and to promise that it would be held in trust by the government for twenty-five years. In addition he spelled out the financial terms for the purchase of the surplus land, including about three hundred dollars for each Iowa to purchase livestock and the materials to build a house. Sayre, appealing to the parents' cupidity, was careful to state that the head of the household would also receive the same amount for each child under eighteen.

Acknowledging that the band would no longer receive the approximately one thousand, two hundred dollars per year from cattlemen leasing pasture, Sayre reassured them by arguing that they would get three times that amount for each of the first five years after they sold their surplus acres to the United States. Then annual payments would be gradually reduced but would total sixty thousand dollars over the entire twenty-five-year trust period. He did not reveal to them that this would amount to a measly thirty-eight cents per acre or, as the commission informed Washington, only twenty-eight cents taking into consideration the fact that payments were staggered over twenty-five years. Sayre did assure them that they would be able to retain ten acres for a church, cemetery, and school. He added that if they accepted the offer they would become "as rich a people as live on earth,"[13] a remarkable perversion of the truth.

Sayre then moved to disabuse the Iowas of any idea they might have held that they could truly bargain about the sale of their property. He told them that the president could take any of their land, but before doing it "had made these generous provisions." But having done that, if they declined to deal, then "he thinks it is right to take the reservation."[14] And take the reservation he could.

Chief Tohee initially reacted to the offer by describing it as "very good."[15] He then began to recite some of the Iowa objections, however, recalling previous cessions in Iowa, Missouri, and Kansas and articulating their fears that this negotiation could mean that in twenty-five years they would be completely landless. He acknowledged that they had been warned they must educate their children to prepare them to live like white people but insisted that Indians were different: "our great father ought to be kind enough to let us have our rights and be as we are." Tohee also objected to the way their children were educated at the Chilocco Indian school. "When we went to see them," he complained, "they looked like servants."[16] This was not an uncommon criticism from tribal leaders, who resented their children's working in the fields and doing housework.

David Jerome ignored the complaint about the education system and stressed the security that the government's offer was supposed to provide. He even had the gall to use the phrase "as long as grass grows and water runs"[17] as a synonym for the security of the title of their allotments. Judge Wilson closed the session with a suggestion that the Iowas return the next day after reflecting on the offer.

The next afternoon they reassembled and the Iowas repeated their objections. The commissioners, who were obviously running out of patience, became more threatening. If the Iowas did not reach an agreement now, they were told, Congress would mandate a settlement. Jerome warned that they would not be permitted to hold unused land. He even recalled his negotiations with the Utes "away back out in 1879 in Colorado"[18] to impress the Iowas. Jerome also reminded them that the 1887 Dawes Act, authored by "a lifelong friend of the Indian,"[19] could be imposed on them by the president.

In that case, he said, the Iowas would be left with smaller allotments than the commission was offering.

Hogarshe then expressed the Iowa lack of confidence bred by a history of disastrous dealings with the United States. They genuinely believed that this would be their last negotiation, and they feared for their children's futures. As Hogarshe phrased it, "we are here watching out for the future and if we make a mislick [sic] with our trade we are gone."[20] But the commissioners were becoming more demanding. Warren Sayre was blunt: "The Congress . . . don't think that you own this land except enough to live on, and the men that elect the men who go to Congress think the same way . . . they think . . . that you are only permitted to live here . . . Congress and the people are wanting to take this land away from you without giving you anything for it."[21]

After three Iowas—Grant, Wilson, and Hogarshe—had made an effort to counter Sayre, Jefferson White Cloud announced that he was ready to sell. "You may go away," he said, "and report to the great father what the majority have said to you, but I want my land." He indicated that he would like 160 acres for each member of his family, twice what the commission was offering. White Cloud also wanted a well dug for him and the house that had been promised. He was one of the few Iowas who had left the village to open a farm, "and now I don't want to loose [sic] all that I have." He concluded, "I would rather live from my tribe and do something for my family."[22] White Cloud clearly had tasted the forbidden fruit.

Jerome, thinking that this was a good note on which to close the meeting, announced that the commissioners would prepare the agreement and make it available for the signatures of everyone over eighteen. He was apparently confident that they would quickly get the required majority. It would be 27 May, however, before the commissioners were able to leave the reservation with sufficient signatures. Councils were held the last two days, Chief Tohee only asking that they be permitted to locate near each other. Judge Wilson assured him that they could, although not spelling out how this could be done with each family on its own homestead. Hogarshe refused to concede, reminding the commissioners that Indians did not accept majority rule: "We have a different idea about that."[23] Despite his stand, thirty-four of the Iowas over eighteen—a majority—did sign the agreement before the commissioners departed.

TAKING INDIAN LANDS

In reporting their success to President Harrison, the commissioners sketched a very unflattering description of the Iowas. They had no regular mealtimes, lived in leaky bark houses, and had "no incentive to energy; to exist is all that is required—a realization of the communist's dream." Nor were the commissioners able to detect any form of government—at least no individual or group appeared to be able to speak for all Iowas. The commissoners dismissed their title to the reservation as being "limited and their tenure even insecure," because it had been created by executive proclamation rather than by treaty or purchase. They told the president that the "standard of intelligence among the Iowas makes it exceedingly difficult to make them understand."[24]

Despite their generally unflattering views of the Iowas, compassion for the blind Chief Tohee inspired the commissioners to include a clause in the agreement providing him $350 and guaranteeing that whether he or his wife died first, the survivor would inherit both of their allotments. That was a surprising note of humanity from commissioners who, with the backing of a powerful nation of sixty million people, had just ridden roughshod over an eighty-six-person fragment of a small tribe. They had managed to purchase, they estimated, 221,528 of the 228,418 acres of the Iowa Reservation for less than twenty-eight cents per acre.[25] The Iowa allotments were for only 80 acres, but then these were the most defenseless wards of the United States that the commission encountered.

Some belated justice was done the Iowas in 1929, when the Court of Claims rendered a decision in a suit they brought charging that they had been underpaid. The court ruled for the Iowas, holding that there had been irregularities, including invalid signatures on the agreement and unfounded representations to the Indians calculated to inspire fear. The Iowas were awarded $254,632.59, sufficient to raise the selling price to $1.25 per acre.[26]

The Cherokee Commission believed that it had completed its Iowa assignment, but there were still some loose ends. It was Interior Department practice to send completed agreements to the Office of Indian Affairs to be vetted before the president submitted them to Congress. An acting commissioner of Indian affairs, R. V. Belt, spotted a problem that would lead to considerable discussion before it was finally resolved. While accepting the agreement in general, Belt maintained that it did not protect the rights of Iowas residing on the reservation that straddled a portion of the

Kansas-Missouri boundary.[27] His caveat was supported by an opinion of Assistant Attorney General George H. Shields.

Shields made a strong case that the interest of the northern Iowas in the Indian Territory reservation should be respected. He cited two Supreme Court decisions to support his opinion, the 1832 *Worcester* vs. *the State of Georgia* and one recently decided, the 1886 *Choctaw Nation* vs. *United States.* From the first he selected Chief Justice Marshall's dictum: "The language used in treaties with the Indians shall never be construed to their prejudice, if words be made use of which are susceptible of a more extended meaning than their plain import as connected with the tenor of their treaty."

From *Choctaw* vs. *the United States* Shields quoted the equally potent: "From their very weakness and helplessness, so largely due to the course of dealing of the Federal Government with them and the treaties in which it has been promised, there arises a duty of protection, and with it the power."[28]

Shields's opinion ultimately helped resolve the issue in favor of the northern Iowas. It is regrettable that the spirit of those two Supreme Court opinions had not guided the Cherokee Commission in its negotiations with the powerless Iowas in Indian Territory. Those dealings were "unconscionable," a term subsequently used by the Indian Claims Commission to describe particularly gross examples of underpayment for land. Had the record been more complete, including a full account of "Colonel Hill" and "Major Dodds," it would have added even more sordid details.

The only references to the colonel and major in the council journal do not identify them fully. Chairman Jerome invoked their names to reassure Chief Tohee that Indian suggestions had been incorporated in the agreement. When an Iowa identified only as "Grant" referred to "a couple of men here as our friends to help us," most likely a reference to Hill and Dodds, Jerome responded with a cryptic, "their work has been different yet they have been very careful and faithful to these Indians."[29] On the last day of negotiations, Major Dodds himself spoke, reassuring the Indians that "this contract is one that neither Congress nor the president can change."[30] In fact Congress could and did revise agreements unilaterally. The fact that Dodds and Hill were permitted to associate themselves with the deliberations is evidence enough that they were not working against the commission. Had they been doing so, they would have been summarily removed from the reservation. Colonel Hill was probably John T. Hill, who also would be working, usually behind the scenes, to facilitate other Cherokee Commission negotiations.

On 28 May, having completed the Iowa Agreement, the commissioners left for the Sac and Fox Reservation. They crossed it from northwest to southeast and concluded that much of the reservation could support agriculture, although "drouth would seem to be the greatest foe,"[31] something that generations of Oklahomans would learn and relearn. Arriving the following day, they met briefly with Moses Keokuk, who had made a favorable impression on Lucian Fairchild and Judge Wilson the previous October. Now the first assistant principal chief, Keokuk agreed to set up a meeting for Monday, 2 June, with the National Council, of which he was president.

The commissioners found dealing with the Sac and Fox much less aggravating than dealing with the Iowas. Keokuk had already developed the acquisitiveness that whites thought a prerequisite for Indian progress. Although he did not speak English, he owned a ranch, a store, and a small inn. He and other leading Sac and Fox had already concluded that a cession was inevitable. Their only concern was how they might shape the agreement to their best advantage.

Jerome opened the first meeting by stressing the need for a land cession to accommodate the increase in the American population: "it requires a state nearly every year to supply them with homes." With a straight face he explained the cancellation of Sac and Fox pasture leases as not done "as an ugly thing to the Indians" but in response to the demands of the great majority of white stockmen who resented the advantage the big ranchers had with their access to cheap Indian grass.[32] Then he got around to talking briefly about the government's desire to help them in "getting a living in a different way from the old way," a euphemism for severalty's replacing land in common.[33]

Principal Chief Maskosatoe began to respond, only to have Keokuk intercede and take over the presentation. Before discussing terms for their surplus land, he wanted to know precisely how much of their land they could retain. Jerome responded by citing the provisions of the Dawes Act: 160 acres for heads of families, 80 acres for single Indians over eighteen, and 40 acres for those under eighteen. Keokuk then stated the terms on which the Indians were prepared to sell: 200 acres per Indian and two dollars per acre for the surplus the government would buy. He also set a third condition that only Sac and Fox residents on that reservation would receive allotments and share in the payment for the surplus. Jerome declared these terms unacceptable and promised to present the government's counteroffer at the next meeting.[34]

Although the commission's journal of the meetings ends abruptly in the midst of the fourth session, Saturday, 7 June, it was 12 June before the National Council approved the agreement. Jerome and his colleagues had tried to hold firm, but Sac and Fox persistence managed to force concessions. Their principal accomplishment—no mean feat—was to obtain allotments of 160 acres per tribal member. That was not the 200 acres they had originally insisted upon but was better than the terms of the Dawes Act that Jerome wanted to apply to them. The commissioners rationalized the 160-acre allotments to the president as being necessary because the Indians demanded that children receive as much land as adults.[35]

The government got its pound of flesh, however, requiring that only eighty acres be held in trust for the full twenty-five years; the other eighty would be in trust for only five years. Jerome and his colleagues anticipated that most Indians would sell eighty acres as soon as possible, and they usually did. For President Harrison's benefit, this was defended as allowing less land to be kept off the tax rolls for twenty-five years as well as giving the Indians valuable experience in the free-enterprise system. Thus the way was cleared for the transfer of more land from Indians to whites.[36]

On price and location the commissioners held their ground. At their second meeting with the National Council, they offered a choice of three packages based on the best land's usually being along the major watercourses, of which there were three on the reservation. One each formed the northern and southern boundaries, and the third roughly divided the reservation on an east-west line. Left to their own devices the Indians would have selected the river bottoms, but the three-package deal militated against this. If the Indians took the first package, they would be restricted to the southern half of the reservation and would receive $485,000 for their surplus, about $1.23 per acre. The second package would still confine most Sac and Fox to the southern area but would permit those who had made improvements in the north to get allotments there. The government, however, would reduce its payment for the surplus to $460,000. According to the third package the Indians would be permitted to select their allotments anywhere on the reservation, but in that case they would receive only $400,000 for their surplus.[37]

Warren Sayre presented the proposals, and he and Judge Wilson defended them. Sayre reminded the Indians that they were being permitted to keep more land than could be done under the Dawes Act and that they had purchased their reservation from the government for only thirty cents per acre. Judge Wilson, folksy as usual, argued that for the Indians now to want to charge the government $2 an acre was "like taking all the meat off the bone and giving the bones to the Government to pick,"[38] an expression he would often use in the next three years. Keokuk, the principal Indian spokesman, made no attempt to respond to the commissioners except to say that the Sac and Fox would discuss the government offer and get back to them.

When they did reconvene three days later, Keokuk reported that the Council wanted not $400,000 but $620,000 for the surplus land if they elected the package enabling them to choose allotments anywhere on the reservation. If they were to be confined to the southern part of the reservation, they wanted $790,000—not the $460,000 offered.[39] This inspired Jerome to give the Sac and Fox a little history lesson on United States Indian policy and how $1.25 per acre had become the usual price the government charged settlers for public land. He concluded the morning session by maintaining that the Indians were being tendered a more generous offer than had been made the "great Sioux Nation" for its surplus land.[40]

Jerome opened the afternoon session with a comment on the "intensely hot weather,"[41] as a result of which he was feeling ill and left it to Sayre and Wilson to make the government's case. They basically rehashed the arguments presented earlier—the pressure of white home seekers and the unlikelihood that the next negotiations would find the Indians getting as good an offer. But Sayre added a warning that in reality the Indians did not have "full power" to set the price on their land.[42] In his conclusion he made crystal clear that this was not an ordinary transaction: "we did not come to barter about prices."[43]

About this time five wagons of Sooners suddenly appeared and went into camp overnight in sight of the commissioners' tents. The intruders reported that many other parties were arrayed along the eastern boundary of the reservation, impatiently awaiting the opening of the area.[44] It is highly unlikely that David Jerome arranged for this intrusion, but it certainly lent credence to the commissioners' warnings of white pressure and possibly undercut Sac and Fox resistance.

Two days later Chief Keokuk led off the session with a lengthy review of the situation and ended by making another counteroffer. This time the Sac and Fox opted to take their allotments anywhere on the reservation and wanted $491,783.75, calculated to be the surplus land at $1.25 per acre. But as the commissioners later informed the president, they "still felt that we ought not to yield the small difference"[45] and would agree to pay only $485,000, or $1.23 per acre. It would seem that indeed they had "come to barter about prices" and balked at paying an additional mimsy two cents per acre. The Indians capitulated, and fourteen of the sixteen National Council members signed the agreement.

Warren Sayre hastened to report to the White House that he and his colleagues "flatter ourselves that [with both the Iowas and the Sac and Fox] we made fairly good bargains."[46] He also emphasized that, being the only attorney on the commission, he had to carry a heavy burden in the negotiations. Neither he nor Jerome had a high opinion of the contributions of Judge Wilson.

The Sac and Fox had entered the negotiations convinced that they would have to sell and then learned that the United States would also dictate what it would pay. Their one significant victory was securing 160 acres for each tribal member, regardless of age. But given that, they still only retained 87,680 acres and ceded 391,189. When the Indian Claims Commission came into being in 1946, the Sac and Fox filed a claim of insufficient compensation. In 1962 the commission rendered its verdict, deciding that the government had not resorted to "sharp or fraudulent practice" nor negotiated in "an unfair or dishonorable manner." It did conclude that the land had been worth $1.75 an acre as opposed to the $1.23 that the Indians received. Nevertheless the payment, while inadequate, had not been "unconscionable," and therefore they were entitled to nothing more.[47]

The Sac and Fox appealed that decision to the Court of Claims, which in 1964 held for the Indians. The court disagreed with the commission on two counts. First, the court held that about $3 per acre was a fair price for the surplus land in 1890. Second, it found that "the coercion and duress exerted by the Government was so strong and overwhelming as to be 'unfair.'" This resulted in an award to the Sac and Fox of $692,564.15. As was its practice, the court made no allowance for accrued interest on the difference between what the Indians had been paid and what they should have been paid.[48]

None of this court action could have been predicted in 1890. According to an account in the *Advocate*, negotiations had been harmonious and the agreement had the unanimous consent of the National Council members present. To show its gratitude, the Cherokee Commission hosted "a great feast" the day following the signing.[49] And then it was on to the Citizen Band Potawatomis and the Absentee Shawnees, where the commissioners would find a more complicated situation.

The reservation occupied by these bands had come into being as a result of an 1867 treaty with the Potawatomis. The treaty, which was part of the effort to move Indians from Kansas to make room for white settlers, provided a reservation for the exiled not to be larger than thirty square miles. Article 3 of the treaty committed the United States to a policy: "After such reservation shall have been selected and set apart for the Pottawatomies [sic], it shall never be included within the jurisdiction of any State or Territory, unless an Indian Territory shall be organized."[50] Congress implemented the treaty in 1872 by authorizing a reservation in Indian Territory.

Shawnees had been in the general area of the new reservation since the 1830s, located on Choctaw and Seminole lands. These early comers were descendants of a people living in the upper Ohio Valley as late as the American Revolution. They were joined over the years by other small Shawnee bands, including one that the United States had removed from Texas in 1859. By 1890 the title Absentee Shawnee referred to over six hundred Indians living on the Potawatomi reservation that Congress had authorized in 1872. Now the Shawnees were divided into two very different bands. White Turkey headed a progressive element, many of whom had already taken allotments. Big Jim led the other band, whose members staunchly opposed allotment whether for themselves or for White Turkey's band.

The six hundred Citizen Band Potawatomis had their own ugly history of removal from the upper Mississippi Valley. Their presence in Indian Territory in 1890 stemmed not only from the United States' efforts to relieve Kansas of its Indians but also from the Potawatomi desire to escape government efforts to acculturate them. Members of the tribe in Kansas had been among the first Indians exposed to the alleged benefits of allotment in severalty. An 1861 treaty provided for Potawatomis to take allotments on their Kansas reservation as well as their per capita shares of any tribal monies in the U.S. Treasury. Such "competent persons" electing to go this route would then become American citizens.[51] From this group came the Indians later designated Citizen Potawatomis. Their agent in 1890 as well as his predecessor described them as mixed bloods, most with French connections, who spoke English, dressed in the style of whites, lived in log cabins, and in some instances were prosperous farmers.

Instructions to the commissioners lumped the Potawatomis and Shawnees with the Iowas and Kickapoos as Indians from whom they should acquire "whatever rights they may have" in their reservations. The commissioners had approached the Iowas as though they had only a limited title to their reservation, and they would treat with the Potawatomis and Shawnees in the same spirit. When they learned, early on, that the Potawatomis claimed to have purchased their reservation, the commissioners sought clarification from Washington. The question was whether the Indians were entitled to anything for the surplus land after they had received their allotments. The Indian Office continued to deny that the Potawatomis owned their reservation, but Secretary Noble later gave the commissioners latitude to negotiate "any fair and reasonable agreement" that protected the interests of the government.[52] In other words, if the Indians insisted, they were not to quibble but to get the land as quickly and cheaply as possible.

The negotiations extended over a week, but no journal has been found for the councils. Although the Potawatomis apparently had a Business Committee, the commissioners could detect no clearly defined governmental structure with which they could negotiate. A first attempt of two days' duration collapsed when the Indians charged that the council was unrepresentative. Six days later, on 24 June, another council was convened at which both the Potawatomis and the Shawnees were represented and the commissioners proposed terms for a settlement. The Indians insisted briefly on amendments that the commissioners refused, and both tribes then quickly capitulated.[53]

There were differences between them as to the areas where they should be allotted. The reservation was roughly divided by the eastward-flowing Little River, the northern half of the reservation containing most of the best land. Because they had been first on the scene, the Shawnees had tended to settle north of the river, as did a minority of the Potawatomis who had already been allotted under the Dawes Act before the arrival of the Cherokee Commission. Jerome and his colleagues took advantage of this to specify in the agreements that the remainder of the Potawatomis and all the Shawnees should be allotted under the Dawes Act rather than receiving the larger homesteads that the Sac and Fox had just been authorized.[54]

The Potawatomis had the advice of an attorney in their deliberations. This may explain the inclusion in the agreement of a statement that these Indians claimed to have purchased the reservation, giving them the option of suing for the $119,790.75 that they said they had originally paid for the land. In their report to the president, the commissioners protested the "ever present Attorney representing the Indians."[55] Given their insistence on buying land at cut-rate prices from Indians uniformly unwilling to sell, the commissioners' criticism of tribal attorneys appears patently self-serving.

Certainly, the commissioners were pleased to report that they had acquired about 325,000 acres at about sixty-nine cents per acre after enough land had been set aside for 1,400 allotments for the Potawatomis and 650 for the Shawnees. The number of allotments for the Potawatomis was inflated to allow for other members of that tribe then living in Kansas but whom the commissioner of Indian affairs insisted had rights in the reservation if they chose to exercise them. For their cessions the Potawatomis were paid $160,000 and the Shawnees $65,000, in both cases distributed per capita.[56] The Indians greatly preferred payment in that fashion to interest received from their money's being held in trust in the Treasury. Deferred gratification not being the Indians' long suit, the prospect of payment in cash as soon as the Congress could act was a factor in their acceptance of the government's terms. The Potawatomis accomplished that by action of their Business Committee, endorsed by the heads of seventy-five families. Chief White Turkey and five councillors signed for the Shawnees, and their agreement was also approved by a majority of the adults. Big Jim, chief of the conservative band, refused to sign.[57]

The House Committee on Indian Affairs, in reporting the bill to ratify the agreement, estimated that the government was paying only fifty-six cents per acre. As it would be selling the land to settlers at $1.25 per acre it should provide the United States a tidy profit—estimated by the committee at $275,000—because "every foot of the land will be occupied immediately upon the opening of the country to settlement."[58] Apparently the committee members had no ethical problem in ratifying such a deal.

In 1968, however, the Indian Claims Commission rendered a decision in a suit brought by the Potawatomis holding that the payment of $160,000 had been "unconscionable." Moreover, the court declared that these Indians had had an exclusive right to the income from the sale of the surplus land, which was actually worth $3 an acre in 1890. This resulted in an award to the Potawatomis of an additional $797,508.99 after deducting "allowable offsets, gratuities, and counterclaims."[59] The Absentee Shawnees were not happy with this decision, but not until 1999 did the Supreme Court finally conclude a 132-year contest between the two tribes by ruling that the Potawatomis indeed had sole proprietary rights in the old reservation.[60]

The commissioners had found negotiations with the Potawatomis and Shawnees vexing on occasion, and they were getting sensitive to criticism from Washington. After both the Sac and Fox and the Iowa negotiations they had been faulted, either by the commissioner of Indian affairs or the Indian Division of the secretary of the Interior's office, for not taking cognizance of the claims of members of those tribes resident in other states. In the closing days of their negotiations with the Shawnees and Potawatomis, Warren Sayre sent a telegram to the president. Speaking for the commission, he complained bitterly of the lack of support and the evil forces with which they had to contend:

> we find cunning, lurking but forceful opposition everywhere. The larger tribes advise smaller ones not to trade until they do. The cattle-men and their friends, lawyers and lobbyists . . . speculators . . . old Indian traders, post traders and adventurers, some hoping to gain somehow, many only intent on mischief, and more that want cultivated indolence continued, unite in opposing anything we do or attempt both here and at Washington . . . The Indians are informed that for want of appropriation the commission expires before June 30th and better chances will follow by law . . . We can buy for ten millions now what Congress will give twenty for in a year from now.[61]

In a follow-up letter, Sayre declared, "I don't like failure." The commissioners were coming to look upon the negotiations as a vital national mission and to impugn the motives of anyone who stood in their way. President Harrison responded and attempted to reassure them: I appreciate the difficulties that beset you in attempting to promote the interests of the government while so many conflicting personal interests are being pressed by those whom you come in contact with. You need not doubt that both [Noble] and myself are anxious to consummate these agreements, and that the Commission will have, in their work, our cordial and earnest support."[62]

The commissioners would get even more frustrated trying to reach an agreement with the Kickapoos, upon whom they descended 27 June. In October 1889 Lucius Fairchild and Judge Wilson had tried to establish a basis for later negotiations with these Indians. Now Chairman Jerome and his colleagues quickly discovered that even that modest objective had not been

TAKING INDIAN LANDS

achieved. The commissioners arrived at the Kickapoo village in the afternoon, but none of the Indians they saw that day would even talk to them. The following morning they sought out blind Chief Wabemashay, who promised to bring three of his headmen to confer with the white men that afternoon, but they never materialized. The local Indian agent and the officer commanding the commission's escort contacted other Indians and advised them to meet with Jerome and his colleagues. Possibly that contributed to a Kickapoo decision to counsel with the commissioners three days later.

The chief and a majority of the Kickapoo men did appear for that morning session. The commissioners delivered their usual opening speeches about the necessity that the Indians change their lifestyles with the assistance of the government and locate on individual homesteads. Jerome presented the chief a draft of an agreement closely modeled on the one concluded with the Iowas, because the two reservations had come into existence on almost identical terms. To the chagrin of the commissioners, Chief Wabemashay acted as if the document were contaminated and after a brief huddle with his headmen insisted upon returning it to Jerome. The Indians then asked for a recess; when they returned that afternoon, they made it clear that they would negotiate no further, fearing to distress the Great Spirit.[63]

The commissioners were incensed: "The Kickapoos are altogether the most ignorant and degraded Indians that we have met, but are possessed of an animal cunning, and obstinacy in a rare degree."[64] The white men were further upset to learn that the Kickapoos had sought advice and counsel from Chief Mayes of the Cherokees and blamed him for the Kickapoos' accusation that the commissioners were really speculators, trying to defraud the Indians. Jerome and his colleagues were so disturbed that they recommended that President Harrison persuade Congress to amend the Dawes Act to shorten the time period for presidential ordered allotment, as the precribed four-year period was to the Indians "almost an eternity" and encouraged procrastination.[65] The threat of invoking the Dawes Act with a much shorter time span for enactment would, the commissioners believed, get the Indians' attention and make them more amenable. As it was, the commission would not have its way with the Kickapoos until they returned for a third confrontation in June 1891.

Under the leadership of David Jerome the Cherokee Commission, in less than two months, had negotiated agreements with the Iowas, the Sac and Fox, the Citizen Band of Potawatomis, and the Absentee Shawnees. Although they had failed with the Kickapoos, they had extracted nearly a million acres from the other three groups. Now the commissioners faced dealing with larger and more intractable Plains tribes, and they were not looking forward to the experience.

4

The Cheyennes and Arapahos
Brought to Terms

WHEN HE SUBMITTED HIS REPORT on the Kickapoo negotiations, Chairman
Jerome requested a break for the commission before taking on the
Cheyennes and Arapahos, citing the heat and unsanitary conditions of a
summer on the plains. Secretary Noble agreed, but only if it were taken after
they had closed with the two Plains tribes.[1] Thus the commissioners found
themselves involved in protracted and difficult negotiations that began in
early July 1890 with a three-week stint and, after a lull, were resumed and
finally completed in October. The deliberations were recorded in journals
totaling 127 pages.

This was the commission's first experience with Plains Indians. Dealing
with the Cherokee Nation and the tiny Iowa band, two extremes in eastern
Oklahoma, did not prepare them for what they now encountered. Although
both the Cheyennes and the Arapahos came under the rubric Plains tribes,
there were significant differences of size and acculturation between them.[2]
The Cheyennes had double the population, 2,272 to the Arapahos' 1,100, as
well as a formidable military reputation, while the smaller tribe was necessarily more accommodating. Together they occupied a reservation of over
4,000,000 acres, mostly grass-covered uplands suitable only for grazing. The
residue was bottomlands along streams, where the soil could support agriculture—weather permitting. Droughts were common, and no rain in May
and June 1890, had blighted the corn and reduced the potential of other crops.[3]

Earlier there had been thousands of cattle on the reservation, although
very few had been owned by the Indians. Trying to put the millions of acres
of grass to a use that would reduce the Indian dependence on government

rations, late in 1882 Agent John D. Miles persuaded the two tribes to lease almost 2,500,000 acres to cattlemen. The income was distributed to all members of the tribe in ten-dollar payments. When the first payment was made, however, some Cheyenne bands refused to accept theirs, and it quickly became apparent that a majority of the Indians opposed the leases. Responding to their complaints and those of white farmers and small ranchers who argued that the big cattlemen enjoyed an unfair advantage, in 1885 President Grover Cleveland ordered the leaseholders off the reservation. Along the way Agent Miles resigned, and his successor soon learned that the Cheyennes were not amenable to regimentation and the Arapahos only relatively so.

Each tribe consisted of several bands headed by chiefs who might or might not accept a course of action proposed in a tribal council. Not that tribal councils occurred often—and when they did, it was difficult to develop the consensus required for action. Before taking up residence on the reservation each band had operated relatively independently on the great expanse of the plains, which was the most practical way to hunt and to find adequate pasture for their large horse herds. It would not be until all bands were forcibly confined to the reservation that, by white standards, true tribal government began to emerge. Washington encouraged this, because it needed a structure through which it could control the Indians. Tribal government was furthered by Washington's favoring cooperative band chiefs in the distribution of annuities and rations and its creation of Indian police forces, which by 1890 had appeared on most reservations.

The Cheyennes and Arapahos generally differed in their reaction to government programs designed to convert them into educated, Christian homesteaders. The Arapahos were more inclined to cooperate, their traditional leaders seeking to accommodate to government wishes while preserving time-honored Arapaho social and political practices. It was a delicate balancing act that led some Arapahos to charge that their chiefs had sold out, but given the relative strengths of the parties, the Arapaho strategy had much to recommend it.

While most Arapaho chiefs were trying to open farms and in other ways take their first steps along the "white man's road," their Cheyenne counterparts for the most part refused accommodation as a policy. Compared with the Arapahos, a high percentage of Cheyennes had participated in the Red River War of 1874–75, the South Plains tribes' last resort to combat to try to preserve their way of life. Once located on a reservation and denied any alternative to that life by the virtual extermination of the buffalo, the Cheyennes still resisted the government's "civilization" programs. As late as 1890 adult males retained firearms and were not intimidated by the agent's small and poorly armed Indian police force. The Dog Soldiers, young and aggressive warriors under the direction of militant chiefs, destroyed the property and threatened the persons of Cheyennes who attempted to open farms and send their children to school.

In August 1890 Agent Charles F. Ashley described his charges as "tenacious in holding to their barbarous customs and vicious habits."[4] Ashley also expressed concern about the impact on the Cheyennes and Arapahos of Wovoka, the newly risen messiah in the Northwest. This "second Christ" was promising his followers that all whites would be removed and the buffalo and other game restored, all without the Indians themselves having to resort to force. They were, however, expected to conduct certain ceremonies, and that had produced a flurry of activity that almost brought to a halt what little efforts were being made to raise crops and tend livestock on the reservation. The messiah movement certainly did not put the Indians in a mood to accept the proposals of the Cherokee Commission.

The commissioners already anticipated problems because of Indian views regarding their title to reservations to which they had been assigned. As early as the 1851 Treaty of Fort Laramie, the United States recognized the Cheyenne and Arapaho claim to about fifty million acres between the North Platte and Arkansas Rivers. Only ten years later by the Treaty of Fort Wise, made under pressure from white miners and settlers, the two tribes ceded those claims in return for a smaller reservation in southeastern Colorado. The treaty even provided for them to take allotments in severalty, although that article proved irrelevant when no Cheyennes or Arapahos took up residence there. Then in 1865, by the Treaty of the Little Arkansas, they surrendered that reservation; in return they were located on some 8,600,000 acres farther east and straddling the 37th parallel, the southern boundary of Kansas. This treaty had no blanket provisions for allotment, and the Cheyennes and Arapahos were authorized to "range at pleasure" between the "unsettled portions" between the Arkansas and North Platte Rivers. However, the Senate amended the treaty to require the removal of the Indians from Kansas "as soon as practicable."[5]

Only two years later, at the Treaty of Medicine Lodge, that portion of the reservation in Kansas was lopped off and the Indians were restricted to

5,024,896 acres south of 37° latitude in the Cherokee Outlet.[6] This was some-what meaningless, as the Cheyennes and Arapahos had settled on neither part of the Little Arkansas reservation. Those few who were willing to try to settle down, however, expressed a strong preference for land farther south that the United States had acquired from the Five Civilized Tribes in the post–Civil War treaties. Advised that this area was indeed better suited for Indian homesteads, President Ulysses S. Grant, by executive proclamation on 10 August 1869, set aside the 4,297,771 acres that became the reservation for which the Cherokee Commission would bargain two decades later.[7]

For no apparent reason except possibly convenience, by 1890 the Interior Department was expressing some doubt about the quality of titles granted by executive proclamation, suggesting that perhaps they conveyed only a right to occupancy as opposed to title in fee simple. At the other extreme, some Indians were claiming that they retained residual rights in previous cessions, particularly in the reservation in the Outlet. That would become apparent when negotiations got underway with the Cheyennes and Arapahos.

The commissioners first met the Indians in council at Darlington, the site of the agency headquarters, on 5 July 1890. The Cheyennes present were led by chiefs Whirlwind, Old Crow, and Little Medicine; all were opposed to ceding any land and were also angry over a contract with attorneys negotiated by other chiefs. This preliminary meeting, arranged to ensure the presence of these disaffected chiefs at the formal opening of negotiations on 7 July, was accomplished with the assistance of Colonel James F. Wade, commandant of Fort Reno near the agency and a man the Indians admired and trusted. Jerome and his colleagues, however, had gotten a preview of the intensity of the opposition they would encounter.[8]

This led Jerome to query Secretary Noble about the provision of the Treaty of Medicine Lodge requiring three-fourths of adult males to validate any cession. Noble's response helps explain the reluctance of the commissioners to make concessions to the Indians. The secretary directed Jerome to get the signatures of three-fourths if possible, "but close with a majority if you cannot get more." Noble reminded Jerome that the Cherokees would claim title to the entire Outlet in which the reservation designated at Medicine Lodge lay, and that the commissioners should not commit the government to paying twice for the same tract. Moreover, the Tonkawas were being paid only thirty cents an acre. "Be careful not to give too much,"

TAKING INDIAN LANDS

warned Noble, going on to argue that the Cheyennes and Arapahos could not claim both the Outlet reservation and the one created by executive order in 1879. Moreover, he declared, the Indians had "only [an] equitable claim" to the 1879 reservation, because it had been created not by treaty but by presidential proclamation; therefore, allotments should be a "large consideration" in settling that claim. The secretary concluded: "But all is submitted to your immediate and just consideration."[9] Despite this caveat, it is little wonder that Jerome clung to his hardline bargaining posture after that communication from Noble.

On Monday, 7 July, the commission met with nearly four hundred Cheyennes and Arapahos. Chairman Jerome and Warren Sayre introduced themselves and their mission to the Indians assembled by Agent Ashley. Jerome had only been in office a year, but in that brief time he had managed to alienate the Indians by his unremitting efforts to carry out Washington's edicts to push the tribal peoples along the white man's road. And, like the Cherokee Commission, he had come along at a time when teachings of the new messiah had further inspired the Indians to resist change.

Jerome opened the council with his standard pitch, telling the Indians that the time had come when they would have to begin supporting themselves by farming and stock breeding. Very quickly he acknowledged, without mentioning the messiah, that there were those among them who hoped for the return of the buffalo. But, Jerome insisted, "the buffalo will never come back . . . and the Indian must live by growing something out of the ground or else he will starve." He also warned them that their annuities under the Medicine Lodge treaty would lapse in seven years. In the first few minutes of his presentation Jerome raised the specter of the Dawes Act: "If you don't do what the President wants you to do, the law of Congress will be put in force . . . you won't have anyone to come and see you as this Commission has done." The president, Jerome continued, "hopes you will do what is better for you than would be done if you wait till force is used."[10]

Then it was time for Warren Sayre, the other member of the tag team, to enter the ring, Judge Wilson having been reduced by this time to a minor role. Sayre reiterated some of Jerome's points and was particularly graphic when describing the pressure of white settlers. He declared that were it not for Colonel Wade and his troops at Fort Reno, "they would trample all over your reservation in a day."[11] Members of Congress, according to Sayre, were elected by white men, not Indians, and already had produced a law (the

Dawes Act) that required Indians to take allotments if the president so mandated.

The only Indians to respond that day—and those briefly—were Cheyennes Old Crow and Whirlwind and Arapahos Left Hand, Tall Bear, Elk Tongue, and Cloud Chief. Opening for the Indians was Old Crow, who was aligned with the opponents of allotment and sale of the surplus. "The Great Spirit," he stated, "gave the Indians all this land and never tell them that they should sell it." And he challenged the commissioners to swear that they had received word to the contrary from the Great Spirit. To loud applause, Old Crow directed the commissioners to "Take the Agent and George Bent when you go and leave Col. Wade."[12] George Bent was a well-known son of fur trader William Bent and a Cheyenne woman. He had served for many years as an agency interpreter, and some Indians charged him with being in the pay of ranchers with cattle on the reservation and receiving illegal payoffs from the agent as well.

After a few other remarks by Old Crow, Whirlwind—a band chief not usually associated with the most militant chiefs—supported Old Crow: "These people all know their minds and . . . what already said is the way we feel." Whirlwind did take the opportunity to respond to a patronizing remark Sayre had made, that "I come to speak to great big stout men and not to children." Whirlwind's rejoinder was, "I am no child, I am pretty good age, you can look around and see all the Head-men and see that they ought to know their own minds."[13] He told the commissioners unequivocally that the Indians did not want to sell their land and the president should be told so. Jerome's reply to that was blunt: "Tell him that the Pottawatomies [sic] thought just like he does but the President ordered them to." Whirlwind fired back, "That is all cut it off," ending Cheyenne participation for the day.[14]

The four Arapaho speakers had very little to say, although both Left Hand and Cloud Chief expressed their willingness to consider the commissioners' message. Tall Bear, the agency chief of police, favored postponing negotiations for seven years until their annuities under the Treaty of Medicine Lodge had expired. Elk Tongue seconded that approach. No other Indians rose to speak, and the meeting was adjourned. The commission was not off to a good start. Jerome telegraphed Secretary Noble that "they are stiff necked but we hope for the best."[15]

When the negotiations resumed Tuesday, it quickly became apparent that an attorney for the Indians, John D. Miles, was present. The former agent for the Cheyennes and Arapahos, he had turned down an opportunity to be a commissioner, perhaps believing that being a tribal attorney would be more lucrative. Despite his presence, Cloud Chief and Left Hand expressed their unwillingness to respond to the commission's offer until the arrival of another attorney, M. J. Reynolds. He and Miles, together with former governor of Kansas Samuel J. Crawford and another ex-agent, D. B. Dwyer, had combined to represent the Cheyennes and Arapahos in their dealings with the government. A first contract, signed 23 May 1889, had been limited to the Indians' interest in the Medicine Lodge Treaty reservation, but a second, signed 20 August 1889, included the executive-order reservation.[16]

Although the contracts purportedly had been negotiated by chiefs and head men representing the entire reservation population, they actually had been negotiated with a few from the third of the reservation's population that was centered around the agency. This one-third was also the most amenable to persuasion by government officials. Both contracts were signed by the same eight Cheyennes and four Arapahos, including Cheyennes Little Chief, Cut Nose, Wolf Face, Little Bear, Starving Elk, Wolf Robe, Cloud Chief, and Leonard Tyler (educated at Carlisle) and Arapahos Left Hand, White Eyed Antelope, Row of Lodges, and Heap of Bears.

In a covering statement for the first contract, the judge who certified it stated that the Indian signers had been "duly appointed at a National Council of the Cheyenne and Arapaho Tribes." That was not the case; the twelve had been selected by Agent Ashley, who—to put the best possible face on it—had been convinced by the attorneys that they could secure compensation for the tribes for any claims they might have in the Outlet reservation.

At the next meeting on Wednesday, Warren Sayre played his customary role, spelling out the details of the government's proposal. For the first time the Indians learned that the commissioners wanted them to give up their claims to the reservation in the Outlet, take allotments on their present reservation, and sell the surplus acreage, estimated to be about 3,000,000 acres. They also became aware that their allotments could not be taken in some areas of the reservation. These included a military reservation of at least 11,000 acres, two sections in every township for schools, plus other land to be set aside for missionary farms and churches. Most disturbing was the news that an entire township of 23,040 acres would be reserved for the agency and that township included the farms of some of the most progressive Indians on the reservation. They would now have to relocate and begin over, generally on less desirable land.

As compensation, the Indians would receive $1,500,000, of which one-third would provide two per capita payments totaling about $145. The remaining $1,000,000 would be held in the U.S. Treasury and would draw 4 percent interest that would be paid out annually on a per capita basis. Sayre completed his presentation with the observation—one used earlier on other tribes—that with this financial settlement, "I can truly say that you will be the richest people on earth: no entire white people on earth will have the home and money that the Cheyenne and Arapaho people will have."[17]

Old Crow was the first Indian to respond, and he vehemently rejected the offer: "As I told you last Saturday . . . I tell you again that we don't propose to give up this land and have it cut into farms." Moreover, he stated that Indians accepting the offer would be punished. Old Crow concluded, "I speak for the Cheyenne Tribe, and that is the sentiment of all."[18]

Jerome immediately responded, citing the president's authority under the Dawes Act to impose allotment and reminding the Indians that the commission's offer was more generous than the law provided. Nor did he ignore the threat against collaborators, warning, "let any Indian try to punish any other Indian for doing what he wants to and the Government will surely punish him."[19]

Old Crow was not impressed: "Now I am going to speak my mind to you if I am killed for it. I have a feeling that God gave me as an Indian and I have not got your ways even if I should be stabbed in the heart. We have been robbed of our land and the worth of our land ever since the white man came into the Country and they ought to be full of it."[20] Other Cheyennes pitched in to support Old Crow. In a typical statement, Spotted Horse declared: "What Old Crow has said are my feelings too and the feelings of all the rest."[21] He also invoked General Philip Sheridan's advice, given during the leasing controversy a few years earlier. As the Indians remembered it, the general had assured them that the reservation was theirs and they should not permit cattlemen and their herds on it. Little Medicine questioned the value to the Indians of cash payments, citing the experience of fellow Cheyenne Wolf Face, who was paid $136 by a railroad that crossed his farm, only to spend it in a few days. Wolf Face himself observed, as many others would in the coming days, that they were still due seven annuity payments from the Medicine Lodge Treaty: "Now you want to spring another treaty on us before the time is up that that one held good for."[22]

At this point Judge Wilson entered the fray—something he was doing less of under Chairman Jerome. He reminded the Indians that the buffalo were long gone and that other game was scarce. Therefore, they should each "get a big piece of land and raise corn and beans and when you get that done I will come and take dinner with you."[23] When that day came, Uncle Alf assured them, they would no longer need their agent, about whom they had been complaining, and could get rid of them all. But encouraged by reports of the messiah, these Indians were doing the Ghost Dance, dancing for the day when they could return to the plains and move freely over that great expanse, as liberated as people had ever been.

Under the circumstances Judge Wilson had little impact on the Cheyennes. Good Bear, Tall Bear, Mad Wolf, and Howling Wolf rose in succession to reaffirm their attachment to their land and their unwillingness to accept the terms offered them. Following that, Jerome closed the meeting and asked that those who had not yet talked make their views known at the next council session. He certainly had had his fill of Old Crow and his supporters.

When they reconvened Thursday, however, Old Crow took the floor and denounced former agent Miles, currently one of their attorneys, as having been "in every deal that was against the Indian, and every scheme that helped the white man." The Cheyenne further declared: "The land is money to us and that is all the kind of money that we want . . . the land and the streams . . . that run through it is all the wealth that I want. I don't expect to see the day that this land wouldn't be my own and when I die I expect to be buried in it."[24]

With some asperity Jerome commented that they had heard from Old Crow on Monday, Tuesday, and Wednesday and now wanted to hear from others. Cloud Chief, who had been to Washington with a delegation and was trying to farm, was the first Cheyenne to break ranks and say something that the commissioners wanted to hear. He dismissed Little Medicine's claim earlier in council that another Cheyenne, Cut Nose, had been "struck dead" for aiding the attorneys in their schemes. Cloud Chief insisted that it had been a natural death and strongly disapproved of "the kind of talk that these people have made."[25] He urged that others go to work as he had.

After a few Arapahos spoke briefly, committing themselves to nothing while voicing some criticism of the Cheyennes for having dominated the proceedings, Sitting Bull, also Arapaho, finally made the day worthwhile for the commissioners: "If these other Indians are willing to take allotments and sell the surplus I will too."[26] But the Cheyennes held firm. Man in the Clouds observed that the commission had previously dealt with tribes to the east who were experienced farmers and he preferred postponing any cession for the seven years until the Medicine Lodge Treaty expired. His fellow Cheyenne, Red Wolf, was the last speaker; he reaffirmed that "the Cheyennes only have one mind on the subject. . . . we were given this land to keep and have seven years more on this treaty."[27]

When the deliberations resumed on Friday, it was obvious that the Arapahos had reached a consensus. Left Hand opened for them, announcing that he was ready to sell, but only if they got $1.45 an acre and 160-acre allotments for everyone.[28] The Cheyenne Cloud Chief endorsed that, as did seventeen Arapahos in succession, beginning with Row of Lodges and White Eyed Antelope. Three other Cheyennes, Starving Elk, Little Chief, and Wolf Robe, also indicated a willingness to settle. All of these Indians were from the Darlington area, the home of the most progressive tribesmen. The commissioners had so far declined to state a price per acre that the government was prepared to pay, but the Arapahos had done some calculating and concluded that it was only about thirty-three cents. Paul Boynton, Carlisle educated and the son of a Cheyenne mother and Arapaho chief White Eyed Antelope, proposed that the United States pay 6, not 4 percent on the tribal funds to be held in the Treasury.[29]

The commissioners must have been delighted that at least the Arapahos and a few Cheyennes had finally agreed to sell, although they were quibbling about the price. But Jerome was warned that the Cheyennes were about to abort the negotiations by pleading hunger and heading back to their camps. He promptly wired Secretary Noble, requesting that Agent Ashley be directed to issue more rations to keep the Indians talking. "Chances for agreement are fair and seem to be getting better," he reported. Noble promptly ordered Ashley to comply with Jerome's request.[30]

At the session the on 12 July Jerome reviewed the government's position and made one concession—the Indians could each get allotments of 160 acres, although only 80 acres could be farmland. He also tried to rationalize the commission's demands by referring to the white people "increasing like the leaves on the trees" and "causing the President and Congress trouble," while he and his colleagues were trying "to fix the Indians so that this great mass of white people cannot be crushing them down."[31]

To justify the commission's low offer for the surplus land, Jerome argued that the government had already had to quiet the title to the area the Cheyennes and Arapahos were selling—and indeed, the Choctaws and Chickasaws had been paid something and would get more, although the commissioners could not have predicted the final settlement. Jerome did note that the government had supplied the Cheyennes and Arapahos with rations worth $2,500,000 that were not specified in the Treaty of Medicine Lodge and said that if the Indians continued to draw rations for another seven years, it would cost an additional $1,000,000.[32]

Warren Sayre tried to impress the Indians by converting the offer of $1,500,000 for their land into silver dollars. He said that that would be like each Indian's getting four hats full, so much that he would have to put it in his saddlebags to get it home. He probably further confused the Indians by spelling out what had already been paid other tribes for the reservation, including thirty cents an acre for the Creek portion and fifteen cents for the Seminole segment. He also specified other government gratuities, including education at Carlisle and Haskell for about one hundred Cheyennes and Arapahos. Jerome then closed the session, telling the Indians that this was the last government offer and that they should return with a response.

Jerome had announced in council that Warren Sayre would be leaving soon to attend a family wedding. Actually, he would be absent about two weeks and would be participating actively in the Indiana political campaign. That would earn him a Democrat newspaper's partisan evaluation as "hardened . . . in political chicanery," something that would not have come as a surprise to Cheyennes and Arapahos.[33]

When the council reconvened on 14 July only Cheyennes spoke, but there were fifteen of them. It was obvious that they had conferred as Jerome had suggested, although he could not have liked the result. The point most frequently made by the Indians was that they had already lost too much land to the whites and would not consent to selling more. General Sheridan's advice that they hold on to their reservation was cited frequently, and they alluded favorably to Colonel Wade while denouncing the incumbent agent and his predecessors.

The commissioners were relatively quiet, although they did remind the Indians that the government had no treaty obligation to issue them rations and there was no guarantee that they would be continued for the remaining seven years of the Treaty of Medicine Lodge. To that Young White Bull responded, "the Government has put this agency here for the purpose of feeding these Indians. . . . we have already counciled [sic] among ourselves and know our own minds and are not going to give up or sell any part of this land."[34] The commissioners were obviously getting nowhere, and Jerome closed the session with an invitation to the Arapahos: "we want to hear talk from you."[35]

With the great majority of the Cheyennes boycotting the meeting 15 July, it was the Arapahos' opportunity to talk. Before any of them got the floor, however, Warren Sayre reviewed the government's offer in detail. Left Hand opened for the Arapahos, announcing that they would continue to press for $1.45 an acre, and Cloud Chief and Starving Elk, accommodationist Cheyennes, endorsed his demand. Jerome reminded them that the commission had conceded to their request for 160 acres for each Indian but $1.45 per acre was more than the government was paying any Indians, and it would be unfair to make an exception for the Cheyennes and Arapahos.

Before the session ended, six more Arapahos insisted on $1.45 per acre. Jerome then revealed his impatience with the pace of the negotiations, observing that for six or seven days they had been telling the Indians that the president and the secretary of the Interior had restricted them in what they could offer, but the Indians kept going back to the issue. Sayre was more threatening, reminding them that the commission was offering a couple and their three children a total of 800 acres, whereas under the Dawes Act they would receive only 280. "Now that would happen," he declared, "if the president would make the order which he can make any day he pleases." Moreover, "if the president would order you to take these allotments there is no provision to pay you any money whatever, if you could not induce Congress, where you can not go . . . it might be years before Congress would give the Indians a single dollar."[36] Unfortunately for the Indians, this was not an impossible scenario. Jerome ended the session by asking them to confer on the commisson's offer and to, "come back in the morning and make the contract and we will sign it."[37]

When the meeting got underway Wednesday, 16 July, it did not look promising for the commissioners. In rapid succession fifteen Arapahos rose and demanded $1.45 per acre. Only Cleaver Warden, who had been at Carlisle for five years, indicated a willingness to accept $1.25, but that was still far more than the government was offering. David Jerome spoke at great length, and it all amounted to a refusal to sweeten the government's offer. If the Indians refused to sell at that price, he threatened them with a loss of rations and the government's imposition of a settlement. "They have the power to make you do it and say what price it will be,"[38] Jerome said, because the Cheyennes and Arapahos had only a right of occupancy and not a full title to the reservation. Nevertheless, most of the Indians continued to hold out for $1.45, with only a few young men joining Cleaver Warden at the $1.25 figure.

The next day's council was very brief. Left Hand again spoke for the Arapahos, agreeing to a deal for $2,000,000, with the money held for them in the Treasury drawing not 4 but 5 percent. Cloud Chief, the maverick Cheyenne, joined him in those demands, but Jerome simply shut the meeting down with a pessimistic, "You must not expect us to raise the amount of money, but if we can do any other little thing that will be for your benefit we will tell you tomorrow morning."[39]

The chairman then wired Secretary Noble the terms of the commission's offer and the Indian response. He added that he thought a deal was possible if he was authorized to pay the attorney's fees for the Indians or to do something similar that would not cost the government much.[40] Noble, however, was inflexible. He described their offer as "most liberal," directed them to offer no more, and concluded with a message for the Cheyennes and Arapahos: "The Indians will lose more than they will gain if you report to the Great Father that they want too much."[41]

Although there were sessions on 19 and 21 July, Noble's telegram had effectively brought negotiations to a halt. Judge Wilson had returned to Arkansas because of illness in his family, but Jerome and Sayre showed up for the last two meetings. Indeed, Jerome offered to raise the interest rate on the $1,000,000 to be held in the Treasury to 5 percent, which would cost the government only $10,000 more a year. The Indians ignored that offer, and Left Hand even insisted that the Indians receive the two cash payments totaling $500,000 with no strings attached, as opposed to a second payment of $250,000 requiring the agent's approval for expenditures. The chairman responded irritably that the Indians would only "spend it foolishly at the stores" and "for whiskey and gambling."[42] That was not well received. Sitting Bull, an Arapaho, spoke for many when he maintained: "All these men that are working for the Government they get paid in cash and when pay-day comes they get cash and see their money and . . . we want to see the money."[43]

The final session of this bargaining period was Monday, 21 July. Within minutes it was obvious that the Indians would again be insisting on at least $1.25 an acre and a cash payment that they could spend as they wished. It was equally clear that David Jerome and Warren Sayre would not meet the Indians' demands. White Bear, an Arapaho, had just expressed the wish that the Great Father be informed that they wanted the $1.25 and that this was the last day they would bargain, when a group of Arapaho army scouts departed in a body.[44] Those Arapahos who remained, along with Cloud Chief, the Cheyenne, sparred briefly with the commissioners, repeating their position. Cloud Chief had the last word—simply that he had no new propo-sition to make. Neither, of course, did the commissioners—after a few more exchanges the fourteen days of deliberation ended with David Jerome's recessing the negotiations. The commissioners had made two modifications in their original offer, both responding to Indian requests. One was to per-mit all Indians to have 160 acres of land, although only 80 acres of that could be tillable. The other was to increase the interest the government would pay on their money in the Treasury from 4 to 5 percent.

The absence of any process by which a chief or chiefs could commit all members of either tribe to a course of action had protracted the negotia-tions. However, it was clear that both Cheyennes and Arapahos had delib-erated privately and had arrived at some positions that they held spiritedly. The Arapahos were probably more united, although on the last day, when the Arapaho scouts suddenly quit the meeting, Left Hand had been shocked and dismayed. "I have been chief among my people and have always been looked upon as chief," he complained, "and this is the first time that they have ever surprised me by turning away from me."[45] It should not have come as a surprise; these Indians were only a decade and a half from the time when they had roamed the plains at will, and the Cherokee Commission had arrived just as they were basking in the messiah's prediction that they were on the verge of becoming free again.

Faced with the fact that the majority of the Cheyennes had begun to boycott the councils, Jerome hastened to communicate the situation to the president by a report to be forwarded by Secretary Noble. The chairman stressed the Indians' insistence on getting the initial $500,000 in cash and justified the commission's refusal on the presumed inability of the Indians to handle that much money. At the very hour that they were demanding $500,000 in cash, to be used as they pleased, he said, hundreds of wagons under the care of the squaws were at the agency nearby getting the rations upon which all were to live during the ensuing week. Five hundred thousand dollars given to such people in money, Jerome said, would be worse than thrown away. He also touched on other impedimenta, including "evil advice from some of the whites who were in attendance daily, and who would have but little trouble in relieving the Indians of the money promptly." He also cited the hopes aroused "by recent reports from Dakota, that the Indian Christ was there and would soon visit the reservation, remove the whites, restore the buffalo and reinstate the Indians in the undisputed control of the country."

The commissioner concluded that a final "formidable obstacle" was the tribes' contract with attorneys, as most of the Indians were opposed to any compensation for them. Jerome stated that the commission had asked attorney John Miles to use his influence to further the negotiations; although he "claimed to exercise a potent power over them," however, there was no evidence that he did. Jerome protested to the president that the commission "can see no good resulting from the Indians having attorneys who are given a prominent standing by having their contracts approved by the Interior Department."[46]

In his covering letter to Secretary Noble, Jerome was even more emphatic about the "baleful" effects of such contracts. He described them, incredibly, as originating "in the false idea that the Commission will probably take some advantage of the Indians." He then warned Noble that none of the Indians would sign if they knew that the attorney fees would come out of their second cash payment. Jerome concluded by informing the secretary that the commissioners would retire to their homes during the "heated term unless otherwise ordered."[47] The chairman had been remarkably blunt considering that he was discussing a contract that involved a former partner of Noble, a contract that the secretary had personally approved.

On his return to his home in Saginaw to await Secretary Noble's reply, Jerome granted an interview to a local reporter. The newsman described him as tanned and about twenty pounds lighter as a result of his work in the Southwest. Jerome recapitulated the commission's work, briefly touching on the negotiations with each tribe. First, however, he dismissed the work of the commission under Lucius Fairchild as achieving "nothing more than visiting the tribes they desired to negotiate with." Jerome singled out the Kickapoos as "pure savages. . . . turbulent and hostile" to any change in their mode of holding land. The Potawatomis he dubbed the most civilized, and he described the Sac and Fox as having the strongest leader in Moses Keokuk. And he praised the wife of Tohee, the blind Iowa chief, as "a very smart woman" who knew English well enough to act as her husband's interpreter.

After "seven weeks of tent life with all the inconvenience and discomforts of bad weather, millions of insects, and intensely hot weather," Jerome told the reporter, the commissioners had found respite in Oklahoma City before proceeding to the Cheyennes and Arapahos, whom he termed "purely savage with few exceptions." The chairman described how he had met Old Crow's threat to quirt any Indians and destroy their tepees and kill their horses if they agreed to the government's terms, with a promise that the president would "give him ten stripes for every one he put on a warrior." The reporter concluded that Jerome was happy to be home after his labors among the Indians, "whose lands we have always coveted and probably always will."[48] Congress confirmed this by appropriating $20,000—but not the $25,000 the president had requested—to permit the commission to continue its work.[49]

While he was in Saginaw, Jerome asked Noble if it would be possible for the commissioners to meet with him and even with the president during the lull between negotiations. He argued that "questions to be discussed are of a nature not practicable to be presented in writing in a very satisfactory manner."[50] Noble did consent to meet with Jerome and Sayre at his vacation residence in upstate New York, while Wilson chose not to attend.

Jerome and Sayre raised three major issues at the meeting. First, they urged Noble to persuade the president not to permit any outside cattle to graze on reservations, because deriving income from the leases would strengthen the resolve of Indians opposing allotment and cessions. Second, they proposed that the Dawes Act be amended to permit the president to require that Indians take their allotments within a specified period of time, in order to deny opponents an opportunity to stall the process. And third, the commissioners pled that if attorneys were stiffening Indian resistance to negotiation, their contracts should be "summarily cancelled," because the government knew the best interests of the Indians and would not take advantage of them.[51]

Immediately following the conference with the secretary, Jerome and Sayre wrote him that Cheyennes Whirlwind, Old Crow, Little Medicine, Howling Wolf, and Little Big Jake "utterly repudiate the attorney's contract. . . . represent a majority of both tribes . . . and they and their followers refuse even to enter upon negotiations while that contract is in existence."[52] Nevertheless, Secretary Noble did not move to void the contract that he had approved. Obviously, adding M. J. Reynolds, his old law firm associate, to their team would appear to have been a very strategic move by John Miles and Governor Crawford. Noble did tell Reynolds that he was "much embarrassed by any personal consideration for you." He also informed him that Jerome found the contract a major obstacle to negotiations and, moreover, believed that even though the attorneys had agreed to the commission's terms, they had done nothing to persuade the Indians to accept them.[53]

All of this did not prevent the secretary from devising a plan by which the attorneys would be paid, but less. Noble cancelled the 10 percent fee the contract had called for and replaced it with a scale that the commissioners could employ to determine a lesser fee. The attorneys met with Noble on 29 September and agreed to the arrangement, which included their earning their fee only in connection with the 1867 reservation in the Outlet.[54]

When negotiations resumed in October there were six sessions, opening the 7th and concluding the 27th. The first meeting was brief and few Cheyennes appeared. For that reason Arapaho chief Left Hand refused to continue the deliberations after Chairman Jerome made his opening statement. The second session, the 9th, was still principally made up of Arapahos, with only a few Cheyennes like Cloud Chief in attendance. Warren Sayre again had the responsibility of explaining the government's terms. Ignoring the Indian demands for more money and even the existence of the Cheyenne majority, which refused to sell on any terms, he opened by stating: "when we ended our talk there was no difference between this Commission and the Indians except that the Indians wanted a certain portion of this money paid into their hands to be disposed of as they saw fit."[55] Sayre then announced that the government was ready to compromise and split the initial $500,000 payment into two parts, with the Indians receiving about $75 at each and only the second requiring approval of the agent for expenditure. After this explanation Jerome proposed that the council be adjourned until the following day. Only Left Hand and Cloud Chief responded, both promising that the Indians would confer on the revised offer.

At the 10 October meeting the Cheyennes opposed to selling were led by their spokesmen Old Crow and Little Medicine. Old Crow still insisted that they would not sell until the Treaty of Medicine Lodge ration provisions, which he continued to believe existed, had lapsed. He declared that the commissioners, by returning after they were told in July that the tribes would not sell, "are trying to confuse some Indians and make them do what they didn't want to do before."[56]

Jerome's response was to state once again that the Indians were deceiving themselves if they thought that the treaty required the government to feed them for another seven years. Judge Wilson was more emphatic, declaring that without rations the Indians would starve before Christmas. Little Medicine, however, was not intimidated: "The Great Spirit knows what you are saying and we don't propose to give up this land and chop it up and take farms for the Indians in this reservation till the 7 years are up."[57] When Jerome urged them to read the treaty themselves, Little Medicine retorted that they had their own views of the treaty and that the book could be wrong.

Other Cheyennes and Arapahos then chimed in, echoing these protests and adding a few of their own. Spotted Horse, a Cheyenne, invoked General Sheridan's assurance that the Indians could hold on to the reservation. An Arapaho, Tall Bear, insisted that "we love our land and do not want to sell even a little bit of it."[58] After seven more Cheyennes expressed their opposition to a sale in any form, Jerome adjourned the meeting.

When they reconvened Saturday, 11 October, and again on the 13th, the Indians present were Arapahos and a few Cheyennes amenable to allotment and the sale of their surplus land. Chairman Jerome promised that the government would protect those who accepted the commission's offer and punish any who tried to intimidate those who did. Sayre tried to make the offer more appealing by informing the Indians that they could rent family allotments. Trying to undercut the opposition, he was blunt: "You can't hunt any more for there is no game to kill, you can't go to war any more because the white men are too strong . . . the Government can't feed you forever and you must get some way to make a living."[59] The fact that the Cheyennes and Arapahos could garden and raise enough cattle to support themselves on an undiminished reservation was not an option the government entertained— or could have, given the demands of its white constituents.

Faced with the adamant stand of the commissioners, the Arapahos began to cave, quibbling only about the nature and timing of the payment.

White Buffalo still wanted his per capita share of the $500,000 in cash: "then I can go with money in my pocket to the white man's place and get my dinner."[60] Bear Feathers and Black Wolf specified that the first payment must take place within two months of Congress's accepting the agreement, and Medicine Dismounted said that he would not sign "unless I see the money piled up in front of me."[61]

Chief Left Hand indicated that he still had questions about what they would actually be selling, and Jerome tried to respond. He stated that the tribes were being asked to sell any rights they might have in both the reservation in the Outlet and the one they were currently occupying. Following that, Left Hand and the commissioners had a lengthy dialogue about other features of the contract, including how the price of roughly fifty cents an acre had been calculated. Finally Left Hand asked for a little more time to study the offer, and Jerome adjourned the council until the 13th.

At the 13 October meeting Jerome concluded his opening statement by saying, "The Commissioners have talked to you a good many days . . . and can do nothing more but ask you to sign these papers."[62] However, he was immediately confronted with some of the same questions that the commissioners had responded to several times. White Eyed Antelope, for example, asked which of the reservations they were selling and whether fifty cents was the price the government would pay. Several Cheyennes, among them Cloud Chief and White Eyed Antelope, grudgingly indicated their willingness to sign. The last Arapaho speakers seemed most concerned with ensuring that Sitting Bull, who had been living among the Northern Arapahos, would be able to take an allotment among the southern branch of his tribe.

Jerome finally announced, "the time has come to . . . sign."[63] He asked Left Hand, as the eldest chief present, to sign first. Left Hand agreed to do so but observed that the opposition still held the majority. Since most of the Cheyennes had been boycotting the meetings, satisfying the Treaty of Medicine Lodge requirement for the approval of three-fourths of the adult males to validate any cession would require a lot of canvasing. Jerome and his colleagues would get help from the attorneys, whose only hope of collecting any fees rested on the Indians' agreeing to sell. Although it cannot be documented conclusively, it is highly likely that it was money provided by the attorneys that persuaded a handful of Cheyennes and Arapahos to persuade enough of their fellow tribe members to sign.

According to the scale devised by Secretary Noble and interpreted and applied by the Cherokee Commission, the attorneys would collectively receive $67,500, a tidy sum indeed at a time when industrial workers were trying to support families on an average of about $600 a year. The secretary would later defend this level of compensation by arguing that the attorneys "made extended oral arguments before the Commission and also furnished the Commissioners elaborate briefs in support of the Indian's claims; also attended the councils on the reservations for several weeks at considerable personal expense."[64] That is almost the precise language Sayre employed in a letter months after the agreement was concluded. During the negotiations, however, the commissioners themselves had criticized the attorneys for contributing nothing toward securing the agreement. Manifestly, their principal contribution was in helping get signatures on the document. Thus the Indians would pay them handsomely, presumably to protect their interests during the negotiations, although the attorneys expended most of their energies getting the Indians to sign so that they might get their $67,500.

Charles Painter, the able Indian Rights Association agent, conducted an investigation in 1892 that provides the best insight into the way that sufficient signatures were obtained. Apparently, educated Indians and mixed bloods were employed to collect signatures in the remote camps and may have fabricated some of them. Painter concluded that George Bent received $250 for his services, although the mixed blood maintained that he had been promised $10,000. At the other end of the scale, a Darlington trader complained that he had been unable to collect from the attorneys the $2.50 for cigarettes that they had asked him to make available to Bent.[65] As an interpreter at the negotiations and a solicitor of signatures, Bent had been a valuable ally of the attorneys.

Others whom Painter identified as agents for the attorneys were Carlisle-educated Leonard Tyler and George Boynton. Belle Balenti, a mixed blood, and her husband, Michael, a white man employed by a local trader, were also of service. Painter lists compensation for Boynton at $150, Tyler at $250, and Mrs. Balenti at $140.[66] Historian Donald Berthrong uncovered an affidavit in the National Archives by which Michael Balenti swore to receiving $200, which he complained was $50 less than his expenses.[67] The man who actually paid Balenti was Gilbert Williams, another ex-agent for the Cheyennes and Arapahos who had been recruited by the attorneys. For his services Williams received $2,200, some of it possibly for having shelved his own plans to ally with another attorney and seek to represent the two tribes in their negotiations.[68]

The signing had begun on 13 October with 91 Indians complying and would take a month to complete. On the 22nd Jerome reported to Secretary Noble that they had only 344 signatures, far short of the three-quarters of the adult male population specified by the Treaty of Medicine Lodge for ceding land. He also advised Noble that some policemen were not cooperating and asked him to wire the agent to "follow our advice in removing such obstructions."[69] As a result Chief of Police Tall Bull was threatened with dismissal, and Painter cited similar tactics employed against Robert Burns, a clerk in the agent's office. Sergeant Chester A. Arthur, a scout stationed at Fort Reno, was threatened with the loss of his stripes for attending a feast sponsored by the commissioners and then refusing to assist them in gathering signatures.

In Jerome's next report to Noble on 25 October, he tallied a total of 416 signatures. He sought and received permission to contact students at Carlisle and Haskell eligible to sign, and that produced 40 more.[70] Jerome and Sayre got some of the army scouts together on the 27th but made little progress. Of those who spoke, almost all responded negatively to the arguments of the commissioners. One Arapaho, Washee, questioned why women were being permitted to sign the agreement: "We never count the women."[71] On 30 October the commissioners were still 50 short, and Jerome appealed to Noble to send the commissioner of Indian affairs to try to close the deal. That was not possible, but the secretary did ask that Colonel Wade be told that his influence would be appreciated, "so far as he can consistently give it."[72] On 12 November Jerome was finally able to wire Secretary Noble that the commission had sufficient signatures. Moreover, they had the signatures of about one hundred wives or widows of intermarried whites who, as heads of families, would be selecting allotments for their children, so their signing had been deemed advisable.

In reporting the completion of their mission to President Harrison, the commissioners made no reference to the understanding that the attorney fees would come from the $1,500,000 the Indians were receiving for their land; nevertheless, that was what was done. When the Cheyennes and Arapahos were paid their second installment of $250,000 in spring 1892, it was short $67,000, that sum having been set aside for the attorneys without consultation with the tribes. In a jocular fashion his friend Reynolds had approached Secretary Noble: "As you are aware, St. Louis lawyers at the beginning of the Summer need a little money." He went on to express appreciation of Noble's assistance, particularly in ignoring "the selfish interest of others who desire to subserve their own personal interest, rather than the interest of the Indians."[73] Noble probably smiled at this reference to other attorneys who had sought to represent the Cheyennes and Arapahos, and he did direct the commissioner of Indian affairs to divert $67,000 from the Indians to the pockets of Crawford, Miles, and Reynolds.

The payment to each Indian was thus reduced from about $75 to approximately $55, or a total of about $100 for a family of five. This was a substantial loss for families, coming on top of other blows. The previous year their beef ration had been cut in half without warning, and the distraction and disruption of the lengthy negotiations were followed by the turmoil engendered by allotment, which many initially refused to participate in. During 1890 and 1891 even the most progressive Indians had lost ground in their attempts at self-support by farming and stock raising.

When the Indians did learn of the diversion of a portion of their cash to pay attorneys, they were outraged. Understandably they could not comprehend how their money was going to attorneys—attorneys whom they had not wanted—to do work on claims they had not made to the reservation in the Outlet. They got up a petition to Washington to reverse the action and meanwhile found allies in John H. Seger, who had been on the reservation for fifteen years, ex-agent Captain J. M. Lee, and Charles Painter of the Indian Rights Association.

Painter coordinated a protest against the manner in which Indian signatures had been obtained for the agreement and also gathered facts relating to the drawing up of the attorneys' contract and the method of their payment. Both Seger and Captain Lee asked Painter to conduct an investigation, and they provided him with information. Others whom he interviewed included General Miles, Agent Ashley, George Bent, Ben Clarke, Colonel Wade, Secretary Noble, and the head of the Indian Division of the secretary's office. In addition Painter was able to persuade two U.S. senators to introduce resolutions in that chamber bringing the matter to the attention of Congress.

In 1893 the Indian Rights Association published Painter's *Cheyennes and Arapahos Revisited and a Statement of Their Contract with Attorneys*. It included summary statements from Captain Lee's own investigation, the last of which was a stunning indictment: "the so-called contract, from its incipiency to its final consummation, was tainted with misrepresentation, fraud, and bribery, and is an outrage upon the Cheyenne and Arapahoe Indians."[74] Painter's own assessment was equally damning: ". . . these men procured a contract . . . with a few of these Indians, and then devoted their energies and expended their money in bribes . . . to induce the Indians to sign an agreement in which they were robbed of at least three-fourths of the value of their property, and their chief interest was to secure a ratification of any agreement which would bring them their fee."[75] Nevertheless, Congress did not revoke the agreement nor demand the attorneys surrender their $67,000. Secretary Noble did devote seven pages of his 1892 annual report to a rationalization of his handling of the issue.

It would be left to the Indian Claims Commission to compensate the Cheyennes and Arapahos. In 1951 the northern and southern branches of the tribes jointly brought suit against the United States before the commission. They sought recovery of the value of their lands recognized as being owned by them in the Treaty of Fort Laramie of 7 September 1851.[76] In 1958 the commission allowed the Cheyennes and the Arapahos to sue separately. Meanwhile, the commission had already concluded that the land ceded in 1851 amounted to 51,210,000 acres and was worth $23,500,000 at the time.

In 1965 the commission also heard testimony on the value of the 1869 executive-order reservation on which the Indians were living when they were approached by the Cherokee Commission. The Indians maintained that the $1,500,000 they received for the land ceded to the United States under the terms of the 1890 agreement was "unconscionable." Apparently the Justice Department attorneys were persuaded of this as well, as the goverment offered to settle all the claims of the southern branches of the Cheyennes and Arapahos for $15,000,000.[77] Within a month all enrolled members of the two tribes were invited to a meeting at Watonga, Oklahoma, to respond to the offer. By an overwhelming 338 to 2, they voted to accept the government's offer. Subsequently they received per capita payments of about $2,600, with $500,000 retained by the tribal governments to fund education.[78]

Although the Cherokee Commission had acquired the Cheyenne and Arapaho land at about fifty cents per acre, the threat of court action by the Choctaws and Chickasaws led Congress to pay them an additional $2,991,450, bringing the total price for acre paid those two tribes to $1.25.

They claimed that when they ceded the Leased District in 1866, they had done so with the understanding that the government would open it to settlement to other Indians, not whites. Their success suggests that it was easier for Indians to obtain compensation for a contract violation than for a contract arrived at corruptly. It certainly had been an experience for the commissioners to deal with the numerous and relatively united Plains tribes. Now they would scatter to their homes to recuperate before meeting their more sophisticated opponents, the Cherokees, again.

5

The Cherokees Revisited

ONCE IT WAS APPARENT THAT SIGNATURES OF THREE-FOURTHS of adult male Cheyennes and Arapahos could be obtained for the agreement, the commissioners began to consider their next objective—either the Wichitas or the Cherokees. After consulting with Secretary Noble, Chairman Jerome informed Principal Chief Mayes of the commission's desire to resume negotiations with the Cherokees at Tahlequah. He expressed the hope that "both parties may be willing to meet the questions, with that spirit of mutual concession, fairness and justice,"[1] something conspicuously lacking in the commission's approach to the Cheyennes and Arapahos.

Jerome, Sayre, and Wilson reached Tahlequah on 25 November and took up residence in the National Hotel. The chairman, who was accompanied by his wife, was described by the Vinita *Indian Chieftain* as "a very dignified and affable gentleman and seems to make friends with all."[2] Apparently Jerome did go to Tahlequah determined to be more conciliatory than his predecessor, Lucius Fairchild.

The *Chieftain* described conditions in the nation that would likely make the Cherokees more amenable to negotiations, conditions brought on by President Harrison's order removing cattle from the Outlet and thus cutting off their $200,000 annual income from cattlemen: "The future existence of the nation seems frightful indeed, for she is at least $100,000 behind. What we are to do is a conumdrum for all. The seminaries and schools will end in a few days without a single cent to pay anything. . . . Banks at Van Buren and Muskogee, and merchants here, are taking salary and school warrants at a large discount and that discount is growing greater every day."[3] Chief Mayes protested the removal of the cattle to President Harrison himself. He invoked memories of the "privations and hardships" of the Trail of Tears and the missionaries' assurances to the Cherokees that "God is a just God and that He is their God and will protect them." The chief concluded with a plaintive, "I ask you to pause and consider . . . and not deprive us of the use of property which we have held and used so long undisturbed by this sacred title and patent from your government."[4] To make matters worse, if possible, a severe drought had devastated crops in Cherokee country. That contributed to the National Council's decision to distribute the last payment from the cattlemen on a per capita basis, as opposed to applying the money to schools and other government functions as Mayes recommended.

On 20 November the chief officially informed the Council of the arrival of the Cherokee Commission. He advised members that "the question will naturally arise as to the value of this property," in which case, he remarked hopefully, "this becomes plainly a business transaction between two parties." Tribes that already been put through the wringer by Jerome and associates could have quickly disabused him of that view. But Mayes even stated that ultimately "we must look to that Government for protection, and feel proud that we have such a strong arm to shield us from danger."[5] Defiance not being practical, the chief's tactic was to appeal to the sympathies of the government that presumably was the guardian of its Indian ward's best interests.

Initially the commissioners had some cause for optimism, the National Council having authorized Chief Mayes to appoint a committee to negotiate. By 2 December the members had met and selected Stan W. Gray, chairman, E. C. Boudinot, clerk, and Captain H. Benge, interpreter. Chief Mayes had already instructed them, emphasizing the importance of what would surely be the last Cherokee cession of land to the United States.

Of the nine-man committee—Stan W. Gray, William P. Ross, Johnson Spade, Rabbit Bunch, L. B. Bell, Stephen Tehee, John Wickliffe, Arch Scraper, and George Downing—only Ross and Bell argued the case for the Cherokee Nation. Both were able representatives of Cherokee interests. Ross had served as interim principal chief on two occasions, although he had failed in each instance to win election on his own. He was a nephew of the legendary John Ross, who had helped him attend a New Jersey preparatory school and Princeton University. Among his other positions, Ross had been the first editor of the *Cherokee Advocate*, clerk of the Cherokee Senate and subsequently a member of that body, and mayor of Fort Gibson. During the Civil War he had first held rank as lieutenant colonel in the Confederate forces, only to switch allegiance when Union troops invaded Indian Territory. After they withdrew and the Confederates again were dominant, they captured Ross, came close to executing him, and did burn his store in Tahlequah to the ground.[6] This perhaps explains his often-expressed hostility to ex-Confederates.

As a Cherokee delegate to meetings at Okmulgee in the 1870s that were a United States–subsidized effort to create a territorial government, Ross demonstrated his political skills by devising a government for the proposed entity. He used these same talents to oppose the railroad companies penetrating the Cherokee Nation, fearing them a threat to Cherokee sovereignty. As interim chief he fought anything that militated against that same sovereignty. In his role as one of the two spokesmen for the committee, Ross persistently but courteously represented his nation's interests. A lawyer, he demonstrated a good grasp of legal and constitutional principles.

L. B. Bell did not have Ross's general education, range of experience, or knowledge of the law. He had served his nation, however, as a member of the Cherokee Senate, a delegate to Washington, and a tax commissioner. In the last capacity he was best known for his aggressive approach to the task, going so far as to confiscate cattle of tax delinquents in the Outlet.[7] Bell might have lacked Ross's polish and grasp of constitutional issues, but his blunt, direct approach left no doubt as to his views.

Ross, Bell, and their colleagues met with the Cherokee Commission in seventeen sessions from 3 December to 26 December, during which all issues were discussed exhaustively, resulting in a journal of 279 pages. The commissioners knew that they were dealing with intelligent and experienced politicians, and they refrained from the implied threats and half-truths they had employed against less sophisticated and more malleable Indian leaders. The first session saw the commissioners and the Cherokees jockeying for position. Jerome had received a copy of the National Council's instructions to the committee that referred to the possible cession of all Cherokee land west of 96° longitude and "the final adjustment of all questions of interest, between the United States and the Cherokee Nation."[8] Jerome and Sayre opened by asking what these questions might be, but the Cherokees insisted that the first order of business should be the presentation of the commission's offer. Jerome maintained that he and his colleagues were bound by the act of Congress that created their commission and specified that their purpose was to purchase land, paying no more than what the United States had paid the Creeks—$1.25 per acre. The Cherokees, however, had decided that the government's interest in the Outlet offered them a last opportunity to seek satisfaction on other issues such as the removal of intruders from their nation and a settlement of Cherokee monetary claims against the United States. On the second day Jerome capitulated and Sayre read the government's offer, promising the Cherokees a copy.

When discussion of terms got underway on 8 December, Jerome described their offer of $1.25 as the most it was charging settlers, while the government's price for land unsold for as much as four years could drop to fifty cents per acre. Jerome also emphasized that the 5 percent the government was offering to pay the Cherokees on their funds held in the Treasury was twice what the government had to pay to borrow money in the current market. He told them that with an annual national income of $376,000 they would be "one of the richest people on earth,"[9] an expression that the commissioners employed freely. The only other item in the United States' offer was its willingness to abrogate the 15th article of the Treaty of 1866 that permitted the settlement of "civilized Indians, friendly with the Cherokees," east of 96° longitude in the heart of the nation.[10] That part of the offer the Indians would be happy to accept. The chairman then turned the floor over to Warren Sayre to respond to issues raised in the Cherokee response and described by Ross as "other questions, that do not relate directly to the sale of land, that we would like to have settled and that are as important to us as the money."[11] On hearing them, Sayre stated that there was only one the commissioners would not even consider—the Cherokee claim to No Man's Land, the Oklahoma Panhandle.

Procedural matters dominated the session on 9 December. However, Sayre took the opportunity to state categorically that the Cherokees would not get the $2.50 per acre they were asking. He did agree to discuss other Cherokee terms and suggested that the money issue be left to the last. L. B. Bell agreed, but a fellow Cherokee, Rabbit Bunch, on one of those rare occasions when Indians other than Ross and Bell held the floor, argued that if agreement on price could not be reached, there was little reason to discuss other matters. Johnson Spade and Stephen Tehee sided with Bunch, and Bell suggested that the Cherokees had "better have a conference."[12]

The commissioners must have also appreciated the break, as they had received some unpleasant news. From the St. Louis *Globe-Democrat* they

TAKING INDIAN LANDS

learned that the Senate had directed its committee on the Five Civilized Tribes to investigate the progress of the Cherokee Commission. The reporter in Washington attributed this to dissatisfaction with the commission's rate of progress. Obviously disturbed, Jerome tried to reassure Secretary Noble: "We have not been idle—the contracts entered into—will do as much good to the Indians—and cost the Government so much less money than has been given and authorized by the direct action of Congress, that we modestly feel, that we ought to be complimented, rather than investigated." Jerome complained that the Senate's action would only encourage the Cherokees to believe that they might get a better deal by negotiating with a Senate committee. Above all, he said, "we earnestly but respectfully ask to be let alone."[13]

With the possibility of an investigation hanging over their heads, the commissioners went back to work the next day. At the beginning of the session Bell announced that the Indians had agreed to set aside their claim to No Man's Land and the price for the Outlet in order to discuss other terms they had proposed. He also took the opportunity to vent some Cherokee frustration: "We know the peculiar situation that surrounds us; we are here in the middle of the world, with millions of buyers and compelled to sell to just one. . . . We are pretty much in the shape of an unfortunate creditor in the hands of an unscrupulous skin-flint; you buy at a price, but offer the price yourselves."[14]

The first new proposal that they wanted to discuss related to the Cherokees retaining title to three salt marshes totaling about 100,000 acres, which they valued as potential revenue producers. The commissioners, however, objected on two counts. The first was that it would create a situation in which United States sovereignty could be challenged by another nation owning land within American boundaries. The other was that there was no reason to burden the agreement with conditions that might lead Congress to reject it. In addition, the commissioners maintained, the salt marshes had yet to generate any revenue for the Cherokees and were unlikely to do so in the future.

To make the latter point Jerome talked about the economics of the salt industry in Michigan, a major salt producer. During a term in his state's senate he had chaired a committee on salt, so he was well acquainted with the topic. Bell was unimpressed, however, rejoining that whether or not the marshes would ever prove profitable was a risk the Cherokees should be permitted to take. The Indians continued to hold their ground, and finally both sides agreed to move on to the next Cherokee proposal—that the railroad crossing the Outlet continue to pay an annual tax of $15 per mile to the nation.

Again the commissioners resisted, Jerome and Sayre holding that if the Cherokees ceded the land, the contract under which the railroad paid the tax would no longer apply. That was met by Bell with a novel proposal: the Indians would simply retain title to the 200-foot-wide right of way. Sayre refused even to consider that possibility and ridiculed the tax on the railroad as a "bagatelle" compared with the greater than $7,000,000 offer made by the United States.[15] Irritated by the the commissioners' consistently negative reaction to Cherokee proposals, Bell fired back: "The title is in us: we don't have to sell. Must you have every square inch . . . If we don't propose to sell do you propose to confiscate?"[16]

Jerome could only say that Congress intended that the commission should extinguish every claim the Cherokees had to the Outlet in order that the homesteaders who moved to the area would have jurisdiction, including the power to control railroads. But Bell was not to be silenced:

> Give us the same opportunity to sell our lands that the monopolies have. . . . The people will flow in just as fast if these railroads have to pay the 15 dollars per mile. The rain will come and the grain will grow. . . . The rivers will flow, people will marry and children be born. . . . We have put behind us our prejudices and traditions when we meet you here in peaceful council and talk about selling the graves of our dead. Now I ask you in the name of justice that you have so often promised and so often failed to give. From the landing of Columbus to the present day the promises of the Government are simply a string of broken promises from beginning to end.[17]

After Bell's outburst Sayre protested that he and his fellow commissioners were only trying to reach "a just conclusion in our negotiations" and described the tone of Bell's remarks as "not diplomatic to say the least."[18] Turning to the Cherokee insistence on continuing to collect the $15 per mile a year from the railroads, Sayre compared Indian and white attitudes toward economic development. He argued that the Indians always opposed it—that if they had their way, the railroads never would have been built and they would still be leasing land to cattlemen for a paltry three cents an acre.

TAKING INDIAN LANDS

Before the session was over Bell had apologized, declaring that he had not intended "anything offensive."[19] Nevertheless, the exchanges on the issue continued, with neither side yielding an inch. Finally Bell interjected, "Let's talk about something else."[20] Having made no progress on the first two issues, they moved on to the question of abrogating the article of the 1866 treaty permitting the government to settle additional Indians in the Cherokee Nation east of 96° longitude.

William Ross reminded the commissioners that the 1866 treaty had been concluded in the wake of the Civil War and "like very many other Indian Treaties it was entered into under circumstances which the Indians could not resist"[21]—an accurate statement. It resulted in the government's locating Delawares and Shawnees east of 96° longitude, a "discordant element"[22] in the opinion of their reluctant hosts. Adding adopted whites and freedmen to that mix, according to Ross, made for too many people for the Cherokees to continue to find sufficient tillable land if they were required to cede over half of their total holdings to the United States.

This prompted David Jerome to deliver a lecture on the development of the government's Indian policy, a subject with which he was thoroughly conversant as a result of his service on the Board of Indian Commissioners. He remembered that when he was a boy the Middle West was still largely Indian country, but the expanding white population kept the government forcing the Indians farther west. He admitted that "abstract right" might have been violated in the process but argued that the government had acted as fairly as it could.[23] Ultimately, he said, this led to the idea of concentrating all Native Americans in Indian Territory. When the Indians from other areas resisted removal, however, the goverment resorted to pressuring them to "bunch up" in order to make room for the growing white population. Jerome maintained that the goverment was not just being "arbitrary"—it was acting through necessity.[24]

Ross did not buy this extenuation of the constant encroachment: "I see no wisdom or justice in importing the thousands and thousands of foreigners . . . and then demand from us our lands for their accomodation [sic]." He urged the government to relieve the Cherokees of being "a constant prey of a change of circumstances," of "bunching us and bunching us again."[25] He concluded by noting their misfortune that "power, and law and means are always in the hands of the United States, and that physically we exist by the breath of their nostrils."[26] It was a moving statement, but when Jerome ignored his plea, Ross could only conclude that "acquisition of money seems to be the ruling passion of the age."[27] Bell then moved adjournment until the next day.

When they reconvened on 11 December, the topic of discussion was the Cherokee Nation's wish to gain access to federal courts, something denied them since the Supreme Court's 1831 edict that tribes were "domestic dependent nations." As usual Jerome insisted that the Indians first present their argument and then the commissioners would reply. Bell made the case for the Cherokees in his customary colorful language. Emphasizing the need for access to the courts, he stated that "it matters not where a man may come from, whether he be Hottentot, African, European . . . so he is not an Indian he may appeal to the courts of the United States for protection."[28] But since the Cherokee Nation could not do that, he observed, it had thousands of squatters to contend with.

Sayre, as always, found the issue "fraught with more difficulties than at first glance would seem to be apparent"[29] and observed that since tribal lack of access to the federal courts was a condition of long standing, it must have merit. He also asked whether, with access, the Cherokee Nation would also become liable to suit and would pay taxes to support the federal judicial system. Finally, he charged that the Cherokees brought the intruder problem on themselves by advertising that they would consider anyone claiming to be Cherokee for citizenship.

Bell could only say that it was difficult to argue with a man who could see the problem but would question every remedy proposed. He did remind the commissioners that the Indians already paid federal excise taxes on tobacco and other commodities. And, he remarked caustically, when the government wanted to buy land it treated them as wards, but when the Indians asked the government to evict intruders they were told to rely on their own laws yet were denied the use of force.[30]

Before the session was recessed for lunch, Jerome asked the Cherokees to draft the language they wanted in the agreement to guarantee their access to federal courts. At that point Ross created a stir by announcing that he and his colleagues had been informed that Chief Mayes had received bids on the Outlet ranging from $10,000,000 to $30,000,000—considerably more than the government was offering.[31] He linked this with the observation that, since the commissioners were opposing every item the Cherokees wished included in the agreement, the Indians had no option but to try to get as

TAKING INDIAN LANDS

much money as they could. That provided Jerome and his colleagues something to discuss during the lunch break, although they probably were not alarmed at this development, since the rule that tribes could sell only to the United States was of long standing.

That afternoon the topic was the Cherokee request for a clause giving their courts exclusive jurisdiction over crimes committed within their nation by their citizens, either by birth or adoption. As matters stood, Judge Parker of the Fort Smith federal court exercised jurisdiction when adopted citizens were involved. Sayre acknowledged that the Cherokees did have a problem and that, had he the authority, he would eject all intruders, "though I had to do it at the point of the bayonet"[32]—an unusual expression of sympathy by a commissioner, particularly this one. Jerome even stated that the commissioners might be willing to include the request in the agreement, recognizing that Congress could reject it. Ross and Bell could congratulate themselves on having at least the appearance of victory on one issue.

The following day the issue on the floor was the Cherokee proposal that they receive an increase in compensation for land they had already sold to the Osages. Their hope was to raise the price to what the Osages had been willing to pay, $1 per acre, although the government had intervened and set it at about seventy cents. This aroused Judge Wilson from his customary somnolence. In a series of sharp questions he drew from Ross the fact that, indeed, the Cherokees had transferred title to the Osages at the seventy-cent figure. He then asked scornfully, "in the name of justice and reason tell me how often you want to be paid for those lands."[33] Ross replied that there was a precedent; the United States had purchased land from the Creeks at one price but later, recognizing an inequity, had made an additional payment.

Wilson then tried a different tack, soliciting the opinions of the other seven Cherokees, who had been content to permit Ross and Bell to articulate the nation's positions. Only Rabbit Bunch responded. Through the interpreter he stated that he had no quarrel with the way Ross and Bell were handling the negotiations—that they were expressing the views of all the Cherokees present—thus stifling that effort to create dissension in the Cherokee ranks.

At that point Bell entered the discussion. He accused Judge Wilson of acting as a lawyer, "seeing nothing at all . . . but his side's interests," and demanded that the commissioners "consider the equities in the case and if we have any give them to us."[34] Wilson was righteously indignant: "I felt an interest in this [Cherokee] Nation before he was half a scholar, before he could cross his galluses behind him: I recollect when he was a little bit of a totling running around here, I recollect associating with his father before he was kittened, and . . . I would do justice to the Cherokees just as soon as to the United States."[35]

Wilson's colleagues must have cringed at his Arkansas good ole boy approach. For the balance of the session they only reiterated their line that the official record documented that the Cherokees had engaged in a legal transfer of title, challenging them to produce any evidence to the contrary. Ross could only say he hoped to uncover some facts and if he could not he would drop the issue. Wilson, however, had the last word: "Now if the President fixed it at 70 cents and the Cherokees accepted it without protest I want to know if that don't end your title."[36] The Indians had lost another round.

Nor would they have any better luck on the next issue they raised when they met the evening of 15 December. This time they complained that two railroads running from Kansas across their nation charged passengers five cents a mile, whereas in Kansas they only charged two cents. The Cherokees wanted a provision in the agreement correcting this inequity. Bell, the principal spokesman on this issue, revealed his populist leanings. He talked of the relative value of gold and greenbacks and of railroads so powerful that Congress would not move against them. Jerome and Sayre countered that the Indians were trying to attach extraneous issues to what was a simple real-estate transaction. The commissioners proposed instead that the Cherokees submit a petition to Congress, but of course what the Indians were trying to do was to use the United States' interest in acquiring the Outlet as leverage to obtain satisfaction on other issues.

Bell admitted this; however, he observed: "We are asked to part with a tract of land that is worth away up in the millions . . . but if we prefer to have these other conveniences in place of money I don't see why they might not be given to us. I may as well state . . . that the money consideration in it is the smallest part to us; if we were left entirely free to exercise our wishes we would not sell it for the 40 millions that has been offered us."[37] But the commissioners would not concede, and they moved on to the next Cherokee request.

Bell identified this objective succinctly—"putting the darkies west of 96"—and he spoke of "about 4,000 niggers"[38] in the nation. About half of them were intruders, but he acknowledged that the others had rights specified in the Treaty of 1866 for former slaves of the Indians. Bell declared them "an ever present trouble in making both social and civil arrangements."[39] The solution he proposed was to include in the agreement a clause granting Cherokee freedmen who were at least eighteen years old eighty acres in the Outlet, and minors forty acres. The United States could then deduct the cost of that land from its purchase price.

That proposal was largely ignored by the commissioners, and in the sessions on the 16th and 17th the Cherokees virtually withdrew it from consideration, along with others including their effort to obtain additional pay for their cession to the Osages. Between them, Bell and Sayre reduced the remaining issues to two categories. One related to the salt marshes and mineral lands. The other had to do with Cherokee access to federal courts, an issue that they clung to through six more sessions, the last one on 26 December. The commissioners were just as adamant in their refusal to incorporate Cherokee Nation access to federal courts into the agreement. Sayre argued forcefully that the Cherokees were asking the impossible, in violation of the Constitution. "[T]hat right," he maintained, "never was given to any state . . . or any city in the United States."[40] He portrayed the commissioners as shocked at the Cherokee position on the issue.

Ross then took the floor to express his surprise at Sayre's presentation. Once again he argued that the Indians were not asking for anything new. The Supreme Court, in its 1886 decision in *Eastern Band of Cherokees v. The United States and the Cherokee Nation* and the Treaty of 1866, had already confirmed that they had the right to determine their own citizenship. His nation now simply sought a way to implement that right. The Cherokees "were brought here under pledges and guarantees as solemn as human words could make them, and we simply ask the proper enforcement of those guarantees."[41]

To Ross's plea for "simple justice" the commissioners offered only the possibility of a commission of Cherokee and United States appointees to judge the intruder claims. Sayre even suggested that if agreement could be reached, the Cherokees would be placed "absolutely secure in possession of what they call the home tract . . . and they can work out their own salvation as they please."[42] He was probably sincere in that statement, unable to forsee that in the next decade and a half the United States would ruthlessly dismantle the Cherokee national government.

Bell quickly demolished the idea that a commission whose acts would be reviewed by the secretary of the Interior was a solution to the Cherokee problem with intruders. He reminded his audience that the secretary had veto power under the present system, yet it had not accomplished the ejection of a single intruder. If they were ordered off the property of an Indian, intruders simply sidestepped and occupied a portion of the Cherokee public domain.

In the last five days of this bargaining period, the commissioners and the Cherokees finally had to recognize that they were hopelessly deadlocked. Even constituting Ross and Sayre as a select committee to try to resolve the question of Cherokee access to the federal courts came a cropper. In the aftermath of that failure, Bell, with his usual bluntness, vented his frustration: "a white man in the Indian Territory may appeal to the courts and the doors are open to him; a nigger may do the same thing, a frenchman—anyone but an Indian. Now I ask in the name of common fairness, why are we excluded?"[43]

Ross employed more elegant language, paraphrasing Ecclesiastes 12:12, to express his distress at the course of events: "If much study is wearisome to the flesh so is over much talk."[44] Nevertheless, he held forth at some length, reminding the commissioners that Cherokees might be brought to trial in Judge Parker's Fort Smith court, but they would not enjoy the right to a jury of their peers, only American citizens being eligible for that duty. And he cleverly rebutted the argument that the Cherokees were singular in trying to ignore precedents in Indian-white relations, noting that in 1871 the United States had unilaterally ceased making treaties with tribes—a practice a century old.

On the day before Christmas the Cherokees presented their most recent draft of measures they wished in the agreement, and the commissioners refused to accept two of them.[45] The first of these guaranteed the Cherokee Nation access to the Court of Claims, with right of appeal to the Supreme Court, on all matters of land and treaty rights. The second was access to a federal court in Indian Territory to secure the exclusion of intruders. Although they carried the discussion into Christmas Eve, no progress was made and they adjourned until the 26th.

When they got back together, both sides seem resigned to admitting failure and anxious to avoid recriminations. Jerome congratulated the Cherokees on their presentations, "one of the most elaborate arguments that I ever

TAKING INDIAN LANDS

had the fortune to listen to," and, choosing to ignore some of Bell's language, lauded the "uniform courtesy" with which they had conducted themselves.[46] Sayre could not refrain from launching into one of his detailed refutations of the Cherokee positions, but even he took the opportunity to express his admiration for "the spirit and pertinacity"[47] with which the Cherokees had advocated their nation's cause. The commissioners then proposed that the negotiations be shifted to Washington.

Ross responded by first reciprocating the kind remarks of Jerome and Sayre. He spoke of the "courtesy and kindness" of the commissioners and, in courtly excess, proclaimed, "we shall all in after life look backward with pleasure to the intercourse" between the disputants.[48] But he could not resist the chance for one more recitation of the Cherokee position, so Sayre felt compelled to respond. That brought Bell to his feet, and he and Sayre engaged in a typically acerbic exchange. It was left to Jerome to close the three weeks of sometimes acrimonious debate on a conciliatory note, voicing the hope that if negotiations did resume in Washington, it would be "extremely gratifying"[49] if the Cherokee participants included some of those present.

That was not to be, although Jerome assured Secretary Noble that the National Council would appoint delegates to negotiate in Washington and that he and his colleagues would be in the city shortly after the arrival of the Cherokees. The Council did appoint two delegates, Richard M. Wolfe and David Rowe, neither a member of the nine-man committee that had negotiated with the commission throughout most of December. Nor did Wolfe and Rowe get instructions to continue the negotiations. Chief Mayes never had accepted the idea of selling the Outlet for what the government was willing to pay, nor did it have much support in the Council. Indeed, the president of the Senate, who presided over the dissolution of the committee with which he had served, was L. B. Bell.

Meanwhile, authorities in the Interior Department continued to act as though serious bargaining would take place there. At the request of Secretary Noble, Commisioner of Indian Affairs T. J. Morgan vetted the proposal made by the Cherokees, concluding that if the government made minor concessions, an agreement could be reached. He based this in part on his belief that there was "a growing disposition in Congress to secure these lands with or without the consent of the Cherokees" and that, given the circumstances, the Indians would respond favorably to a modest improvement in the offer of $1.25 per acre.[50]

Secretary Noble did request that David Jerome and Warren Sayre come to the capital for what he hoped would be a successful renewal of negotiations, but when they arrived they were quickly disillusioned. Wolfe and Rowe informed them that they had no instructions to negotiate.[51] The commission's third effort to purchase the Outlet had failed. It had, however, occasioned a commendable change in the bargaining posture of the commissioners. Although they had not markedly altered their offer, they had made every effort to win their points with logic and facts, as opposed to the bullying tactics employed against less-educated tribal representatives.

Lucius Fairchild
State Historical Society of Wisconsin, #WHi (D485)6813

David H. Jerome
State Archives of Michigan, #02886

Warren G. Sayre
State Archives, Indiana Commission of Public Records

Alfred M. Wilson
University of Arkansas Library

John W. Noble
Collections of the Library of Congress

William P. Ross, Cherokee
Archives and Manuscripts Division of the Oklahoma Historical Society

Joel B. Mayes, Cherokee
Archives and Manuscripts Division of the Oklahoma Historical Society

E. C. Boudinot, Cherokee
Archives and Manuscripts Division of the Oklahoma Historical Society

L. B. Bell, Cherokee
Archives and Manuscripts Division of the Oklahoma Historical Society

Robert L. Owen, Cherokee
Western History Collections, University of Oklahoma Libraries

Little Soldier, Ponca

Western History Collections, University of Oklahoma Libraries

White Eagle, Ponca
Western History Collections, University of Oklahoma Libraries

Moses Keokuk, Sac and Fox
Archives and Manuscripts Division of the Oklahoma Historical Society

Towakonie Jim, Wichita
Archives and Manuscripts Division of the Oklahoma Historical Society

Whirlwind, Cheyenne
Archives and Manuscripts Division of the Oklahoma Historical Society

Cloud Chief, Cheyenne
Archives and Manuscripts Division of the Oklahoma Historical Society

Iseeo, Kiowa

Archives and Manuscripts Division of the Oklahoma Historical Society

Big Tree, Kiowa

Western History Collections, University of Oklahoma Libraries

Big Bow, Kiowa
Archives and Manuscripts Division of the Oklahoma Historical Society

Lone Wolf, Kiowa
Western History Collections, University of Oklahoma Libraries

Tabananaka, Comanche
Archives and Manuscripts Division of the Oklahoma Historical Society

Howeah, Comanche

Western History Collections, University of Oklahoma Libraries

Quanah Parker, Comanche, and two of his wives, To-pay and To-narcy
Western History Collections, University of Oklahoma Libraries

Eagle Chief, Pawnee
Western History Collections, University of Oklahoma Libraries

6

Agreements with the Wichitas, Kickapoos, and Tonkawas

AFTER THEIR FAILURE TO RESUME NEGOTIATIONS with the Cherokees in Washington in February 1891, the commissioners returned to their homes, not to take the field again until early May. Meanwhile, on 3 March Congress appropriated $15,000 to enable them to continue their work. When the commissioners returned to Oklahoma, their focus would be on the residents of the Wichita Reservation, created in 1859 to house several small tribes that settler hostility had driven from Texas. Collectively referred to as the Wichitas, these included 545 Caddos, 95 Delawares, and 175 Wichitas. Confederated with this last tribe were 150 Tawaconis, 35 Wacos, and 66 Kichais.[1]

The Delawares were a remnant of a widely dispersed tribe that had once been a potent force in the Northeast, but the other tribes were native to Texas and adjoining areas. Coronado had found Wichita farming villages on the upper Arkansas River in 1541, and survivors of the DeSoto expedition had met Caddos on the Red River a year later. Wichitas and Caddos had similar cultures, based on mixed hunting and farming economies. Once strong confederacies, they had been courted by early white explorers and traders.[2]

Despite the Wichitas' long residence in the area between the Red and Canadian Rivers, when the United States was seeking land in that area on which to resettle Indians from the Southeast in 1818 it purchased the land not from the Wichitas but from the Quapaws. In turn, after the Chickasaws and Choctaws were located on the land, the United States prevailed on them in 1855 to lease the portion of their reservation west of 98° to provide homes for the Wichitas who more recently had been living in East Texas. At Fort

Arbuckle in 1859, the Wichitas agreed to move to a new agency in what would be called the Leased District.

Representing the United States at the Fort Arbuckle council were Elias Rector, in charge of the Southern Superintendency, and Robert S. Neighbors, Superintendent of Indian Affairs in Texas. In his report to Washington, Rector described how they had informed the Indians of their new home and assured them that "after removal they would occupy a country . . . where none could intrude upon them; and they would remain, they and their children, as long as the waters should run, protected from all harm by the United States."[3] Unfortunately for the Wichitas, this commitment was not embodied in a treaty, so it would carry no weight when the Cherokee Commission came to call.

Before that took place, however, the Indians would suffer badly in the Civil War. They were forced to abandon their homes and flee to Kansas and did not return until 1867. That same year the United States negotiated a treaty with the Kiowas, Comanches, and Apaches that assigned those tribes a reservation in the Leased District south of the location of the Wichitas. Only two years later President Grant, by executive order, also placed the Southern Cheyennes and Arapahos on an adjoining reservation that inexplicably included the area occupied by the Wichitas.

Recognizing the concerns of the Wichitas at finding themselves wedged between such fearsome neighbors as these Plains Indians, in 1872 the government brought a Wichita delegation to Washington to reassure them by enlarging their present reservation and confirming it by treaty. Unfortunately, the agent who had been assigned the task of selecting the delegates had botched the job, neglecting to ensure that they were truly representative and properly empowered to negotiate for their tribes. As a result, even though a treaty was drafted to add 569,000 acres to the Wichita Reservation, making a total of 743,610, leaders back on the reservation repudiated what had been transacted. They objected particularly to a sweeping article stating: "the said Wichitas and other affiliated bands hereby cede and relinquish to the United States all right, title, interest, or claim of any nature whatsoever in and to any lands in Texas, Louisiana, Indian Territory, or elsewhere."[4] Nevertheless, the government proceeded for nearly twenty years to act as though Congress had ratified the treaty and the Indians were able to enjoy access to the entire 743,610 acres.

TAKING INDIAN LANDS

In their instructions, David Jerome and colleagues had been told that they should negotiate "with the Wichitas and affiliated bands for any right or claim they may have to the lands now occupied by them in the southeast corner of the Cheyenne and Arapahoe Executive Order Reservation, by virtue of the unratified agreement of 1872, or otherwise."[5] To this end, between 9 May and 4 June they held seventeen sessions with the Indians, recording their deliberations in a journal of 162 pages. During their first three sessions Jerome and Sayre made their customary presentations. The Indians were told that the Cherokee Commission was but one of five traveling to reservations to implement the new policy laid down by the Dawes Act and designed to ensure their future as self-sustaining farmers and stockmen. Since they had enough land to provide 700 acres per Indian, they should accept smaller allotments and sell the surplus to the government.

The spokesmen for the Wichitas quickly made their opposition to the plan clear. Towaconie Jim reminded them that he had met the commissioners the previous fall, when they were negotiating with the Cheyennes and Arapahos. At that time he had advised them that the tribes at the Wichita Agency would want to be represented by attorneys, yet none were now present. Therefore, Jim proposed that the Indians, who had already wasted two days, should go back to planting sweet potatoes while the commissioners summoned the attorneys.[6] Jerome replied that the commissioners regarded attorneys as a waste of tribal funds and cited the example of the Potawatomis, who had attorney fees of $30,000 but had received the same price for their land as the Shawnees, who had no legal counsel.[7]

At their next session on 11 May, Caddo Jake delivered a rather meandering statement, the thrust of which was that the Wichita Agency Indians would not be ready for allotment until their children were educated. To that Jerome responded that what the children needed was to learn how to farm. He also had the temerity to describe Indians in the "native condition" as living by hunting and fishing.[8] That hardly could have impressed the Wichitas, whose ancestors were farming when Coronado observed them three and a half centuries earlier.

Nor did Jerome's statement that the Wichitas did not need 700 acres each meet a warm reception. Towaconie Jim first asked why the government would let Comanches have 320 acres, as their 1867 treaty allowed, yet offer the Wichitas only 160. Moreover, he ridiculed the commissioners' argument that 160 was all the Indians needed: "white people try to get lots of money, more than they can spend . . . and we don't tell them that they can't use it. . . . So it is with our land."[9] Kewaitsidde (Wichita) and Bull Wilson (Delaware) also expressed their unwillingness to take allotments and sell the surplus. The Wichita referred to the earth as his mother, and both he and Wilson recalled the much larger area that had belonged to them. As Wilson phrased it, "the Government took it away from us and put other Indians there and never gave us a cent."[10]

Caddo Jake, a preacher who frequently invoked God, then went back in history with a reference to a treaty that Columbus, "a tall, slim man," had made with the Indians.[11] In this version Columbus said that if the treaty was not observed the sun would halt in its course and the streams cease to flow. Jake also observed that he already knew how to farm and had learned to milk cows as a boy. He then referred to, among other things, the forced migrations of the Indians and a treaty that they had signed with Sam Houston. He concluded his diffuse monologue with what must have been an accurate observation: "Judge Sayre . . . keeps looking at his watch."[12]

The next day Sayre spelled out the terms the government was offering: the standard 160 acres, at least half of which must be grazing land. The land would be held in trust by the government for twenty-five years, and no taxes would be levied on it for that period, nor could it be seized for nonpayment of debt. The United States would pay $286,000 for the surplus land after alloting the estimated 1,060 Indians. For a family of five that would mean nearly $1,500 and 800 acres, "ten times as much land as any Indian has in cultivation on this reservation."[13] There also was a provision for two payments of $50 each in cash, the second to be spent only with the approval of Indian Service personnel. The balance of the $286,000 would be held for them in the Treasury and would pay 4 percent interest. Since 5 percent was the usual interest rate, this was apparently a bargaining ploy.

The only Indian to speak after the presentation was Towaconie Jim, who did not comment on the offer, only reiterating his concerns that the negotiations were keeping the Indians from tending their crops and that they also needed something to eat if they were to stay around the agency. Jerome promised that rations would be issued at the end of each day's session—but no freeloaders: "we do not want you to invite anybody to come here simply to get rations that don't talk in the council."[14]

At the following session the Indians began to react to the proposal, Caddo Jake first. He promptly ruffled a few feathers, declaring that "when Christ was on this earth the white people treated him cruel and nailed our own Christ to the cross."[15] As a result the Indians could not put their faith in the commissioners' professions that they would be considerate of the Indians. Despite Jerome's protestations, Jake continued in this vein. He maintained that the rations they received were actually payment for the buffalo "the white people killed and only took their hides and leave the meat lying around,"[16] a reference to the profligate slaughter by the hide hunters in the 1870s. He also charged the United States with violating several treaties, concluding that the Indians did not want to be allotted and he wanted to go home.

Chairman Jerome could not let that pass unchallenged. He declared that "what we say to you we say with a straight tongue" and expressed the hope that "this is the last time that you will say, seem to say, disrespectful things to the Government."[17] He also informed Jake that Columbus had never made it to this continent and therefore could not have made a treaty with the Indians. Jerome then discussed how much better their offer was than what the Indians would get from the Dawes Act, urging them: "Act like white men and act like smart men would and don't talk about what Columbus did but about what will happen to your families tomorrow."[18]

The chairman did not intimidate Tawaconie Jim, who maintained that the Wichitas would be even more difficult to negotiate with if they had treaties like those of the Five Civilized Tribes; nevertheless, they would not take allotments. He attributed their small numbers to casualties suffered when they were allied with American troops against other Indians. Moreover, the price offered for their land was too low. Despite this, "if you want to trade with us all you have to do is to telegraph to Washington and have the [attorneys'] contracts approved."[19]

Sayre attempted to rebut Jim by stating that the attorneys would cost them $28,000 (10 percent of their sale price) or, put another way, $27 would be deducted from one of their $50 per capitas. Nor, he declared, would the attorneys be able to provide them with another acre or another dollar. Sayre quoted President Harrison as saying, "the Indian has no more use for a lawyer than a pony has for 5 legs." And, the commissioner concluded, the government "knows much better what is good for the Indian than the Indian does himself."[20]

Jim was not fazed by the commissioner's eloquence. He continued to insist on having an attorney present: "Is it not a law that a man can have a lawyer if he wants it?"[21] He then observed that the commissioners had yet to inform the Indians of the price per acre the government was offering, which elicited the response that for the land declared surplus after allotment the government would pay about fifty cents per acre. Sayre defended that figure by pointing out that the Indians would have first pick of the land, leaving the sand hills for the government. He also observed that fifty cents was about what the United States had paid the Cheyennes and Arapahos and the Potawatomis and Shawnees, and that the Iowas had received less, about thirty-eight cents. According to Sayre, the Creeks and Seminoles had received more because they had ceded land in a block without reserving allotments of the best land. Finally, the commissioner reminded the Indians that the Cheyennes and Arapahos and the Choctaws and Chickasaws also had claims to the Wichita land that would have to be quieted. But Towaconie Jim remained adamantly opposed to selling. He argued that one reason the Cheyennes and Arapahos had sold for such a low figure was their awareness that they were selling land that belonged to the Wichitas.

That exchange occurred on 15 May, and little changed in the five sessions over the next ten days. Warren Sayre left for Indiana on personal business, going by way of St. Louis, as he was able to confer there with Secretary Noble, who was visiting the city. Presumably Sayre filled him in on the obstinate refusal of the Wichitas to complete any agreement without the presence of their attorneys.

In Sayre's absence Jerome shouldered most of the burden, although Judge Wilson played a more active role, using the vernacular that he believed to be most effective in communicating with Indians. When Sergeant Tom (Caddo) protested that eighty acres of crop land was insufficient, Wilson declared that he had only forty acres himself and "I make my corn and beans and everything to live on."[22] When the Caddo complained of the fifty-cent offer, the judge observed, "you have a right to set a price but the Commission ain't a going to pay you more than four bits."[23] Because the Indians would presumably take the best land by allotment, Wilson complained, resorting to his favorite bromide, "you take all the meat off and leave us the bone."[24]

Towaconie Jim continued to be the commissioners' most vocal opponent. He constantly harped on the need for attorneys, arguing that even the

Cheyennes had been permitted them despite having killed many whites. He also made the point that he could raise twenty-five bushels of corn on an acre and sell it for fifty cents a bushel, yet the government was offering only fifty cents for the whole acre. Jim then got in a dig at the commissioners by complaining that the Indians were being forced to neglect their crops as the negotiations dragged on, but the commissioners were drawing ten to fifteen dollars a day and actually profiting from the prolonged discussions. He observed sarcastically that if the Indians were being paid at the same rate, "we could stay here too."[25]

Jerome rebuked him for bringing up the commissioners' salaries and attempted to give an air of inevitability to what they were proposing. He referred again to other commissions operating in the Northwest, cited the wishes of the president, and invoked the names of senators Henry M. Teller and Henry L. Dawes as friends of the Indian and staunch proponents of allotment. Furthermore, Jerome declared that the size of the government's offer had been fixed by "higher authority" (Congress) and that the Dawes Act, with its less generous terms, was their only alternative.[26]

Jerome's eloquence had no impact. Caddo Jake indicated, apologetically, that while Jerome had earlier rebuked the Indians for criticizing the government and the commission, he still wanted to defer allotment and sale of the surplus land until the children had been educated. Returning to the fray when Jerome proposed that the council be adjourned until the following Tuesday, May 26, Towaconie Jim queried the chairman as to whether his lawyers would be present. Getting a negative response, he stated bluntly that the Indians had nothing more to say and would not be attending the session.

Nevertheless, when that day rolled around, Tawaconie Jim was in attendance, because the long-awaited attorney, Luther H. Pike, had reached the reservation. Probably it was with the approval of Secretary Noble, secured after he had learned from Warren Sayre that it was either deal with the attorney present or abandon efforts to negotiate with the Wichitas. But now it was all sweetness and light as Chairman Jerome announced Pike's arrival-with "great pleasure."[27] It would be two days, however, before he appeared at a council session, and then it was to report that he had been meeting with the Indians to determine their objectives and to prepare a paper incorporating them. Pike revealed that the delay in formulating the Wichita position had been caused by their reluctance to accept allotment, although "I presented every view that I possibly could to get them to accept that proposition."[28] No wonder Jerome had welcomed Pike with "great pleasure."

Luther Pike was the son of Albert Pike, who had represented the Confederacy in negotiating alliances with tribes in Indian Territory. The son had been acquainted with the Wichitas for many years. He first met them at the Fort Arbuckle council in 1859, and he worked with the Indians in 1883 to strengthen their case for compensation for land lost to the United States when the government created the Cheyenne and Arapaho Reservation. Pike was a native of Arkansas and Judge Wilson knew him well, asserting that "if the Indians have a friend in America it is Pike."[29]

At his first full meeting with council on 30 May, Pike announced that "my position is nothing but that of an attorney between these Indians and the Government and persuading these Indians to take allotments."[30] That was a strange position to take, since the Wichitas and not the government would be paying his fee. Pike did aver that the Wichita claim to much of the area occupied by the Cheyennes and Arapahos and the Kiowas, Comanches, and Apaches was "well founded." Indeed, in 1883 Pike had invested considerable time in preparing the Wichitas to contest their case. He also drafted a constitutional form of government for them and researched the history of Wichita-white relations in order to establish their residence since Coronado. Nothing had come of that enterprise, but he had retained his research notes, which would be incorporated in new Wichita efforts to be compensated for lost territory.

At this session of council Pike gave a synopsis of Wichita history and professed complete confidence in their claims to aboriginal occupancy and ownership: "They understood at Arbuckle [1859] . . . that what is now known as the leased district was theirs as long as the grass grows and the river flows."[31] Although the commissioners had maintained from the beginning that dealing with tribal land claims was not part of their mission, Jerome was inclined to indulge Pike in this recital if it made the Indians happy. After hearing the attorney, the chairman announced that he was adjourning the council until that afternoon in order to permit the commissioners to react to the paper Pike had presented them.

One of the Wichita demands was that a north-south line be drawn through the reservation, with one of the two resulting divisions containing enough land to equal the size of all of the allotments—and that one the Indians would occupy. When Pike presented the paper to the commissioners, he assured them that he had told the Wichitas the government would never consent to simply creating a smaller reservation. Again, this was a strange stance for an attorney whom the Indians were paying to represent their interests.

When the session got underway that afternoon, Jerome quickly made the point that the commission was not created to entertain Wichita land claims. Nor did he respond favorably to most of the points in Pike's memorandum, in which the Wichitas agreed to sell the surplus land, but at a price of $1.25 an acre as opposed to the fifty cents offered by the commission. The Indians also wanted both of the initial payments to be made with no strings attached, rather than the second one requiring government approval as to how it was spent. And the Wichitas wanted the remainder of the purchase price to be held in the Treasury only until the end of the twenty-five-year trust period and then distributed among them.

Jerome and colleagues were more favorably inclined to three other proposals in Pike's memorandum. They were willing that the Wichitas pursue their claims against the government, but only after the trade had been completed. They were also agreeable to trying to work out a procedure to permit allottees to purchase additional land, for $1.25 an acre, to give them full access to the river when their surveyed line touched it at some point. Finally, Indians could take adjoining allotments, but the land could not be held in common.[32]

Following the recital of government views, Jerome announced that they would adjourn until Monday, 1 June. Chief Niasto (Towaconie) proposed that the adjournment carry over to Wednesday to enable the Indians to try to cope with the weeds threatening to take over their crops. This the chairman was unprepared to do, arguing that council business was more important than the men's hoeing their corn, which could be left to the women and children.[33]

When they did reconvene Monday, Jerome and Sayre rehashed the government's rationalizations for offering only fifty cents an acre. The Indians— so the argument went—were taking the best land for their allotments, and the Wichitas' title was faulty as they held the reservation neither by treaty nor by executive order. Towards the end of the session Judge Wilson offered one of his down-home bits of wisdom as to how the Indians might exploit their allotments: "get in the shade and rent it to some white man."[34]

The meeting the next day was aborted by Pike's failure, because of bad weather, to consult previously with his clients. The breakthrough came on

3 June. Towaconie Jim opened with a brief statement that since the commissioners and the Wichitas could not agree on a price, it should be left to Congress, and he then presented their terms.[35] Obviously with Pike's coaching, they had agreed to accept the agreement proposed by the commissioners except for the price, which they opted to leave to the determination of Congress.

After reading the Wichita proposal, David Jerome quizzed Pike about its details, "inasmuch as he prepared the Paper."[36] The chairman got statements from him that the Indians were agreeing to each of the government's terms except the price and that Pike himself would make the Wichita case to Congress, earning another tidy fee. Jerome was concerned that in subsequent dealings, other tribes might try to use this as a precedent. He also insisted that Congress had already "determined to open the lands to white settlement"[37] and had mandated the price. To that Pike rejoined: "Treating these people here as human beings the offer to negotiate assumes that they have a voice in what is done." What they wanted was to "leave it to the conscience of Congress,"[38] a frail reed for the Indians to depend upon. Like the Cherokees and others, these Indians believed that they had friends in Congress who would make them a better deal than the Cherokee Commission was offering. Jerome finally conceded that if the Wichitas wanted Congress to set the price, the commission would consent.

The following day, 4 June, Sayre opened the council by reviewing the articles in the revised draft. The commissioners then signed three copies and invited the Indians to come forward and record their Xs. Ultimately 152 of 227 adult males, including every chief and headman, signed. The agreement allowed for 1,060 allotments of 160 acres, leaving 3,600 homesteads of the same size for the whites.[39]

In their letter of transmittal to the president, the commissioners went out of their way to justify their fifty-cent offer, thus undercutting the Indian case for a higher figure. The Indians, they held, had no treaty confirming their right to the reservation, not even a presidential proclamation establishing it. The commissioners made no mention of the promises made at the Fort Arbuckle council in 1859, although they did estimate that the United States had given the Indians more than a million dollars' worth of rations, clothing, and farm equipment. In addition Washington was informed that the Indians would take the best land for their allotments and that the fifty-cent figure had been good enough for tribes with better titles than the Wichi-

TAKING INDIAN LANDS

tas had. The commissioners had the gall to conclude by declaring that they were not recommending a price but just making "observations in justification of our own determination in the matter."[40]

Not until 2 March 1895 did Congress finally ratify the Wichita Agreement. Nor was that the end of it. The Indians continued to protest that they had been swindled and filed suit. The Court of Claims would have the case for another four years before rendering a decision in 1899. It then held that the Wichitas were entitled to their allotments but that the Choctaws and Chickasaws should receive the payment for the surplus land. On appeal to the Supreme Court, however, the attorneys for the Wichitas got this judgment overruled. The Court of Claims finally determined that the Wichitas should receive $1.25 an acre, a total of $673,371.91. In May 1902 Congress appropriated the sum, with the proviso that $43,332.93 would be deducted for the attorneys who had represented the Wichitas before the Court of Claims and the Supreme Court. Congress had earlier appropriated $15,000 for the heirs of Luther Pike, deceased.[41] White advisors always seemed to be taken care of before the Indians who had sold the land.

At the conclusion of negotiations with the Wichitas, Jerome, Sayre, and Wilson returned to their homes. They had instructions to deal with the Mexican Kickapoos next but were not eager to do so. The prospect of protracted discussions with the recalcitrant Kickapoos in the Oklahoma summer heat was depressing. The commissioners were convinced that the conditions were so bad that they needed a physician assigned to them: "The weather will be extremely hot, the water unfit for domestic purposes and liable to cause disease when used. To these is added malaria of the extreme type."[42] Jerome went so far as to attribute their failure with the Kickapoos the previous summer partially to impaired health of the commissioners. The army, however, while willing to provide an armed escort and camping equipment, would not supply a physician.

Despite reports from their agent and the governor of Oklahoma Territory that they were ready to negotiate, the roughly three hundred Kickapoos showed no sign of it when the commissioners reached them. They appeared to be the same intransigents that Lucius Fairchild and Judge Wilson had encountered in October 1889 and David Jerome, Warren Sayre, and the judge the following June. An Oklahoma Territory newspaper described them as "defiant and arrogant" but "neither dangerous nor mischievous, although they are by no means desirable neighbors."[43]

The negotiations were relatively brief, with only four sessions resulting in a journal of fifty-seven pages. The Indian daily attendance was usually less than fifteen, and at the first meeting, 16 June 1891, Chief Wabemashay announced that he and four headmen—Washehove, Okanokasie, Keshokame, and Parthee—would do the talking for his people.[44] For their part, the commissioners stated their mission and immediately brought up the Dawes Act that the government would impose if the Indians failed to accept their terms.

The commission's proposal to the Kickapoos called for allotments of only eighty acres and a per capita payment of $220 for the land remaining after allotment. Once Sayre had explained the terms and given the Kickapoos a copy of the government's proposal, Jerome suggested that the Indians retire to consider it and return that afternoon. Parthee, who had been a headman for many years, gave the commissioners an inkling of how negotiations would proceed: "It is a fact that sometimes we have a piece of property that . . . we don't like to dispose of . . . because we like it: we are all like that . . . both Indians and white people."[45]

Jerome countered that even if a white man owned property that the government wanted, it could force him to sell, and it could do the same with the Kickapoos. He then displayed the volume of *U.S. Statutes at Large* containing the Dawes Act, which, Jerome said, required the Indians to take allotments. Okanokasie then introduced a new element to the negotiations by insisting that the Great Spirit owned the land and that they were where they were because he had so arranged it.[46] Okanokasie had the last word that session.

The next day the Kickapoos displayed a united front. Keshokame announced that Chief Wabemashay had selected him to speak for the Indians and that their decision, made in council the previous night, had been not to sell the land. He then turned the floor over to Okanokasie, who again spoke at length about the Great Spirit being all-powerful and decreeing that the Kickapoos should not sell. He included an apocalyptic vision of an eminent doomsday: "when you destroy the Indian Reservations the Great Spirit will come down and destroy the earth."[47] After repeating the warning several times, Okanokasie observed that the book Jerome had brought to the council appeared to be the work of the devil, "to make bad feeling."[48] But he closed on a more conciliatory note, maintaining that, as the government had demanded, they had settled on a reservation and were trying to support themselves; however, they still would not sell.

Judge Wilson had the chore of replying first to Okanokasie. He ignored the discussion of the Great Spirit, choosing to emphasize the failure of the Kickapoos to use but a small fraction of their reservation and the inevitable growth of a white population demanding homesteads. He maintained that the commissioners were not trying to buy their land, "we simply want to give you money to give you a start in stock so you can make a living without the buffalo."[49] Since it had been fifteen years since a Kickapoo could have seen a buffalo, few of the Indians were likely to have been impressed by that argument.

It was left to Warren Sayre and David Jerome to match Okanokasie's insights on the wishes of the Great Spirit. Sayre held that the red, white, and black men all had the same god and that while he provided the natural setting, all people had to labor to have anything, from firewood to crops and livestock. Jerome asked, if the Great Spirit opposed allotment, then why had the white settlers prospered? Moreover, queried the chairman, if the Great Spirit would be angry at the Kickapoos' taking allotments, why had he not destroyed the Iowas, the Sac and Fox, and the other Indians who had been allotted? Jerome defended their bringing the statutes to the council on the grounds that Parthee had said the Kickapoos would not sell. That prompted the Kickapoo to interject, "I said we don't want to trade, leave us alone we want the whole reservation."[50]

Only one of the Kickapoos, Che-quam-o-ko-ho-ko said anything that the commissioners wanted to hear during the Wednesday session. He had returned from Mexico nearly twenty years earlier and claimed that he remembered Americans who had arranged his return, alerting the Indians to the possibility of eventual change in their reservation status. He also deplored the lack of young men at the council and declared, "I would be very glad to have the Commission succeed."[51] Overall, however, the session ended with Jerome still trying to counter Okankasie's version of the desires of the Great Spirit with his own statements about the universality of the human heart.

The session on 18 June was brief. The commissioners made one last effort to convince the Kickapoos of the necessity that they accept allotment and sell their surplus land. Jerome asked them to think of the welfare of their wives and children. Sayre predicted that without the protection of soldiers they could not hold the reservation against the flood of settlers and reminded them that, only three years ago, the Kickapoos had had to request troops to evict a band of Shawnee squatters. But the Indians were not moved, repeating that no deal was possible. Okanokasie closed the session with, "This is the last day that we come together and we will shake hands and go in peace."[52]

The commissioners did managed to attract the largest number of Kickapoos yet to a council on Friday, 20 June, but if that encouraged the commissioners, they were quickly disillusioned. Jerome and Sayre made one last presentation of the government's proposal and then asked those present to come forward and add their Xs to the three already affixed to the agreement. At that moment one of the Kickapoos rose and told those Indians who did not want to sign to line up behind Chief Wabemashay, who had just entered accompanied by Parthee. To the chagrin of the commissioners, all of the Kickapoos except for the three signatories joined their chief. Wabemashay abruptly terminated the council with a mocking, "Now we are about done, ain't we, you see how it turns out. Good Bye."[53]

The outcome could not have surprised their agent, who, in his annual report that year, testified that the failure of their crops in 1890 had led to the starvation of a few Kickapoos. Yet after he had finagled emergency rations for them, many of the Indians refused to accept them for fear that it was a government ruse to sign them up for allotments. The agent still expressed confidence that the Kickapoos would ultimately have to capitulate, and when the commissioners left they promised to return promptly if the Indians had a change of mind. They could not have been confident of that's happening at the time. In their report to the president they attributed their failure to the Kickapoos' being "obstinate to a degree rarely met with in any Indians today" and to encouragement that the Kickapoos had received from Big Jim's Band of Potawatomis.[54]

Information as to what happened after the June negotiations lacks significant detail. We do know that the commissioners scattered to their homes and that in the next two months the Kickapoos held some councils, one John T. Hill appearing in the role of advisor. A white man married to a Creek, Hill was acquainted with the Kickapoos because he had pastured cattle on their reservation and had served as a federal marshall enforcing the ban on liquor for Indians. A. M. Gibson, author of an able Kickapoo tribal study, attributes much of Hill's standing among the Indians to his being, in their eyes, the embodiment of the law.[55]

In 1890 Hill persuaded the Indians to employ him as an advisor, although he was not an attorney. Indeed, his handwriting and spelling offer little evidence of formal education. But Hill, who had an eye on the main chance, would later intervene, to his profit, in the commission's negotiations with the Kiowas, Comanches, and Apaches and would seek to represent the Chickasaws and Choctaws in their land claims.

On 16 August 1891, fifty-one Kickapoos—presumably all the adult males—put their Xs to a statement witnessed by Hill and Joseph Whipple. The latter was a mixed-blood Cherokee and an adopted Kickapoo who served as interpreter despite his being illiterate. The statement granted Okanokasie, Keshokame, and John Hill "full power to deal with the Government or commission," although it did not specifically authorize them to sell land or go to Washington.[56]

The delegation that met the commissioners in Oklahoma City consisted of Whipple, Okanokasie, Keshokame, and five other Kickapoo headmen. Three of the Indians, including Okanokasie and Keshokame, had been vocal opponents of the Cherokee Commission during the councils in June. Nevertheless, their Xs appear with those of the other delegates on two statements prepared 29 August in Oklahoma City. The first statement was signed by Jerome and colleagues, Okanokasie, Keshokame, and John Hill. It declared that the tribe had agreed to sell their surplus land on the terms offered them but refused allotment, preferring to hold their remaining land in common. To resolve this difference the Kickapoos would send Okanokasie, Keshokame, and Hill to Washington to lay their case before Secretary Noble for final judgment. The second statement, signed by Whipple and the other five Kickapoos, simply attested to their knowledge and approval of the first statement.[57]

By telegram, Jerome secured Noble's consent to bring Okanokasie, Keshokame, Hill, and Whipple to Washington. The Kickapoos later would maintain that Hill had gotten the tribe's approval under false pretenses, promising to help them obtain money for claims they had against the government. Okanokasie also remembered his shock at seeing Jerome and his colleagues on the train bearing all of them to Washington.

The Kickapoo delegation and the commissioners arrived in the capital on 2 September, and the following day the Indians met Secretary Noble. According to the commissioners' version of events: "A full and free discussion of the question was had between the Indians and the Secretary, whereupon he took the matter under advisement, and on Wednesday, September 9, 1891, decided that the Indians should take allotments and hold the title in severalty. Thereupon the agreement . . . was executed.[58] It would have come as a great surprise had the secretary ruled otherwise, given the government's commitment to eliminate the Indian practice of holding land in common. Holding out the hope that he might do so was a devious tactic on the part of the commissioners and John Hill.

By the terms of the agreement to which the Kickapoos were now committed, each Indian would receive only 80 acres and the remainder of the reservation would be sold to the United States—enough for 160-acre homesteads for some 1,200 settlers. In his 1893 annual report the Interior secretary described the cession as "magnificent land. . . . no land heretofore opened surpasses it in value for agricultural purposes."[59] For that "magnificent land" the Indians would receive a total of $64,650, less than thirty-five cents per acre. The preface to the agreement described it as "entered into on the Kickapoo Reservation . . . on the 21st day of June, A.D. 1891 . . . and completed at the City of Washington, D.C. this 9th day of September, A.D. 1891."[60] As the commissioners had left the Kickapoo village with only three signatures from the fifty-one adult males, it was grossly misleading to claim that the agreement was "entered into on the Kickapoo Reservation." It did, however, have appended to it the names of all the adult males whose marks had been on the document drafted at the Kickapoo village on 16 August 1891. Although there are variations in the name spellings, they are sufficiently similar to be recognized and some of the name groupings are identical.

A day after the agreement was signed, Okanokasie and Keshokame, in a statement attested to by Warren Sayre, asked that $5,172 be withheld from their $64,650 to pay John Hill's fee.[61] When the matter was brought before the House Committee on Indian Affairs, it spoke glowingly of Hill's "nearly two years of residence and labor with them, suffering many privations," and argued that but for his "knowledge . . . of their customs and habits, and the long acquaintance he had with the Indians, and their confidence in him no agreement could have been made."[62] This was a remarkable assessment of the contributions of a man who was apparently unknown to the commissioners until he surfaced after their failure in June 1891. It would be more accurate to say that he was just another in a long line of white and mixed-blood go-betweens who enabled American officials to dictate treaties and agreements while maintaining the facade of pure negotiation.

As ratified by Congress in March 1893, the agreement differed in a few details from the original. The option that the Indians might choose to receive the payment for their land per capita was deleted. And, of course, the $5,172 for Hill was not part of the original agreement. Commissioner of Indian Affairs T. J. Morgan, when he vetted the agreement at the direction of Secretary Noble, also advised against the Indians' being permitted to get the entire payment per capita, but he did say that any change would require the approval of the Kickapoos—advice ignored by Noble.[63]

Before the agreement had even been presented to Congress, it had become a heated issue back on the Kickapoo Reservation. On their return the tribal delegation hosted a village council and feast, with beef provided by the government. According to Okanokasie and Joe Whipple, nearly all those present then approved the delegates' actions. Shortly afterward, however, 226 of 284 Kickapoos joined the third member of the delegation, Keshokame, in repudiating the contract.[64]

Once Congress ratified the agreement in 1893, Secretary Noble authorized $50 per capita, possibly to facilitate the next step—getting the Kickapoos to register for allotments. Most flatly refused to accept the $50 and sign up for allotments. As was the practice, however, those who refused to accept allotments had them chosen for them. Elizabeth Test, a member of the Society of Friends and a field matron in the Indian Service working among the Kickapoos, reported in August 1894 on their condition. Only a "very few," she stated, had understood that they were selling their land; many still refused to occupy their allotments and had moved to a remote part of their reservation, trying to maintain their old lifestyle.[65]

One of the irreconcilables, Pa-pa-shekit, appeared in Washington in the winter of 1892–93 and sought help from Charles Painter, the Washington agent for the Indian Rights Association who had questioned the performance of the Cherokee Commission in dealing with the Cheyennes and Arapahos. Painter, who now championed the cause of the Kickapoos, began to gather information on the manner in which the agreement had been drafted. When a Kickapoo delegation went to Washington in February, he helped them make their case to the House Committee on Indian Affairs. He also devoted seven pages to the Kickapoos in his annual report to the Indian Rights Association in 1894.

Part of Painter's report was based on interviews with the Kickapoos on their reservation in November 1894, and he listed Keshokame as one of the informants. Painter composed a scenario that did nothing to improve the images of Secretary Noble and the Cherokee Commission. He denounced Noble for having inspired the creation of the commission in order to make more Indian land available to settlers, a commission that "put back the cause of civilization in that Territory more than fifty years." In its dealings with the Indians, Painter fulminated, the commission, "by trickery, coercion, threats, and cunning, over-reached and defrauded . . . these dependent and trusting wards of the Nation."[66]

Nevertheless, the Kickapoos were unable to block the passage of the agreement into law in March 1893. Their chronic unrest did finally lead Congress to reexamine their status in 1907. The Senate published a report compiled by its Subcommittee on Indian Affairs that included a deposition by the proprietor of the hotel in which the Kickapoo delegation had been housed in September 1891. He swore that Joseph Whipple, the interpreter, had confided in him that "Hill was to be paid $5,000 for fooling the Indians into a treaty, and that Hill had agreed to pay him $500 and give him a good time in Washington for helping to fooling the Indians."[67] The subcommittee stressed that the Kickapoos had been paid less than 32.5¢ per acre for their surplus land, although the government had turned around and sold it to settlers for $1.50 per acre.

To compensate the Kickapoos for the obvious underpayment in 1908, Congress appropriated $215,000, but $26,875 was deducted from that for one Martin J. Bentley for services to the Indians. Bentley was another of those con men who preyed on the tribes. His disgraceful manipulation of Kickapoo factions after the Cherokee Commission finished with them is detailed in A. M. Gibson's *The Kickapoos.*[68]

In their letter to President Harrison reporting the Kickapoo Agreement, the commissioners suggested a schedule that would carry them into the summer of 1893. Unlike Lucius Fairchild, they were obviously in no rush to get back to their normal occupations. Alfred Wilson was in his early seventies and no longer practiced law. David Jerome was in his early sixties and apparently retired from active participation in his hardware business, while Warren Sayre, in his late forties, showed no regret at being away from his law practice. Indeed, Sayre would soon be seeking a federal judgeship in Oklahoma Territory and, failing that, aspired to a seat on the District of Columbia federal bench. But according to him, being a member of the Cherokee Commission paid better than being a federal judge, so all three were pleased to continue as long as possible. Life in the field could be rugged and demanding; however, there were intervals of weeks—even months—between negotiations, and meanwhile their pay continued.

At least a month elapsed between the completion of the Kickapoo Agreement in Washington and the resumption of their work in Oklahoma. When Jerome returned, his wife accompanied him. She would remain in Oklahoma during these negotiations.[69] This time the commissioners' focus would be on the Ponca Agency's six reservations, housing the Poncas, Tonkawas, Osages, Otoe-Missiouris, and Kaws. All of these tribes had been moved to the eastern end of the Outlet as part of the post–Civil War effort to concentrate Indians in order to free up more land in Kansas and elsewhere for settlers. In the instructions the commission had received in 1889, all six tribes were now to be allotted and the United States would purchase the surplus land.

As early as September 1890, President Harrison had authorized the allotment of the Tonkawas, Otoe-Missouris, Pawnees, and Poncas. The allotting agents began with the smallest of the tribes, the Tonkawas. Each of them had been assigned 160 acres by the time the Cherokee Commission arrived. These Indians were a remnant of a Southern Plains tribe that in the 1840s numbered over six hundred. Although generally allied with the Texans against the Comanches, they had suffered badly at the hands of the white men. In the early 1850s the government located the Tonkawas, together with the Wichitas and affiliated tribes, on the Brazos Reservation in Texas. When Texans forced the closure of that reservation in 1859, they were shifted north to the Wichita Agency in the Leased District. As Southern sympathizers in the Civil War they had come under attack from U.S.-affiliated tribes, who in 1862 massacred 167 Tonkawa men, women, and children. After the war the survivors clustered around army posts, and the men acted as scouts for the cavalry. In 1884 the government finally located them on the reservation recently abandoned by the Nez Percé, who had been permitted to return to their homes in the Northwest.[70]

This is where the Cherokee Commission found the tiny band of sixty-seven Tonkawas when it arrived at the Ponca Agency in October. No journal of the negotiations has been uncovered, but the commissioners quickly obtained an agreement. The Tonkawas did produce a letter from the commissioner of Indian affairs in 1885 promising a title if they agreed to remove to the reservation. Regrettably, Congress took no action to fulfill this commitment, leaving the Indians with neither a treaty nor an executive order to buttress their claim to the land.

The commissioners, however, believed that the Tonkawas needed some payment to help them get established as homesteaders. So they included in the agreement, "under guise of buying from them what they thought they owned," the payment of $30,600, or about thirty-six cents an acre, for the surplus 84,710 acres. Per capitas of $25 and $50 would be paid each Indian, and the remainder of the $30,600 would be placed in the Treasury to draw 5 percent.[71] David Jerome characterized the settlement as "thrifty," as indeed it was.[72]

Within ten days of the execution of the agreement, all seventeen of the adult male Tonkawas who had signed it had put their Xs on a letter to Secretary Noble protesting the "pretended settlement."[73] They accused the local Indian agent of threatening to withdraw their allotments if they did not accept the agreement. The Tonkawas also claimed that they had demanded $1.25 for land for which they had been paid thirty-six cents an acre. They had contracted with a law firm to represent them, but a resulting protest to the Interior Department was in vain. The Fifty-second Congress considered the agreement in 1892 and ratified it 3 February 1893. No member of Congress rallied to the support of the tiny group. Indeed, Senator Henry L. Dawes, often described as the best friend the Indians had in Congress, dismissed the Tonkawas as "a little body of seventy Indians" with "no real title to that property."[74] Dawes even supported a move to spend the interest on the $30,600 promised the Indians, on roads, bridges, and schools that otherwise would have to be supported by tax-paying Oklahomans. That would have been a radical step, but fortunately for all Indians, Dawes and the Senate Committee on Indian Affairs did not get sufficient support to set that precedent.

In Congress pressure was mounting to open more Indian land to settlers. For their part, Jerome and his colleagues appeared to be becoming more cynical, more ruthless in their treatment of small tribes that resisted allotment and sale of their surplus land. The commissioners tended to explain their difficulty in discharging their mission by references to conniving whites—of which there were plenty—and to Indian troublemakers from neighboring tribes. But they themselves employed unscrupulous characters such as John Hill and Joseph Whipple and fostered tribal factionalism by their divisive tactics.

TAKING INDIAN LANDS

The day the Tonkawa Agreement was wrapped up, 21 October 1891, David Jerome had notified Secretary Noble by wire. Noble responded with congratulations and a reminder that a Senate committee would be visiting the Cherokees early in November and that the Cherokee Commission should go to Tahlequah to touch base with the senators. A fourth attempt to purchase the Outlet was about to get underway.

7

A Cherokee Agreement at Last

UNDER PRESSURE FROM SECRETARY NOBLE, David Jerome and his colleagues had reluctantly left the Ponca Agency early in November 1891 to travel to Tahlequah in order to meet a senatorial committee. Once in Tahlequah they decided to try to reopen negotiations with the Cherokee Nation. The commissioners called on Chief Mayes to inform him of their desire, and on 11 November they made a formal request for the resumption.[1]

The passage of a year had not improved the Cherokee bargaining position. Their government was in serious financial straits, and members of Congress were getting restive under the pressure brought by thousands of white home seekers living in tents and shanties along the southern boundary of Kansas, just over the line from the Outlet. Business leaders in Kansas City and St. Louis, as well as railroad promoters added their weight to the agitation for opening the Outlet—with or without the consent of the Cherokee Nation.

In February 1891 the House Committee on Territories issued a report reflecting the pressure for an opening. The committee recommended appropriating a sum suffcent to pay the Cherokees $1.25 per acre for the Outlet and incorporating it into the Oklahoma Territory without further consultation with the Indians. To justify this the committee stressed the perceived inequity of millions of acres in the Outlet's lying vacant when they could provide 160-acre homesteads for 37,626 poor families.[2] Meanwhile, the 25,000 Cherokees could continue to hold their over-five-million-acre estate east of 96° longitude, the equivalent of five hundred acres for each family of five.[3]

If the committee's bill were enacted into law, the Cherokee Nation would receive almost $7,500,000 for the Outlet, with about $2,500,000 of that sum being paid immediately per capita—a tactic designed to attract support from at least some Cherokee citizens. The remaining $5,000,000 was to be placed in the Treasury to earn 5 percent that would be disbursed to the Indians annually. Added to the income the Cherokees received from over $7,600,000 of their funds already in the Treasury, that would afford the nation an annuity of nearly $389,500. "Under such financial conditions of lands and money," declared the committee, "there is no room for sentiment in our dealings with them, justice is all they can claim."[4] Regrettably, they would have trouble getting that.

Such a settlement would be fair, the committee reasoned, because it regarded the Cherokee title to the Outlet as badly flawed. The report cited opinions of the attorney general, the assistant attorney general assigned to the Interior Department, and Secretary Noble to that effect and further stated: "Your committee is irresistibly driven to the conclusion that the Cherokee Indians were never given . . . anything more than an easement . . . to travel over . . . the Cherokee Outlet to the great hunting grounds of the West, which easement is now forfeited by non-use, not having been travelled upon since A.D. 1855 for hunting purposes . . . by the Cherokees."[5]

The committee also argued, incredibly, that as "the alleged owners can not settle, can not improve, can not lease, and can not sell to any person other than the United States," the government's offer of $1.25 per acre was appropriate, even generous.[6] It cited the initial government evaluation of Outlet land at 47.49¢ per acre and, subsequently, at 70¢. To undercut Cherokee demands for more than $1.25, the committee quoted National Council instructions to its delegates, 1873–81, indicating that at that time they wanted to sell and would accept less than $1.25. The committee observed that when the Cherokee Nation first leased to cattlemen in 1881, its new appreciation of the value of the Outlet was promptly reflected in instructions to the delegates the following year to accept no less than $1.25 per acre.[7]

The report repeated the canard that Chief Mayes himself had sought the creation of the Cherokee Commission and exonerated its members of any responsibility for unproductive months of negotiations. The report also questioned "whether American civilization shall be stayed in its onward progress and a desert of desolation in the heart of the country be perpetuated." Why? Because a few hundred white men with a little Cherokee blood want to "maintain themselves in luxury, as leaders of less educated and intellectual members of their so-called Cherokee Nation of Indians."[8] The commitee believed that if it were possible "to reach the ordinary Indian free from the influence of Chief Mayes and his fellows, and submit the proposition directly to the great body of the Indians, a speedy solution . . . of the Cherokee Outlet problem would be had." But since the congressmen did not think this possible, the only thing was for Congress to recognize that the Indians were wards of the government and to legislate a settlement at $1.25 per acre, "a fair price for these lands."[9]

Two decisions of Oklahoma Territory judges upped the pressure on the Cherokees by ruling that the Indians had only an easement right to the Outlet and by nonuse had forfeited even that. Citing a judge who upheld the removal of cattle from leased range, a newspaper in the territory observed, "A Texas longhorn cow has long enough been considered better than a poor man wanting a home."[10] The paper also reported that a meeting of Boomers was to be held in Arkansas City, Kansas, with possible attendees including Representative Charles H. Mansur of Missouri, who had introduced the bill discussed above, and two members of the Kansas congressional delegation. These were Senator William Alfred Peffer and Representative Jeremiah Simpson, both spokesmen for the struggling farmer class.

In the executive branch it was Secretary Noble who was most intent on the government's acquiring the Outlet. His 1891 annual report contained a self-congratulatory item regarding the success of the current administration in opening about 23,000,000 acres to white settlement. As Noble smugly observed, unlike European nations that competed with each other for colonies on remote islands and continents, "our country is so fortunately situated that within its own boundaries are vast tracts of fertile land heretofore unused, on which communities can establish themselves in a single day."[11] As an illustration, he offered the opening of the surplus lands of the Sac and Fox and the Iowas in September. At noon an estimated 20,000 people had rushed over the line at the signal, and before sunset the roughly 5,500 quarter sections had all been claimed. Presumably, the unsuccessful thousands would try again elsewhere, including the Outlet when it was opened.

Noble had a problem within his own department—Commissioner of Indian Affairs T. J. Morgan. The head of the Indian Office did espouse the conventional wisdom that allotment in severalty was essential in order to expose the Indians to the stimulating virtues of private property, which— by limiting the Indians to 160-acre allotments—would also open vast areas to white settlement. "Whatever right and title the Indians have . . . is subject to and must yield to the demands of civilization," Morgan argued.[12] He maintained, however, that the Cherokees were correct in describing their title as one in fee as opposed to one of occupancy based on a treaty or executive order. Having a title in fee meant that, like any property owner, the Cherokee Nation could refuse to sell except at its own price.[13] Morgan's temerity in adopting a position contrary to that of his boss was in vain. Congress was unmoved by the Indian commissioner's logic, and he had only further alienated Secretary Noble.

Nor was Congress persuaded by a memorial submitted by the Cherokee delegates Richard M. Wolfe and David Rowe protesting any congressional move to bypass negotiations and acquire the Outlet on dictated terms. In the document the Cherokees carefully reviewed the history of their nation's claim, stressing the terms by which the Outlet had been acquired and the federal court decisions upholding the Cherokee title. Wolfe and Rowe concluded, "surely those representing the United States Government cannot afford to occupy the questionable position, having driven away all our other purchasers to force on us a dishonorable and unfair bargain."[14] The memorial was reprinted in the *Advocate* just as the 1891 Cherokee election campaign was about to get underway.

The *Advocate* worked to keep its readers informed of the Outlet situation by publishing the reports of their delegates to Washington and stories on the mood of Congress. The gravity of the Cherokee situation was a factor in making the 1891 election, in the editor's judgment, "the hottest ever conducted in this Nation."[15] Three parties ran slates of candidates, all three acknowledging that they must sell the Outlet while insisting that the Cherokees should be able to set the price.

There was also a growing concern among the Indians about the wisdom of continuing to hold their land in common indefinitely. Members of Congress were increasingly vocal about the size of Cherokee landholdings. The report of the House Committee on Territories, cited above, declared that, including the Outlet, it was 17,707,279 acres, an average of 3,116 per Indian. "This is a situation," warned the committee, "not borne with toleration or looked upon with equanimity by the poor people of the country seeking for homes, and . . . should be remedied by the Government at the earliest hour possible."[16]

During the 1891 campaign the National and Liberal Party candidates favored their brand of allotment, simply dividing the public domain equally among the Cherokees and leaving no surplus for the United States to purchase. This proposal was justified on the grounds that individual citizens of the nation were monopolizing thousands of acres, a case in point being Colonel Robert L. Owen, the former Indian agent, who, according to his biographer Kenny Lee Brown, "controlled" about 10,000 acres.[17] Another Cherokee complained of in the *Advocate* was "old Zach Foreman, near Webber Falls," who had "colonized nearly one hundred worthless Alabama negroes" to cultivate "several thousand acres of the best agricultural lands in the Cherokee Nation."[18] Another writer in the same issue concluded that the time was fast approaching when good farmland would be unavailable to young Cherokees seeking to establish homesteads. Nevertheless, the Downing Party, the third competitor in the 1891 campaign, opposed allotment while it claimed that it would end such aggrandizement. On that platform the Downing Party candidate for principal chief, Joel Mayes, easily won reelection. That could not have been good news to the Cherokee Commission, given Mayes's steadfast opposition to sale of the Outlet on the terms it was offering.

In the weeks before Jerome and his colleagues reached Tahlequah, the *Advocate* carried a letter by Colonel Owen advocating a bold solution to the Outlet problem. He proposed that the National Council launch a preemptive strike by dividing the entire Outlet among the Cherokees and issuing patents in fee: "when Congress is confronted by twenty odd thousand patents, there is no danger of a law being passed to ignore the right of the people owning this land. The title is clear. Let us act at once."[19] Owen distributed several hundred copies of his pamphlet, *A Plan For Saving the Cherokee People Millions of Dollars.* He assumed that his fellow citizens would sell their Outlet properties and realize more this way than by sharing the sum being offered by the United States. The *Advocate* commented that the scheme "is well worthy of serious thought." The paper even suggested that the new Democrat-controlled Congress, elected in reaction to the late Republican "Billion Dollar Congress," would be so reluctant to spend money that it might step aside and allow Owen's plan to bring the Outlet into the market.[20] There is no evidence, however, that Chief Mayes and the Council gave Owens' scheme serious consideration. The colonel professed to be advocating the plan in the interest of the general welfare. Nevertheless, he was able to take advantage of the government's proposition by becoming the agent for sixty of the sixty-two Cherokees ultimately granted eighty-acre allotments in the Outlet under Article 5 of the agreement.[21]

Chief Mayes did not refer to the plan in his annual address, delivered at Tahlequah on 4 November. He did make a strong statement about the indisputable Cherokee title to the Outlet, "by patent in *fee simple*, now a matter of record in the General Land Office in Washington." Mayes warned that another effort by the government to buy the tract could be expected, and it should be at a fair market price. "I do not believe," declared the chief, "that the power exists anywhere to take these lands from the Cherokee without their consent, unless by an act of robbery."[22]

The chief did respond promptly to David Jerome's request for a resumption of negotiations. Seven Cherokees would represent their nation—E. C. Boudinot, J. A. Scales, Roach Young, George Downing, William Triplett, Thomas Smith, and W. W. Hastings. Only Boudinot and Downing had participated in the previous round of discussions, Boudinot as secretary. This time he would be the sole spokesman for the Cherokees. Trained in the law, he most recently had been editor of the *Advocate*. A nephew of Elias C. Boudinot of *Cherokee Tobacco* fame, he had gained considerable notoriety by killing the editor of another Indian Territory paper—in self-defense, as determined by a jury in Judge Parker's court in Fort Smith.[23] Boudinot would prove to be a forceful and articulate representative of Cherokee interests, and his reputation may have helped guarantee him a respectful audience.

The commissioners and the Cherokees met on seventeen days between 18 November and 19 December 1891, usually for morning and afternoon sessions. Their meetings were held in an office in the Cherokee capitol, with their transactions recorded in a journal of 206 pages. In their letter to Chief Mayes the commissioners had expressed the hope that the progress made on some issues in the 1890 talks would be taken into account,[24] and at the first meeting Jerome declared, "we are here to renew the work that has been discussed, more or less, very elaborately heretofore."[25] E. C. Boudinot made clear, however, that the Cherokees would not be bound by the positions taken by their predecessors. It could not have encouraged Jerome and his colleagues that Boudinot had to ask for a copy of the 1890 proceedings.

The negotiators would indeed find themselves rehashing most of the arguments employed a year earlier. Initially the tones were conciliatory, and

Jerome proposed that their meetings be opened to the public. The Cherokees declined this suggestion, although Chief Mayes did put in an appearance twice. Jerome and Sayre did almost all the talking for the United States, and Judge Wilson was absent for a brief period towards the end.

On the first day of deliberations Boudinot requested that the commissioners present their proposition in writing, which they did in the next session. They adjourned early to give the Cherokees an opportunity to consider the offer. On 23 November they reconvened and the bargaining began. The commissioners had proposed to buy all Cherokee claims west of 96° longitude, but the Indians wanted the western boundary defined as 100° in order to preserve any claims they might have to No Man's Land, the Panhandle. They also wanted the acreage estimated, which would enable them to arrive at the price per acre being offered by the United States. At the afternoon session the commissioners complied, but it quickly became apparent that the Indians were not happy with the U.S. proposal of a new tribunal to pass on intruders' claims to Cherokee citizenship.

Jerome and Sayre subjected Boudinot to a rigorous examination regarding the Indian position, beginning with how it defined intruders. In response, Boudinot excluded those individuals brought in under contract to work on Cherokee farms, as well as government and railroad employees. He then explained the process by which citizenship might be obtained. For example, intermarried men and women could be adopted by action of the National Council, as could individuals capable of convincing it of their Cherokee blood. The Council was the ultimate authority, and it could also strip any adoptee of citizenship for misbehavior. Moreover, no one could have property rights in the Cherokee Nation without citizenship. Boudinot sought to exclude freedmen from the discussion, maintaining that those recognized as citizens were already covered and those seeking citizenship were the subject of judicial proceedings then underway. When asked if the Cherokees would prefer the United States to leave the intruder problem exclusively in their hands, he responded sharply: "The government of the United States for the last twenty years has failed to remove these intruders although it is promised in every treaty, and they having accumulated we would rather the government would clear the country before turning it over to us."[26]

At that point Jerome invited Chief Mayes, who had appeared in the chamber, to comment on the difficulty of evicting intruders. The chief attributed it to neglect on the part of the government and sketched the way in which it had gone wrong. He maintained that the National Council had enacted a law requiring the intruders to dispose of their property and leave within three months of notification, but Interior Secretary William F. Vilas requested that the intruders be given an additional three months and Mayes complied. Vilas then issued orders for removal, but before they could be carried out a change of administration in March 1889 saw Vilas replaced by Noble and the new secretary declined to act. The chief speculated that Noble refused out of undue concern for the intruders' property rights to any improvements they might have made.

Chief Mayes then denounced the insolent behavior of intruders who would occupy and fence Cherokee land, build houses and barns with Indian timber and stone, and then defy eviction orders from his government. Without permits they even opened stores in the towns. "[W]e can't control them," the chief complained, "and the government won't put them out and the courts will do nothing."[27] He attributed the United States' inaction to the influence of the Cherokee Indian Citizenship Association, founded by William Jefferson Watts, which hired lobbyists in Washington. All that any intruder had to do to join the association was to state that he or she was a Cherokee and pay a membership fee of five dollars.[28]

David Jerome acknowledged that it was "a startling state of things: that there is an organization in your country . . . defying the laws." Having said that, however, he then used the gravity of the situation as an argument for a new tribunal, one in which the Indian members would be outnumbered two to one. Boudinot quickly tried to counter: "why create a tribunal to decide over what was finally decided by our tribunals. To create a new tribunal to try the right now would be an admission that they had not been finally dealt with and that they could put in a claim for their improvements."[29]

The debate on the intruder issue continued on 24 November and into the 25th. The commissioners spoke at length of their government's concern with the property loss intruders would suffer if they were expelled unceremoniously. Jerome observed gravely that "the magnitude of it is so very appalling"[30] and described it as involving six thousand people and millions of dollars in property. He even managed to invoke the memory of John Brown, suggesting that if the old abolitionist had had six thousand men at Harpers Ferry, he would not have ended up on the scaffold. Nor, he maintained, would Congress now suffer thousands of people to be deprived of millions in property without proper trial. "The government is so tenacious of the rights of its citizens," Jerome proclaimed, "that it will do anything to protect them."[31] The rights of the government's wards he ignored.

The commissioners did have precedent on their side. The United States, from its inception, had been torn between safeguarding Indian title until it was extinguished on the one hand and not infringing on the property rights of its citizens who squatted on Indian land on the other. On countless occasions the implementation of orders to remove intruders had been delayed in order to give them time to harvest their crops and round up livestock. President Harrison's delay in implementing his proclamation to remove cattle from the Outlet was, at least partially, a recent manifestation of this phenomenon.

Boudinot tried to make it clear that the intruders had had their day in court and that the Cherokee Nation had jurisdiction, as attested to by the Supreme Court. They were clearly trespassers and should be treated as such. As for their improvements, nine-tenths of them, Boudinot estimated, had been made after they had been ordered to remove. And when Judge Wilson raised a hypothetical case of an intermarried white man whose Indian wife died, following which he had married a white woman, the Cherokee disposed of it quickly. He stated sarcastically that the white man had forfeited all improvements, as he was no longer a citizen by virtue of his marriage to a Cherokee—he had chosen "to be governed by his heart rather than his improvements."[32] Having failed to reach an understanding on the intruder issue, the conferees moved on.

On 27 November the Cherokees presented a written response to the government's proposal; it was detailed and a shocker, consisting of a draft of an agreement with eight articles that essentially held:

1. The United States must remove all trespassers from the Cherokee Nation.

2. The trespassers must leave in place all buildings, fences, crops, and orchards. Article 15 of the 1866 treaty must be abrogated.

3. Cherokee courts should have exclusive jurisdiction in civil and criminal cases that involved only Cherokees.

4. The United States should provide an accounting of money and lands due the Cherokees under a series of nine treaties, and provide them access to federal courts to rectify any errors uncovered. In addi-

tion, the Cherokee Nation might sue the United States for money or land due it of a valuation of at least $5,000, and the suit would go to the head of the docket.

5. The United States would pay the Cherokees a sum equal to that they would have received from the railroads for crossing their land.

6. The United states should pay the Cherokees $400,000 for loss of revenues from Outlet leases.

7. The United States should compensate any Cherokees who would lose improvements in the Outlet.

8. The United States should pay $3 an acre for the Outlet.[33]

On the day that Boudinot delivered this manifesto, Warren Sayre wrote a letter to his friend in the White House, enclosing a copy of Chief Mayes's Thanksgiving proclamation. In a statement accompanying it, the chief had called on all Cherokees to "ask Him to continue to the Cherokee people that civil liberty they have enjoyed from time immemorial, and ask that they may continue in the peaceful possession of their land and homes."[34] Sayre described the chief as "Your ward," fifty-eight years old, weight 265 pounds, a one-eighth Cherokee who does not speak the language and is seeking in his proclamation protection "from the rapacity of you, his guardian."[35] Sayre suggested that, left to their own devices, the Cherokee masses would sell the Outlet, but the few in authority might refuse to deal.

Sayre also offered an explanation for the slow pace of the Cherokee Commission: "The indian [sic] is the slowest animal on earth—time is of no possible importance to him—and gratitude to the government for protection and care and very expensive conduct of indian affairs is unheard of." And, he added, "I believe Congress should enact that no person shall be denominated an Indian who is not possessed of at least one-half Indian blood."[36] He concluded by proposing that Congress appropriate $30,000 for the commission so that it might complete its work.

When negotiations resumed 1 December, David Jerome complained of a "night of pain and distress," to which the Cherokee memo of 27 November must have contributed. Although he said that he was in no condition to concentrate for long on anything, he felt that the "magnitude" of their mission compelled him to speak at least briefly.[37] He then criticized the Cherokee draft for introducing entirely new issues. Jerome said that he had searched his memory of forty years in business for a "parallel that would furnish me with a reason as to what was activating you."[38] He had been set off by Cherokee demands for what he regarded as unlimited access to federal courts in order to sue the United States. In addition the Cherokee price of $3 an acre for their land was, he declared, about three times what it was worth. Obviously distraught, he said that his remarks had been so "rambling" that he would ask Warren Sayre to clarify them.[39]

Sayre opened by declaring that the rumors circulating that claimed the commissioners had asked for additional time in order to seek instructions from Washington were unfounded: "we are here . . . without any instructions save our judgment and the act of Congress which created us."[40] He did not choose to reveal their instructions prepared by the Office of Indian Affairs. The evidence does indicate that the commissioners were now much less inclined to seek guidance from Secretary Noble or even to keep him regularly informed of their progress. Between Noble and Jerome there was not the bond of Civil War combat experience that was so important to veterans such as the secretary and Lucius Fairchild, and the secretary was having health problems that occasionally kept him out of the office.

Having made clear the relative independence of the commission, Sayre went on to state its positions forcefully. He advised the Cherokees that they were dependent upon the government and that Congress, by enacting a law of no more than four lines' length, could remove them from the protection of the Trade and Intercourse Acts, and they "would be simply ruined."[41] The actual removal of that semblance of security was highly unlikely, but he did not exaggerate the effect if it were to occur.

Sayre reviewed most of the issues from price through the additional considerations the Cherokees had demanded. He derided their request that Congress compensate the handful of Cherokee settlers in the Outlet for their improvements. As for the recommendation that Congress pay damages for Cherokee losses suffered when President Harrison cancelled their leases in the Outlet, Sayre said that the commissioners were "unwilling to dignify it even by discussion."[42] He chose to interpret the Cherokee language on this issue as disrespectful to President Harrison. Judge Wilson chimed in that the Indians must have forgotten that the majority of the commissioners were Republicans loyal to the president. As for the $3 an acre, Sayre said flatly that "we will not at any time agree" to pay more than what had already been offered—about $1.32 an acre.[43]

Boudinot did his best to answer the flood of objections. Repeating some of the arguments other Cherokees had used in 1890, he held that they were only asking a price commensurate with that of comparable land in contiguous areas. As to the other Cherokee demands for "concessions," as the commissioners insisted on calling them, Boudinot observed caustically, that it would not be a concession for the United States to deliver on commitments promised in the Treaty of 1835 and every treaty since. The Indians, he declared, had not intended to be disrespectful of President Harrison; they knew no other way than to go to Congress for redress. As for their postponing transfer of title until all conditions in the agreement had been met, "we have . . . some promises of the government that have been delayed generations and have not been carried out yet."[44] When Sayre asked if that applied to the intruder problem, Boudinot replied sharply, "You have about guessed it, we want the intruders out before we sell."[45]

At the next two sessions, Boudinot tried to get the commissioners to admit that the United States, on occasion, had paid more than $1.25 per acre for Indian land. Early on, Jerome moved to quiet the Cherokee by reminding him that "you gentlemen know that you have only one market"[46] and that every day the land remained unsold they were losing $1,100 in interest. Boudinot did elicit some interesting rationalizations for what had been paid to other tribes. Sayre stated that the United States had actually overcompensated the Cheyennes and Arapahos, the Iowas, the Kickapoos, and the Absentee Shawnees because all of them were "blanket Indians" and needed help. In contrast, the government felt no need to be charitable to the Sac and Fox, who owned their reservation, or to the Potawatomis, "intelligent men, white men as a rule and fewer examples by far of the Indian than you will find even [in] the Cherokee Nation."[47] Sayre concluded 4 December with the proposal that the matter of price for the Outlet be left to Congress.

On 5 and 7 December the discussions focused on attempts to narrow the differences between the contending parties, and some real progress was made. As Sayre summarized it, the United States had ceased trying to insert provisions protecting freedmen and making the Cherokee Nation a defendant in lawsuits involving leases. The Cherokees, for their part, had given up the idea of collecting damages for Outlet grazing leases that the government had invalidated and dropped their demands for compensation from the railroads as well as their right to sue in federal courts for sums over $5,000. The commissioners repeated their willingness to include abrogation of the article in the 1866 treaty permitting the government to settle other tribes in the Cherokee Nation proper. But, as Sayre pointed out, the Indians were now demanding that the government recognize claims of the very few Cherokees in the Outlet.

When his turn came, Boudinot volunteered that the Cherokees would cease their efforts to include land claims that might cast a shadow on settlers' titles and prevent them from selling or even securing loans on their land. Nevertheless, he found it necessary to proclaim that if the Cherokees had a good title, "it matters not to us if there are ten thousand citizens on it."[48] (A century later, similar sentiments would be expressed by Indians in the Northeast.)

On 4 December Secretary Noble had difficulty contacting Jerome by telegraph and finally was forced to ask help from the governor of Oklahoma Territory. Noble passed on a request by President Harrison for information on the status of the negotiations. By the following day Jerome had received the telegram and had replied, stressing the "unreasonable conditions and exorbitant price demanded" by the Cherokees. Jerome informed Noble that he and Sayre were trying "to accomplish our mission by making liberal concessions and more than liberal money consideration." Nevertheless, he concluded that the Cherokees "by new and increased exactions . . . will make it a hopeless task." He promised to report within a few days when "our work closes."[49] Clearly, Jerome was deeply pessimistic.

Sessions on 7, 9, 11, and 12 December were devoted to haggling over details of payment—if a bargain were struck. In response to the commissioners' queries concerning inclusion, in the list of payees, of freedmen and of Delawares and Shawnees whom the Cherokee Nation had adopted earlier, Boudinot stated that they would all be treated like adopted white men and would not share in the payment. The Cherokees also rejected the commissioners' proposal that the government distribute the payment among the Indians as opposed to the National Council's performing that function. Boudinot declared that the Cherokee situation was different than that of other Indians, and if the National Council was competent to sell the land, it was competent to receive the payment.[50]

On the 11th the Cherokees essentially accepted a draft of an agreement, except for the price of $1.32 per acre, for which they substituted $2. David

TAKING INDIAN LANDS

Jerome could hardly contain himself as he denounced the figure as "extraordinary" and "extravagant."[51] Boudinot further exasperated him by announcing that the Indians had a copy of the secret instructions the commissioners had received from the Indian Office in 1889. Moreover, Boudinot declared that the Cherokees would not be bullied into capitulating: "We may be told that the "boomer" will overwhelm us; the Secretary of the Interior may say that we have only an easement right there and other arguments may be used without end to convince us that our hold upon the land is not secure still we shall take the ground that it is ours and we shall treat it as such throughout this negotiation."[52]

The parties devoted the remainder of that day's deliberations to defending the positions they had staked out on the price. Boudinot indicated that it was unfair for a guardian to take advantage of a ward, but Sayre held that—despite Chief Justice Marshall's dictum—history demonstrated that the United States had made treaties with the tribes "as though they were a foreign power." In situations such as the present negotiations, he maintained, "the suggestion of guardian and ward is unfitting and out of place."[53]

At a brief meeting on the 12 December, Sayre suggested a way of protecting the claims of a limited number of Cherokees in the Outlet and proposed again that it be left to Congress to determine the price for the Outlet. He emphasized that the agreement could be worded so that the Cherokees would be guaranteed they would not receive less than the $1.32 already offered them. Boudinot, however, would only agree that the Indians would take the offer under consideration, and he said that they would not respond before the 14th.

When they reconvened Boudinot presented a counteroffer, but discussion was postponed because of the death of Chief Mayes only a few hours earlier. Not until 16 December did they get together again, and then Jerome and Sayre (Wilson was in Arkansas) made appropriate statements about the loss of a great Cherokee leader. Jerome's certainly rang true when he described the chief as being "endowed . . . with a large mind and . . . a tenacity of purpose that would make him rank high in any station."[54] Indeed, Mayes had never wavered in his determination to hold the Outlet until offered a fair market price. Boudinot also offered a few remarks on their loss. He drew on the tribute to Brutus, from Shakespeare: "His life was gentle and the elements so mixed in him that nature might stand up and say to all the world, this was a man." As Mayes was exclusively the product of Cherokee schools, Boudinot could not refrain from adding, "I hope our country may continue an existence that has shown we are capable of producing such a man."[55]

For the next day and a half the commissioners tried to convince the Cherokees that they were overpricing the Outlet, but Boudinot held firm, declaring, "for this time and this place we made you our last offer."[56] To that Jerome and Sayre responded with the warning that the next Congress would be dominated by Democrats determined to reduce government expenditures, aided and abetted by members of the Farmers' Alliance. When Boudinot expressed concern that the Cherokees would soon run out of good land for their growing population, Jerome had some advice, unrealistic as it might be: "I believe that your road to the highest prosperity is not to weight your people with so much land, but put your land into money and your money into factories and make your own things instead of buying them outside."[57]

When the negotiators recessed on 18 December, the prospects for an agreement appeared dismal. Both sides had declared that they had made their last offer. When they reconvened on the 19th, Jerome reviewed the situation: "You say now that you have nothing more to say until we say something. If we say nothing more the one thing left is for us to bundle up our baggage and leave Tahlequah." He then announced their willingness to try to break the impasse by a "peace offering."[58] It was an additional $80,000 obtained by restoring a deduction that the commissioners had made to compensate the United States for a payment to Cherokee freedmen. This had been mentioned in the negotiations, and Jerome seized on it to demonstrate their willingness "to exhaust every possible resource." He warned, however, "This is the extreme limit to which we can go."[59] After further remarks by the commissioners, the Cherokees recessed to consider the government's new offer.

When they returned, the Indians declined the offer and countered with one of their own, "the last one we shall make you"—$8,595,736.12. After a noon break Jerome announced that while he was satisfied the positions he and his colleagues had taken were "sound . . . yet I think we have staid [sic] here long enough and placing the additional responsibility on you we have decided to accept your proposition."[60] A subcommittee of Sayre, Boudinot, and J. A. Scales (one of the Cherokees who had sat silent the entire period) was delegated to draft the agreement, by which the United States purchased an estimated 6,022,754 acres.

In their report to the president the comissioners calculated that in their four efforts to obtain the agreement they had spent a total of twenty-three weeks in Tahlequah and additional time in Washington, in travel, and in preparations for negotiations. The commissioners defended their accepting the several Cherokee conditions as necessary to close the deal, and discussed each, beginning with what they said the Indians referred to as "the blighting curse of intrusion."[61] In citing these conditions the commissioners adopted an objective tone quite removed from the combative stance they had taken during the negotiations. Referring to the price they had finally consented to, they would only say that "it was finally acceded to by the commission because it could do no better."[62]

The commissioners did express some surprise at how the Cherokees had responded to the threatening environment in which they had found themselves. The white men were clearly taken aback by the Indians' failure to panic when the government deprived them of any use of, or financial return from, the Outlet. Indeed, observed the commissioners, those actions somehow only inspired confidence among the Cherokees that justice would ultimately triumph. Similarly, the hostile ruling of a territorial judge only made them even more sanguine about taking their case to the Supreme Court.

Jerome and his colleagues thought it necessary to defend their acquiescence to the Cherokee demand that the entire purchase price be paid to the National Council instead of the usual procedure of Indian Service personnel's distributing payments to the tribal members. "[I]f the Cherokees shall ever become competent to deal with their own funds," they declared, "they are competent now." The commissioners were confident that after generous per capita payments, the Indians would set aside appropriate amounts for their governmental functions, particularly education. "If there is any universal purpose among them it is to maintain a high standard for their schools," the commissioners observed.[63]

In his report to the president on the agreement, Secretary Noble was able to contain his enthusiasm. He included the differing opinions of Commissioner of Indian Affairs Morgan and Assistant Attorney General George H. Shields on the validity of the Cherokee title to the Outlet. Morgan credited the Indians with holding a title in perpetuity, whereas Shields found it at best to be only an easement to the plains for hunting—one that had been lost through nonuse. On this issue Noble sided with Shields, although he said that since it had taken two years to get the Cherokees down to the price in the agreement, the government might as well settle for that.

The secretary did find fault with specific provisions of the agreement. He did not think that any individual Cherokee claims in the Outlet should have been countenanced. Nor did he think that the money should be paid in a lump sum to the National Council or that the Shawnees, Delawares, and Cherokee freedmen should be excluded from sharing in the government's payment. But after listing these and other drawbacks, he grudgingly recommended the agreement as presented. He had provided ammunition, however, which would be used against Cherokee interests in the ratification procedure in Congress.[64]

Once the terms had been agreed upon, most Cherokes were anxious to see the agreement implemented. The National Council quickly ratified the document, and a majority of voters endorsed it in a special election 4 January 1892. The new chief, Johnson Harris, promptly appointed two delegates to represent the nation's interests in Washington. One was E. C. Boudinot, coming off a fine performance as the spokesman for the Cherokees during the negotiations. The other was Thomas M. Buffington, who had served as Senate clerk, and then as acting chief before Harris assumed office.

Boudinot took the lead in making himself available to congressional committees, reporters, and even a church group, seeking any venue to pitch the case for the Cherokees. On 4 March 1892, he made a presentation to the House Committee on Territories, using maps to illustrate areas the Cherokees had once held, including portions of Kentucky, Virginia, Tennessee, Alabama, Georgia, and the Carolinas, and a second map depicting "the last vestiges we have left."[65] Boudinot also addressed the intruder issue and opposed a bill introduced by the Oklahoma Territory delegate to create a new state including the domains of the Five Civilized Tribes. But he was happy to report that, "as everyone should," the delegate could see, "that there is nothing wrong about it [the agreement] and it will be to the advantage of all concerned."[66] One can only speculate as to how much pride of authorship may have influenced Boudinot's judgment.

At the insistence of the Cherokees, the agreement had concluded a 4 March 1893 deadline for congressional ratification, or "it shall be utterly void." Bills to ratify were introduced in the Senate by Henry L. Dawes and in the House by Samuel W. Peel of Arkansas. They were referred to the Indian committees that responded in reports to the House on 13 June and to the Senate on 26 July. The House committee simply recommended ratification as submitted and proposed pricing the land so that the government might recover its costs and guarantee that "honest homeseekers" would not be thwarted by "professional land-grabbers and claim-jumpers."[67] The agreement, the committee declared, would "make splendid homes for thousands of our homeless and most deserving people, and at the same time make the Cherokee people the richest of all their brethern and place them upon the high road to American citizenship."[68]

The Senate committee report offered some serious objections. Using the army to force up to seven thousand people to abandon their homes and other improvements was "too harsh a proceeding to be contemplated with equanimity."[69] The senators proposed an amendment assuring that the improvements of intruders who had been on the land before 11 August 1886, should be appraised and that the Cherokee Nation would compensate such intruders accordingly. The rationale for this was that for fourteen years prior to 11 August 1886 the Interior Department had authorized the local Indian agent to issue certificates legalizing intruders who provided sufficient evidence to convince the agent of their qualifications. The fact that this had been done over the vigorous protests of the Cherokees was ignored.

In their report the senators included comments and a recommendation that can only be regarded as irrelevant to the mission of Jerome and his colleagues. Possibly inspired by Senator Dawes, the committee observed: "The anomalous condition of five separate, independent Indian governments within the Government of the United States must soon, in the nature of things, cease."[70] The senators argued that the policy of "treating with the Indians as independent and foreign nations" had stopped in 1871 with the end of treaty making, and they predicted that very soon the tribes would be absorbed.[71] While the legislators considered the Cherokees to be the Indians best qualified for allotment in severalty and citizenship, they expanded their proposal to include the remainder of the Five Civilized Tribes. To this end the committee recommended an amendment to the agreement providing the consent of the United States to allotment in severalty of the five tribes, with American citizenship to be granted the allottees.

The recommendations of the House committee reached the floor in January 1893. Approval of the agreement was strongly urged, particularly by representatives from the neighboring states of Arkansas and Kansas. The House

Committee on Appropriations, now chaired by William S. Holman of Indiana, a Democrat considered the watchdog of the Treasury, warned that the bill would be blocked unless the agreement was amended to defer payment for the Outlet. Against this the Cherokee delegates lodged a protest, but the House sent the bill on to the Senate with the understanding that some such action would be taken.

In the Senate there was more opposition to be overcome, and concern was expressed about the use of cavalry to evict intruders. Senator Anthony Higgins of Delaware, who had visited Tahlequah back in November with a colleague and met with both Cherokees and intruders, supported the latter. He charged that the leaders of the Indians were white and that it was "simply amusing and grotesque for them any longer to be posing as wards of the nation."[72] Only Senator Butler of South Carolina rallied again to the support of the Cherokees. Henry Dawes, presumably the great friend of the Indians in the Senate, defended the intruders and argued for acceptance of the agreement as "the entering wedge for a surrender of all their tribal government."[73]

The flamboyant Kansas populist, Senator Peffer, denounced the intruders east of 96° longitude, but championed the thousands of Boomers awaiting the opening of the Outlet who were lined up along its Kansas boundary. His fellow populist from Kansas, Representative Simpson, urged his colleagues to open the Outlet because a large body of uncultivated land there helped generate the heat that plagued Kansas farmers. A cultivated Outlet, he proclaimed, would contribute to increased rainfall in the area—the rain-follows-the-plow theory popular in the West at the time.[74]

Congress was facing a deadline to ratify the agreement and moved with dispatch. The Senate added an amendment that would require the Cherokees to compensate those intruders who held the certificates issued by the Indian agent up to an aggregate of $250,000 for their improvements. Another change called for the opening of the Outlet to occur whether or not the Cherokee Council accepted the amendments. The altered bill was sent back to the House, which refused to concur, and a conference was required. Representatives and senators conferred throughout 3 March, trying to reach a compromise. Finally, on 4 March—the last day possible—agreement was reached and the bill was enacted into law.

The law differed in a few respects from the agreement drafted in Tahlequah. The two most significant differences concerned the intruder problem

TAKING INDIAN LANDS

and the method of payment to the Cherokees. As the Senate committee had recommended, a tribunal would make the final judgment as to who were intruders and the Cherokees must compensate them for their improvements. The House conferees accepted that Senate proposal, while the senators agreed to a House plan to delay full payment. On ratification the Indians would receive only $295,736 up front, the remaining $8,300,000 to be paid them in five annual installments, with the deferred payments drawing 4 percent interest. However, a sum equivalent to the shares of the Shawnees, Delawares, and freedmen enrolled in the Cherokee Nation would be withheld by the Treasury until the rights of these three groups had been determined by litigation. An additional provision enabled the Cherokee Nation to pledge the money due them by issuing bonds for the entire $8,300,000. Presumably the 4 percent interest would cover any interest that the Cherokees would have to pay on the bonds.[75]

When the Cherokees were finally paid in the summer of 1894, each citizen received $265.65. By that time the Outlet had been opened in the most spectacular of the Oklahoma "runs," which included the surplus land resulting from agreements with the Tonkawas and Pawnees. Registration for the run totaled 115,000, and at stake were 40,000 homesteads of 160 acres. In the enabling legislation, Congress recognized variations in the value of the land and assigned it to three price categories. The eastern section with the highest rainfall was priced at $2.50 per acre, the middle at $2.00, and the most westerly at $1.50—all prices substantially higher than that paid the Cherokees.[76]

The Cherokee delegates' report to the Council on the ratification appeared in the *Advocate*. W. W. Hastings and M. V. Benge, who had succeeded Boudinot and Buffington during the long ratification process, detailed the parliamentary maneuvering that produced the final legislation and their own actions, including hiring a Washington lobbyist and appearing all of fifteen minutes before a Senate committee. They concluded with an ominous "unless the Five Tribes are cautious, diplomatic and vigilant, and unless they act in concert a change of conditions is likely to be forced upon us."[77] Hastings and Benge saw allotment and possible dissolution of the Indian governments on the horizon.

Land tenure was an increasingly controversial issue among the Cherokees themselves. During over a year that had elapsed between the signing of the agreement in Tahlequah and ratification of an amended version in

Congress, the *Advocate* carried several pieces relating to citizens who were monopolizing land. The paper managed to maintain a relatively objective view of prospective changes. Editorial comment even asserted that "the growing necessity for allotment . . . lie[s] mainly with ourselves, try as we may to place the blame elsewhere." The writer attributed the nation's inability to prevent a citizen from controlling thousands of acres to a phobia about doing anything that might open the way to a change in the tradition of holding land in common. The result was: "Hundreds of our young men want homes and can't get them, because only the refuse of our public domain is left to select from."[78]

Although the Cherokees were understandably bitter at being forced to sell at less than the fair market value of the Outlet, they took comfort from the agreement promising an end to the intruder problem. The president did appoint a three-man board to evaluate the improvements of those to be expelled from the nation. The Cherokee member was Clement V. Rogers, a prosperous mixed blood and the father of Will Rogers, the humorist. Chief Harris submitted a list of 5,273 intruders to Washington, but after eight months the board had located only 385 sets of improvements and recommended compensation for only 117.[79] Board members were also disturbed to find that more intruders continued to arrive and these newcomers as well as those already in place proceeded with their planting, fencing, and throwing up structures, confident that they would not be expelled. And most of them were not. Just as the board was wrapping up its investigation, Congress ordered that the removal of intruders should be delayed until 1 January 1896 to give them an opportunity to harvest their crops and remove their livestock.[80] Meanwhile, a commission headed by Henry L. Dawes had appeared on the scene.

Created by Congress at virtually the same time that it ratified the Cherokee Agreement in 1893, the Commission to the Five Civilized Tribes, popularly known as the Dawes Commission after its first chairman, was given the task of persuading those tribes to accept allotment and dissolve their governments. The *Advocate's* gloomy prediction had come to pass. Although the tribes refused to cooperate in their own extinction, Congress was not to be thwarted. In 1896 it gave the commission authority to draw up tribal rolls for allotment, which meant that not the Cherokees but the Dawes Commission would determine who, including intruders, would be classified as Cherokee citizens. Congress also directed the commission to investigate the

TAKING INDIAN LANDS

monopolization of land that had helped rationalize the government's allotment crusade, following this with legislation that ended the jurisdiction of tribal courts. The dissolution of the governments of the Five Civilized Tribes was underway. On the new rolls compiled by the Dawes Commission were the names of people whom Cherokee authorities had determined to be intruders. The Indians had congratulated themselves on holding out until the Cherokee Commission included a requirement that the United States remove intruders in the agreement. Now they understandably felt betrayed.

Not until 1961 would the Cherokees be vindicated for positions they had taken in the negotiations with the Cherokee Commission. That year the Indian Claims Commission rendered a decision in *Cherokee Nation* v. *United States*, Docket #173, that was a scathing denunciation of tactics the commissioners employed. It held that the United States had applied "duress" throughout the negotiations, terminating cattle leases that it had tacitly condoned for years and threatening to take the land at $1.25 per acre by congressional fiat.[81] The commission singled out Lucius Fairchild, describing his conduct as "petulant" and noting that he had threatened to have Comanches and other Plains Indians moved into the Cherokee Nation.[82] It did not observe that Fairchild had the complete backing of Secretary Noble in every tactic he employed to try to force the Cherokees to the negotiating table.

The Indian Claims Commission declared that the $1.29 per acre the United States paid for the Outlet, excluding the land the Cherokees had earlier sold the Osages and five other tribes, was "unconscionable." It estimated that the land, as of 1892 was worth on the average $3.75 per acre, even more than the highest price the Cherokees had asked during the negotiations.[83] The Indians had received only $7,795,328.14 for the 6,022,754.17 acres, which were actually worth $22,585,384.14, less such offsets as the commission would recognize. These amounted to $425,000, so the Cherokees finally received $14,364,476.15.[84]

In its Findings of Fact, the Indian Claims Commission had some well-deserved compliments for the Cherokees' spokesmen. William P. Ross and L. B. Bell, who took the lead for the Indians in 1890, were described as "able and well informed men."[85] E. C. Boudinot had articulated the Cherokee positions in 1891, and he and his colleagues were described as "able, astute and dedicated. . . . well-informed with respect to the real estate market in areas adjoining the Outlet and in the capabilities and adaptability of the lands being bargained for."[86] The Cherokees had indeed made a convincing case; unfortunately, the outcome of the negotiations at Tahlequah was determined not by facts or abstract justice but on the perceived needs of thousands of white homeseekers plus businessmen and railroad developers, all of whom were enfranchised and could bring pressure to bear on the government.

When Oklahomans celebrated the centennial of the opening of the Outlet in 1993, the Cherokee Nation responded. It issued a sixty-page document whose conclusion opened with a damning but accurate summary: "The sale of the Cherokee Outlet was no sale; it was acquiesence to Presidential, congressional and bureaucratic extortion to appease the clamor of white greed for land. The Outlet was not taken by physical force but was acquired through the blatant abuse of the trust relationship of Congress with the Cherokee Nation."[87]

8

A Frustrating Eleven Weeks with the Poncas

SHORTLY AFTER THE SIGNING OF THE CHEROKEE AGREEMENT, the commissioners dispersed to their homes. Chairman Jerome and his wife arrived in Saginaw late Christmas Day 1891 "in a Pullman which covered ground at the rate
of almost 40 miles an hour," according to a local reporter.[1] The reporter
interviewed Jerome the next morning and found him to be optimistic about
the completion of his mission. Jerome mentioned only a few tribes in the
eastern part of the Outlet as still being without agreements. That sanguine
estimate ignored the large reservation of the Kiowas, Comanches, and
Apaches in southeastern Oklahoma and the stubborn resistance to negotiations already displayed by some of those tribes in the Outlet.

   One of the commissioners, Warren Sayre, was getting restive. The latest
appropriation was nearly exhausted, and—while funding might be
renewed—he possibly felt that it would be well to line up other employment
while he still had a friend in the White House. In mid-January 1892 he wrote
a long letter to President Harrison. An Oklahoma Territory judgeship was
about to be vacated, and the incumbent had suggested to Sayre that he might
wish to apply. Although observing that the Cherokee Commission paid better, Sayre indicated his interest in the judgeship and cited his familiarity with
the area: "My official dutes have, for more than two years, taken me over and
across and through and around the whole country. . . . I have also been in
every town and city in the Territory, and know the people very well and they
know me. The work done by the Cherokee Commission has also, in a manner, endeared us in the affection and respect of the people."[2] That last could
not have included the Indian population, but of course they had no voice in
the matter.

The president did not commit himself in his response. He did observe that his selection of a governor for the territory had been influenced by the Oklahomans' strongly expressed preference for a local resident. Because of Sayre's time in the territory, Harrison joked, "they may recognize you as a sort of step son!"[3] Sayre did not score that time, but he would try again later. Meanwhile, the commissioners would be endeavoring to convince the Poncas that they should accept allotments and sell their surplus land.

The Poncas would prove to be a hard sell—not surprising given their bad experiences at the hands of the United States during the previous twenty years. A small tribe living dangerously near the powerful Plains Sioux, they had lost lives and property to those consummate raiders in the 1860s and 1870s. Not only had the United States failed to protect the Poncas; in 1868, by a blunder that defies explanation, a federal commission assigned the Ponca homeland in Nebraska and Dakota Territory to the Sioux. The remedy the United States offered eight years later was not an unusual one for the government—shift the weaker tribe elsewhere. Although Congress specified that this should be done only with the consent of the Poncas, in 1877 they were coerced into a tragic removal with all the usual attendant suffering. Their first destination was the Quapaw Reservation in northeastern Indian Territory. Miserable in that situation, the following year they were permitted to relocate to Cherokee land in the eastern end of the Outlet under the terms of the Treaty of 1866 for refugee tribes.

But the conditions at the new location were initially only marginally better and were slow to improve. Early on, the death of an infant son led Chief Standing Bear to defy authority, slip away from the reservation with a party of his fellow tribesmen, and head north. The chief's hope was to inter the bones of his child in a traditional Ponca burial site in Nebraska. Intercepted along the way by troops, the Poncas, now prisoners, attracted vocal white sympathizers who publicized the case nationally. With legal representation provided by their supporters, the Poncas had their day in court and won release, the judge ruling that Indians were "persons" as defined by the Fourteenth Amendment and entitled to full rights under the law.

Standing Bear was permitted to remain in Nebraska, but those Poncas in Indian Territory were not allowed to return. In December 1880 they consented to an agreement with a contrite United States providing that they should be compensated to the amount of $140,000, $50,000 of which should be used to provide them a title "in fee-simple" to the reservation that they were occuping in the Outlet.[4] Congress did appropriate the money requested, but it did not ratify the agreement and only specified that the appropriation would be used "to secure to them lands in severalty."[5] Once again, the Poncas had been betrayed by their guardian.

When the Cherokee Commission got around to the Poncas in late 1892, efforts were already underway to allot them, although the Indians had refused to cooperate. More than two decades of neglect and abuse by the United States had understandably left the Poncas highly suspicious and pre-disposed to resist any Washington initiatives. The Cherokee Commission had made an attempt to conclude an agreement with them in over two weeks of negotiations in October 1891, for which there is no journal. That effort was aborted by Secretary Noble's ordering the commissioners to Tahlequah. The second attempt would take place during eleven weeks in the spring of 1892, producing a journal of 333 pages.

When the first meeting got underway on 17 March, Chairman Jerome was on his own, Judge Wilson being ill and Warren Sayre one day late in arriving. The Poncas were not in a receptive mood. Of the nearly six hundred residents on the reservation only a few had selected allotments, although the surveying had been completed. When Jerome opened the negotiations, he spoke to a sparse audience. He made the usual presentation about the Great Father's wanting his red children to take allotments and sell their surplus, and he reminded them that the previous October the Poncas had insisted that the commissioners finish with the larger tribes and then come back to them. Now Jerome was able to announce that the commission had finally obtained the Outlet from the Cherokees and was prepared to treat with the Poncas. When he completed his statement, the only Ponca to respond was Big Goose, recently appointed by the agent to be a judge on the tribal court. He volunteered that muddy roads might account for the poor turnout, and he thought that if the agent sent out his police, men with "badges on their breasts," attendance would improve.[6]

For the thirty-five sessions held, attendance was generally poor. Due to the ever-changing composition of their audience, Jerome and his colleagues found themselves having to repeat their presentations on specific points and respond time after time to the same questions. A few of the chiefs and head-men were fairly consistent in their attendance, but the young men, if they offered any excuse for their absences, pled their need to get their planting done for the season. Jerome tried scheduling sessions every other day, and in the afternoon and early evening, but nothing worked. The Poncas were voting with their feet.

For the second meeting Jerome was joined by Warren Sayre, who had been in Washington consulting with President Harrison and Secretary Noble. Together the commissioners tried to convince the Poncas that farming and education were the only ways that the Indians could improve their standard of living. To be efficient farmers they would need plows, teams strong enough to pull them, as well as drags, reapers, and mowers. To obtain these essentials the Indians could sell their surplus land. By the commissioners' calculations the Poncas themselves were making use of only about two thousand acres of a total of over one-hundred thousand. They had, however, leased sixty thousand acres to cattlemen, bringing in some income. Sayre described the president as anxious that the Indians do well: "His only wish is to put you in a condition so that you will live better and we are sure that you will live better if you will take his advice and ours."[7]

At that point, after inviting the Indians to return the next day with any questions they might have, Jerome was about to close the session when Chief Standing Buffalo and then Chief Frank LaFlesche took the floor. They proceeded to hold forth on a trip they had made to Washington a few weeks earlier and the conference that they had had with the then acting commissioner of Indian affairs, R. V. Belt. Standing Buffalo, the second-ranking chief after White Eagle, was about sixty years old and had served on the tribal court. That appointment was usually an indication that the agent considered him a man of influence in reservation affairs and prepared to accept some direction from the agent. LaFlesche, about fifty and the third-ranking chief, had also been on the court and on the occasion of his appointment had been described as "very intelligent," wearing citizen's dress, and "favorable to white man's ways."[8] Neither he nor Standing Buffalo, however, spoke English. The two chiefs described having been selected by their fellow Poncas and being presented with travel funds to visit Washington and determine whether the Cherokee Commission had the power to force them to accept allotments and sell their surplus land. Both Standing Buffalo and LaFlesche maintained that Acting Commissioner Belt had assured them that the Poncas had indeed purchased their reservation with $50,000 and therefore could not be forced into either allotment or sale of the surplus.

Chairman Jerome hastened to correct the chiefs. He said that many times during the councils of last October the commissioners had told the Indians that they would not use force to get the Poncas to sell. As for allotment, the president had issued an order in 1890 that the Indians should take allotments, and an agent was even then prepared to register their claims. Jerome concluded by announcing a session the following day, something he described as more important than planting potatoes.

At the third session Jerome tried to discourage the Poncas about their ability to continue the status quo. Unlike Indians, he observed, white men were "very peculiar . . . they want to get on every piece of vacant land," and they elected the members of Congress who made "laws that . . . govern the whole country."[9] The chairman also took the opportunity to deny Standing Buffalo's charge that the United States had not completed purchase of the Ponca title to land in Nebraska and in Dakota Territory.

Sayre followed this up by telling the Indians that while they could not be forced to sell their land, they would have no peace until they did. Nor was leasing large pastures to cattlemen any longer practical: "white men are not going around a big cattle pasture but they are going through it."[10] He also reminded them of the theft of pasture fence by intruders. That very morning he had learned that a mile of fence had been taken, and the previous fall six miles had disappeared. There was no evidence, however, that the commissioners were being heard. Following this meeting, Jerome wired Secretary Noble for a copy of the president's order for allotment of the Poncas. To his chagrin he learned that no specific order for them existed. Nevertheless, the commissioners would continue to refer to the president's issuing such an order, even alluding to it in their final report.

Meanwhile, the meetings would drag on, five more sessions in the period 20 March to 28 March. On the 21st Sayre read the Dawes Act, prefacing it with information as to how it had come about and stressing the concern that Dawes had felt for the Indians. According to Sayre, the senator had concluded that the reason the Indian was poor was that he resided on a reservation and "lived as he pleased and roamed about as he pleased and that the right way to make an old Indian better off was to put him on a farm."[11] For the Poncas, Sayre declared, the time had come; the land had been surveyed and the allotments were ready. They also learned for the first time that an amended Dawes Act specified only 80-acre allotments of farmland, in contrast to the 160 authorized a head of family under the original legislation.

The commissioners constantly reminded the Ponca fathers that they would control the allotments of other members of their families. Thus a family of six would have 480 acres, and the father could cultivate a little of this and rent the rest. Jerome went so far as to say that given those circumstances, they might "work as much as pleases yourselves and rent the rest of it."[12] Doing so would have vitiated the principal argument for allotment—that it would provide the stimulus to work that was missing in a system of communal ownership. In time, however, regardless of what David Jerome had said, unless they were physically incapable of working their allotments they would learn that government policy was to discourage leases to whites. This was simply another example of the commissioners' pulling out all stops in their effort to acquire Indian land.

Jerome and his colleagues had other arguments to make in their effort to break down Ponca resistance. Here, as elsewhere, they talked of the flood of immigrants and the necessity of making land available to them. The chairman observed that most immigrants were also handicapped by being unable to speak English and, unlike the Indians, they did not have the help of children who had been to school and had learned English. Indeed, many Ponca children were in school, as most parents did not discourage attendance.

The Indians had their own arguments, which speaker after speaker invoked. Beginning in the negotiations the previous October, they had insisted that they were not ready to deal and that the commission should first treat with tribes such as the Cherokee, which was larger and better prepared for allotment. Since the Cherokees had accepted an agreement, the Poncas now most frequently offered the Osages as better prepared for the transition. Another generally held Ponca view was that they needed to keep the entire reservation to enable them to provide land for children yet to be born. Hairy Bear, who had signed the 1880 Agreement in Washington, spoke to this point. He worried about where these children would go: "the young ones would be just like a bird, fly off to some other place."[13] To a people who attached so much value to family and clan, this was a frightening prospect.

Peter Primeaux was also concerned about the Poncas' future if they accepted the government's proposal. He was a mixed blood who could speak English but nevertheless was one of the more outspoken critics of the commission. Primeaux expressed his unease regarding the possibility of their not realizing real benefits from any cash payment for the surplus land. "If you have plenty of money it goes like a high bank caving in but the land will

TAKING INDIAN LANDS

stay,"[14] he declared, and he was worried about tax collectors descending on the new allottees. He cited the plight of Omahas, who a few years earlier had been allotted only to have to hide in the brush to escape county officials trying to tax their personal property, which was not tax exempt unless issued them by the government. Black Buffalo Bull couched his warning about tax collectors in an allegory. It featured a bird that could speak "Ponca, Pawnee, and Omaha with great fluency" and envisioned the Ponca's livestock being seized for taxes.[15]

Overland, who would prove a real thorn in the flesh of David Jerome by his persistent opposition, reported that he had seen a white man crying as his property was seized for nonpayment of taxes. He warned his fellow Indians that land was the only secure thing and they should hold on to it. He ended his comments that day by complaining of the interruption of his farm tasks: "I get ready every day and hitch my horses to the plow but I hear your bell and finally I will have to eat my seed potatoes."[16] The often expressed fear of tax collectors was not irrational. That same year they descended on the allotted Potawatomis, half of whom retreated to Creek or Cherokee country to save their personal property from confiscation. Their agent summarized their dilemma: "they seldom keep money on hand, in fact obtain so much credit as they can prior to an annuity payment, and taxes could not be collected without selling their property, and the consequence would be discouragement to the Indian in the ownership of property and an inclination to remain in poverty rather than submit to be taxed."[17]

After hearing the commissioners use the flood of immigrants as an excuse to sharply reduce Ponca landholdings, White Eagle, the nominal head chief, had a ready solution: "all the increase coming from over the big water would stay on their own reservation."[18] As the occupants of the continent for thousands of years before the arrival of the white men, the Indians were not impressed that the acceleration of immigration was used as justification for a drastic reduction in their own landholdings. Four years earlier, at a Lake Mohonk Conference meeting, Senator Dawes had described White Eagle as "the clearest head of all the Indian tribes." And Dawes had to admit that the Ponca chief opposed allotment, because White Eagle did not feel able to compete with the white men who "would strip me bare as a bird in a month."[19]

Nor were the Poncas persuaded by the argument that, aside from being harassed by tax collectors, the other newly allotted tribes were doing well or that those who had been able to avoid allotment were doing badly. Standing Buffalo cited the Fox of Iowa, who still held their land in common, as prosperous, while Southern Cheyennes who had been allotted were "hard up."[20] Bear's Ear offered the Cheyennes as an example of a tribe reduced to making moccasins to buy bread.

But most aggravating to the commissioners were the Poncas' continual references to Standing Bear and Frank LaFlesche's version of their interview with Acting Commissioner Belt. As Standing Bear once put it: "I can not read or write but I have a real good head and I have all the words Frank and the commissioner said in my head."[21] Finally, on 26 March, Jerome wired Secretary Noble informing him that the Poncas refused to take allotments and sell their surplus land and that they justified their inaction by citing the interview. Before Noble could respond, Jerome proposed that they continue the negotiations even though they had made no progress, because he was not willing to give up yet. The secretary did arrange to have a stenographic copy of the Washington meeting forwarded to the commission.[22] With that ammunition at hand, Jerome determined to persevere.

Twenty-six more sessions were called to order by the chairman, but the positions already staked out by the parties remained essentially unchanged. To acquaint the Indians with the actual dimensions of an 80-acre plot, Jerome resorted to a tactic employed before—staking out two such plots and marking their parameters by flags. To his disappointment the Poncas declined invitations to wagon rides around the plots, White Eagle declaring that he already knew the size of 80 acres.[23]

A report that four unnamed Poncas were willing to accept their allotments precipitated some quarreling among the tribal members. Understandably, no one was willing to admit in open council that he was ready to break ranks on the issue. A few, including White Eagle, countered that they would be willing to accept 160-acre allotments, but that was a safe stand for them because the newly amended Dawes Act limited allotments of arable land to 80 acres. Under no circumstances were they willing to sell any land declared surplus after allotment. No Ear, who described himself as a full blood who still wore leggings, denounced selling land as "like throwing my children into a red hot fire."[24]

On 1 April Sayre read to the council the newly arrived transcript of the controversial interview the Ponca chiefs had had with Acting Commissioner Belt. It failed to sustantiate the Indians' claim that Belt had assured them they could not be allotted against their will. LaFlesche was unimpressed: "It is only three or four weeks since we were there and I have not forgotten my words."[25] Nor did Standing Buffalo back down: "Some of my words are all right and some of Frank's are all right and some are different and some are there that we did not say."[26] Even a telegram from the acting commissioner to Standing Buffalo, ordering him to use his influence to get the Poncas to take their allotments, produced no results.

Because of the constantly changing attendance, a few days later Sayre read the transcript again. Afterwards he spoke of the advantages of a written record, stating that Big Goose, who had just had the floor, could not repeat exactly what he had just said. However, Sayre declared, the stenographer had taken down every word Big Goose had uttered and "can read it to you today, this year or next year, he can tell you every word that Big Goose said."[27] Nevertheless, the Indians would not accept the accuracy of the transcript. Given that everything the Indians and R. V. Belt had said or heard went through an interpreter, the possibilities for misunderstanding were abundant. At a minimum there was the natural tendency of each party to hear what it wanted to hear. Even after hearing negative reactions from the Poncas, however, Jerome assured Secretary Noble that "we are confident that the stenographic report" of the Washington conference "will afford us material assistance."[28]

David Jerome's impatience with the lack of movement was beginning to show. Particularly frustrating was the poor attendance, and at one point he threatened to get the Indians to the councils "if it takes the whole army."[29] When Peter Primeaux, the mixed blood, appeared after missing several sessions and then proceeded to question the veracity of Jerome and Sayre, the chairman was furious. He told Primeaux to leave and not return until he apologized.[30] The Ponca chose not to return. That, in turn, led an unintimidated Thick Nail to charge, "You white men are using us like Texas cattle."[31] That was a telling remark to his audience, who leased pasture to ranchers and well understood the difference between their care of the imported breeds and their leaving the Texas longhorns to fend for themselves.

Not until 12 April did Warren Sayre finally spell out the government offer in all particulars. Each Ponca would receive an 80-acre allotment, "8 or 10 times as much land set off to him as he has now."[32] In addition, thirty days after Congress ratified the agreement each Indian would receive $20 cash, and Sayre emphasized that for a family of five that would mean $100. That payment would be part of the $69,000 (roughly $1.25 per acre) that the government would pay them for their surplus land. The balance of the purchase price would be placed in the Treasury, where it would earn 5 percent interest, which would be paid annually at the rate of $10 to each tribal member. Should the Indians wish to withdraw the principle in the future, each Ponca family of five would receive a "whole box" of money—$1,000.[33] Sayre added that if they accepted this offer, the Indians could "live as you please. You can visit as much as you please."[34] That was a remarkable statement, coming from a representative of the government that was trying to discourage intra- and inter-reservation visitation as prejudicial to the proper care of Indian property.

Both White Eagle and Standing Buffalo were highly critical of the government offer. The latter was particularly unhappy with the size of the allotments, declaring that when some of the young men learned that it was only 80 acres, "they almost fainted; even a simple man would know that 80 acres was not enough to make a living on."[35]

The 23 April session suggested the depth of Ponca resistance and the inability of the commissioners to extract any concessions. At one point Little Soldier, one of the young men, replied thoughtfully to the argument that if they sold the surplus they would have money to spend: "The land is worth more than gold, the money will be spent and gone in a day, the sod every year will raise a crop, it will last forever. We know these things and have them in our heads and we know that the [reservation] is very small so we do not think about taking allotments and selling the surplus land."[36]

In an effort to end the stalemate, Jerome tried to get Little Soldier simply to choose between two methods of determining the location of his allotment—making the choice himself or letting the allotting agent do it. But Little Soldier refused to fall into that trap, and several exchanges later he was still unalterably opposed. Finally an exasperated Jerome declared that if he could not get an answer from the young men, he must ask Principal Chief White Eagle. That dignitary promptly passed the buck: "Ask Overland."[37] Jerome did query that recalcitrant as to whether he had been adequately informed about the Dawes Severalty Act, and the young man denied ever having heard it read, adding, "if you would read it I would not hear it at all."[38]

After further futile exchanges and Overland's final refusal even to respond to a question, White Eagle intervened to suggest that the chairman quiz Standing Buffalo. The second chief quickly replied that he also did not have a preference as to how his allotment should be selected. He did say, however, that Jerome's line of questioning seemed designed to precipitate a quarrel among the Indians. Standing Buffalo then neatly encapsulated the Ponca position: "This land was bought by us for these young men so they could live upon it all their lives; it was bought for the young ones that are coming and so they want to hold it in common."[39]

Three days later Standing Elk, another young man, informed Jerome that he considered the other tribes that the commission had been able to persuade to consent to allotment and the sale of their surplus to be fools, "but I am not."[40] That contemptous rejection provoked Jerome to recall other Indians who had refused his offers, the Nez Percé and a Ute tribe. Chief Joseph had talked as Standing Elk was now doing, and "the result today is that Joseph has no home. . . . had a war and lots of his people got killed." As for the Utes, "they talked just like Standing Elk talks . . . they lost their [Colorado] reservation by it, they are way over in Utah and have not nearly so good a home."[41]

The one Ponca to respond to Jerome's recollections was Hairy Bear, who had earlier reminded the chairman that while Jerome might be tired, he was "earning a good deal but when I am tired I am not earning anything."[42] Hairy Bear then informed Jerome that, "Some of your words are real good to listen to, but most of them are like this wind that is blowing real hard"—hardly a flattering comparison.[43]

That exchange took place on 26 April, and there would be eight more sessions, with David Jerome carrying the burden for the commissioners. Warren Sayre went back to Indiana and then on to Washington in late April. While Judge Wilson put in an appearance at three of the sessions, he was in poor health and unable to make much of a contribution. Indeed, given the commission's failure to make any headway against a united Ponca front, one can only speculate as to why Jerome persisted. Since Congress was facing a decision as to whether to continue funding the Cherokee Commission, perhaps he thought it necessary to show some activity.

There were no major developments in the last two weeks of the negotiations, although some exchanges are worth noting. Standing Bear, the second chief, took occasion to discuss his relations with White Eagle, the first chief. Years earlier, in a fight with another tribe, he had saved White Eagle's life when that chief's horse became mired, taking him up behind him on his own horse, "but now we are getting old and not caring much for each other."[44]

For his part Jerome remembered his service on the Board of Indian Commissioners: "I gave five long years of my life to working among the Indians and never got or expected to get a cent for it." Moreover, to discharge his current assignment, he said "I have left a great business of mine in Saginaw and in Marquette . . . to come down here and try to do you good."[45] He had been compensated only for his expenses during his years on the Board of Indian Commissioners, but he was certainly was being well paid as a member of the Cherokee Commission.

The chairman tried to convince the Indians that by their obduracy they risked losing the government support that they enjoyed. Congress was about to act on Indian appropriation bills, and he reminded them of what they had at stake. Aside from annuities due the Poncas for earlier cessions, Congress was being asked to continue to provide $14,000 a year to furnish the tribe a school, blacksmith and carpenter shops, a mill, farm implements, and fencing. "Congress," he warned, "can get along without the Poncas but the Poncas can not get along without the Congress."[46]

In that same session, 10 May, Jerome invoked the example of the Civil War after hearing Standing Elk loudly proclaim that he would neither take an allotment nor sell the surplus land: "A long time ago when Hairy Bear and Standing Buffalo and White Eagle were boys 13 of the states said that they would not mind the laws of Congress. They raised armies and had a great many soldiers but the Government went right on and killed a great many and after four years fighting . . . the 13 states had to give up, and I do not think that a few Poncas can stop the Government."[47]

Samuel Himman, a son of White Eagle who had earlier rejected the commission's proposals now entered the breach again. He inquired whether there was a law that required an Indian with 160 acres to sell it and, if he did not chose to, "was the law made to have a war with that person."[48] Jerome ignored the part about war and expounded at length on the power of Congress to do whatever it willed with the land: "The title to the Ponca's land and the land of every tribe is in the United States."[49]

The day after that session Jerome alerted Secretary Noble: "Negotiations with the Poncas drag on with little satisfaction or hope of success."[50] Nevertheless, he would call two more sessions, on 12 and 13 May. The chairman guaranteed that he would have an audience for the first by sending out the Indian police with a list of chiefs and headmen. His intention was to try one more time to get White Eagle and Standing Buffalo to support the commission. He seemed to believe that White Eagle wanted to do so and that if he could be prevailed upon to take a stand, then Jerome would try to get the Indians to choose between the chiefs. All that he got, however, were the usual rejections. Thick Nail stated that since they had moved to Indian Territory the Ponca chiefs "are not the ones to say what we should do, the land belongs to all the men, women and children and they have a right to say what shall be done with it."[51] Jerome could only comment that he had heard enough lectures from Thick Nail.

Then Buffalo Head, who had a wife and six children, had a suggestion that must have been like music to the ears of David Jerome: "My plan about this is for the chiefs to go to Washington and settle this matter because then we could not do anything about it"[52]—a remarkably frank statement describing a favorite government tactic. The chairman asked the Ponca if he really meant that, and Buffalo Head responded affirmatively but then launched into a rambling monologue that ended by his raising the old issue of the Indians' getting 160-acre allotments instead of the 80 the government was offering.

One of the last speakers that session was Little Dance. His principal comment was that he did not believe he could make it on an allotment: "God made me red and even if you took a razor and peeled me I would be red still."[53] Jerome did not attempt to respond; his intention was to set the Poncas against each other, not to respond to every comment made by an Indian.

When the session opened on 13 May, Jerome expressed the hope that he would hear from chiefs favorable to the government's proposition. The first Ponca to speak, however, was Overland, who was in his usual negative mood. Thoroughly annoyed, the chairman interrupted him, exclaiming that he had heard Overland's views "half a dozen times and it does no good. . . . I have heard you talk all that I want to."[54] Jerome went on at length about the government's not sending the commissioners "to coax" the Poncas to do anything, saying that he was tired of listening to those who opposed government policy.[55] The only response came from White Eagle, who asserted his claim to be *the* Ponca chief but admitted that he was not prepared to give any direction to his people on the issue. Rather, the chief said, he was waiting for them to declare for the government's plan, although he had seen no movement in that direction.

Jerome then closed the eleven weeks of negotiations by expressing his belief that "the great body of the Poncas are mistaken in their position . . .

but there are a great many of the old men that think the words spoken [by the commissioners] are good words."[56] If they shared their view with the young men, Jerome suggested, the other Poncas could be convinced. He told his audience that Judge Wilson, who was still there, had been too sick to come to the councils but must now go home and that Warren Sayre had been summoned to Washington. He himself had been called home and would be leaving for the train station in a few minutes. Jerome expressed the hope that before the commission returned, the Poncas would have selected their allotments and decided to sell the surplus land of their reservation.

It had been a most unproductive eleven weeks for the Cherokee Commission, although the local Indian agent put the best possible face on it: "The Commission all through these councils displayed wonderful sagacity, forbearance, and persistency . . . and retired gracefully from the field."[57] The strong Ponca stand had reflected an unusual degree of tribal unity that thwarted the desire of Chief White Eagle to lead them down a path they found so repellent. The commissioners would be back the following spring, but for the near future their attention would shift to the Kiowa, Comanche, and Apache Reservation.

9

The Kiowas, Comanches, and Apaches Fight a Delaying Action

WHEN IT BECAME APPARENT THAT NEGOTIATIONS with the Poncas were going nowhere, Secretary Noble decided it was time to establish guidelines for the Cherokee Commission concerning which tribes it should treat with and in what order. In May 1892 he advised Chairman Jerome that he should next approach those tribes in the Outlet still without agreements, although "I would not protract the labor." With the Cherokee Agreement under its belt, the commission "has done a very great work and has been successful in its main object." With the small tribes it should move expeditiously, "with as little discussion as their interests require." The secretary emphasized that the Indians should be made to understand that allotment and the sale of their surplus land were in their best interests, in line with the "liberal treatment that the Government has given all Indians"[1]—a generalization that none of them would have employed. With those tribes taken care of, the commission should turn to the Kiowas, Comanches, and Apaches by or before September.

Jerome and his colleagues did not respond with alacrity. Indeed, they did not return to work until late September. Undoubtedly they had no desire to experience another summer on the Southern Plains. Nor did their pay arrangements strongly motivate them. In September 1891 Secretary Noble had ruled that since the commission "gives its whole time to the duty required by law," the members should be regarded as continuously employed and paid accordingly. Even the voluminous evidence normally required of government employees to justify their travel expenses was largely dispensed with. The commissioners had complete latitude "to choose the routes of travel as best adapted to the proper conduct of their business."[2] These same liberal arrangements were extended to other commissions, although none had the lengthy tenure of the Cherokee Commission. For most, tenure was measured in months, not years.

In mid-July Congress appropriated another fifteen thousand dollars for the Cherokee Commission to continue its work, and in late September Secretary Noble asked the War Department to arrange with Fort Sill to provide the type of escort and camping equipment that Fort Reno had been supplying. To get negotiations with the Kiowas, Comanches, and Apaches off on the right foot, Noble also directed the commissioner of Indian affairs to order their agent to issue rations to Indians conferring with Jerome and his colleagues.[3]

The three tribes with which the commissioners were preparing to negotiate were Plains Indians whose lifestyles were in most respects similar to those of the Cheyennes and Arapahos. Like them, the Kiowas, Comanches, and Apaches had roamed freely over the plains until the rapid expansion of Texas settlements and the California gold rush seriously impacted them. They fought back, and in 1865 and 1867 the United States negotiated treaties with the tribes. The second of these, the Treaty of Medicine Lodge, committed them—at least in the government's interpretation—to locate on a three-million-acre reservation in the Leased District obtained from the Choctaws and Chickasaws.

One main Comanche political division, the Quahadas, refused to move to the reservation, and hunting and war parties from all three tribes freely left it and returned at their convenience. Some brought back horses and captives—Texan and Mexican women and children—usually offering to release the captives to government authorities in return for ransom. They also drove off herds of Texan and Mexican cattle and sold them and unransomed captives to the Comancheros—the Pueblos and Mexicans who brought trade goods to the plains.

By the early 1870s, however, the Plains Indians were facing a genuine threat to their staff of life. White hunters began to make substantial inroads on the great herds of buffalo, and the Indians struck back. This precipitated the Red River War in 1874–75, which ended with the defeat of the Indians, so that even the Quahadas were finally forced to enter the reservation. Between 1875 and 1878 small parties would slip away to hunt, and on a few occasions rations were so short that the agent arranged with the army to have them escorted on hunts. But by 1878 the buffalo had virtually disappeared, and the Indians were "stranded," not even able to slip away and survive.

From 1875 until the arrival of the Cherokee Commission in late September 1892, the Kiowas, Comanches, and Apaches made little progress down the white man's road. The great majority were still heavily dependent on government rations, the misguided efforts to turn a hunting and gathering people into corn farmers having failed in an area not suitable for that crop. In 1892 there were thousands of cattle grazing on the reservation, but almost all of them belonged to Texas ranchers leasing pasture. That produced some slight income—"grass money"—for the Indians, and they were also annually issued about thirty thousand dollars worth of clothing, household goods, and farm tools under the terms of the Treaty of Medicine Lodge. Unfortunately, many of the items were of poor quality.

In his yearly report on the reservation written in August 1892, Agent George D. Day summarized the situation. By his account there were 1,014 Kiowas, 1,531 Comanches, and 241 Apaches.[4] Most of the Indians still lived in tepees, although they were now made of canvas, not buffalo hide. A few of the more adaptable were living in small houses constructed by the government. The Indians still dressed distinctively, with the blanket as the most prominent remnant of the old style, and the men continued to wear their hair long and in pigtails. Multiple wives were not uncommon, and a peyote-based religion was conspicuous on the reservation, although the agents did not advertise either the peyote or polygamy in their reports. Among the Comanches the old tribal divisions, such as Yamparika, Quahada, and Noconie, persisted.

Agency headquarters had been moved from Fort Sill to Anadarko after its jurisdiction had been expanded to include the old Wichita Agency. Nevertheless, the Cherokee Commission's first councils were held at Fort Sill, a more central point for the three tribes. Later the sessions would be moved to Anadarko. In the period from 26 September to 17 October, councils were held for eleven days and generated a journal of 140 pages.

Before David Jerome could get the initial session underway, Howeah (Gap in the Woods) presented him with a copy of the Treaty of Medicine Lodge.[5] A Yamparika Comanche, Howeah had been one of the tribe's ten chiefs and headmen to sign the treaty in 1867. His action at the beginning of the council foretold how much significance the Indians would attach to the treaty during the negotiations.

Jerome offered his usual introductory presentation, briefly describing the commission's origin and mission. As always, he stressed the benevolence of the United States, but he cautioned them that "the time that the Government furnishes you food and clothing is drawing to an end."[6] And he quickly got to the bottom line—the Indians had more land that they could use, and the commission was offering them an opportunity "to sell to the great father all the land that you can not use for homes for his white children." The money they would receive would assist them "in fixing up your houses" so that they might "live in comfort such as you have never known."[7] Jerome then turned the floor over to Judge Wilson and Warren Sayre. As usual, Sayre spoke at greater length and took a harder line, citing the existence of the Dawes Act and the power it gave the president to allot reservations at "any time."[8] He also informed the Indians that they did not own the land in the same sense that a white man owned his farm; they could not sell an acre of the reservation nor lease any of it to cattlemen without government permission.

Jerome then invited the Indians to ask for clarification of anything the commissioners might have said. He made it clear, however, that "We do not want to shut any Indian off from what he wants to say but we want to talk business."[9] Tabananaka (Hears the Sun), another Yamparika chief, was the first to respond. He was pessimistic about the chances of a trade in the near future and was concerned about the interests of the young Indians. He also stated that Lone Wolf, a leading Kiowa chief, "is with me."[10]

Then the commissioners had an opportunity to hear from the principal Comanche chief, Quanah Parker, and he lived up to advance billing. The son of a Comanche warrior, Peta Nocona, and white captive Cynthia Ann Parker, Quanah was a member of the last large Quahada band to surrender at Fort Sill in the spring of 1875. He had promptly inquired about his mother, only to learn that she had died a few years after her recapture by Texas Rangers.[11]

Quanah arrived on the reservation prepared to accept the new way of life and make the most of it. Intelligent and a born leader, he managed to maintain the respect of more conservative Comanches while being sufficiently cooperative with white authorities to rise rapidly in the reservation power structure. By 1892 Quanah was recognized by the local agent as the leading Comanche chief. Moreover, he had developed mutually profitable relationships with prominent Texas ranchers who leased over a million acres of reservation pasture. With their financial help he became the owner of a large house and had a white sharecropper to operate a one-hundred-acre farm. He also owned a herd of several hundred cattle and 150 horses, all of which he pastured on a private range that enclosed some 40,000 acres of the reservation. Quanah, however, was also blessed with five wives, and that put him at odds with Commissioner of Indian Affairs T. J. Morgan. That official would insist that Quanah be removed from the local Court of Indian Offenses, which happened to have the elimination of polygamy on the reservation as one of its objectives.

The Comanche principal chief had first gotten wind of the Cherokee Commission in the late summer of 1889. He promptly sought, but failed to obtain, permission to go to Washington to discuss the commission with Commissioner Morgan. The following February the local agent again refused to permit him, this time with a group of Kiowa and Comanche chiefs, to visit the capital. Two months later the agent reversed himself, recommending that Quanah be permitted to make the trip. Finally, in June 1890, still without authorization from the Indian Office, Quanah showed up in Washington accompanied by one of his wives and a white son-in-law. Apparently the expenses of the party were taken care of by Texas ranchers concerned about losing access to reservation pastures.

In March 1892 Quanah again appeared in Washington, this time with a wife, Chief Lone Wolf of the Kiowas, and Chief White Man of the Apaches. They were accompanied by an attorney representing the cattlemen. The trip, paid for by ranchers Daniel W. Waggoner and Daniel Burk Burnett, was a good investment. They held leases about to expire, and Secretary Noble agreed to extend them for a year. Waggoner and Burnett would be major figures among the coalition of Texas cattlemen working to defeat or at least delay the implementation of any agreement the Cherokee Commission would offer the Kiowas, Comanches, and Apaches.

Clearly the members of the three tribes had been discussing the expected visit of the commission and how to avoid allotment and sale of their surplus land. They listened patiently while Jerome made his opening remarks. Quanah's first words to him and his colleagues were that he had cautioned his fellow Indians: "do not go at this thing like you were riding a swift horse . . . do not go into this thing recklessly."[12] He went on to refer to his visit in

March with Indian Commissioner Morgan and their discussion of the impending visit of the Cherokee Commission. According to Quanah, Morgan told them that the commissioners "have not got any money but want to buy it with mouth-shoot." Quanah then went right to the bottom line: "how much will be paid for one acre, what the terms will be and when it will be paid."[13]

When Jerome responded that he would be told "bye and bye," Quanah pressed the issue. He said that some of the Indians were in a hurry to sell, "but I want a thorough understanding and thought it would be better to wait until the expiration of [the Treaty of Medicine Lodge]."[14] The chief then announced that he would not be in council the following day, because he would be at home overseeing construction of an impressive two-story porch for his new home.

That observation did not sit well with the commissioners, and Judge Wilson asked Quanah when he would be back. Quanah replied, "in a few days," adding, "I just want to talk about business, talk to the point."[15] Jerome promptly observed that the business at hand was more important than building houses and asked the chief about his remark indicating that the commissioners had no money to close a deal for the surplus land. Quanah explained that he had meant that Congress had not appropriated funds for the purchase, which had a more acceptable ring than "mouth-shoot."

The chairman then launched into a closing statement, providing some information as to how the commission would proceed. Jerome proposed that the land on the reservation be divided into three classes—mountainous, corn, and grazing—and that the Indians be permitted to choose between corn or grazing or perhaps a combination of the two. In time, however, that would be modified to a requirement that the Indians take at least some of their allotment in grazing. There was no incentive for them to take 160 acres in the Wichita Mountains, a series of granite peaks jutting from the prairie on a line running west through the middle of the reservation. Jerome also pointed out that their annuities of clothing and other useful items would expire in five years and reminded them that there was no provision in the treaty for the rations that they had been receiving for twenty-five years. Those could be terminated any time, and if they thought otherwise he offered to read them the entire treaty.

The meeting on 27 September saw the commission spell out its offer and the Indians, with one exception, express their desire to postpone negotiations until the Treaty of Medicine Lodge expired. Stumbling Bear, a Kiowa who had signed the treaty in 1867 and whom the agent regarded as generally cooperative, was the first Indian to speak. Describing himself as an old man who did not have long to live and was concerned about his descendants, he called for suspending negotations until Medicine Lodge expired.

He was followed by Big Tree, a Kiowa chief in his early forties who was aligned with Lone Wolf, the head of the conservative wing of his tribe. Big Tree spoke in images, describing the Indian reluctance to deal as being like Indians who, while traveling, would always look for the "good places to cross. . . . They do not care to jump across a big gap."[16] He also spoke of the reservation as being like a valuable workhorse that they did not want to give up: "If I were to come to your house . . . and attempt to buy something that you prize very highly, you would probably laugh at me and tell me that you were not anxious to sell it. So I tell you, I am not anxious to sell the useful horse."[17] Big Tree further observed that the Cheyennes and Arapahos had sold their land and were now poor.

Howeah, the Comanche who had spoken at the first session, now raised the spirits of the commissioners. Speaking of how he had trouble when land on which he had opened a farm was included in a rancher's lease, he came out for allotments, offering them as a means of keeping the young men out of trouble. "I feel like shouting with joy at the chance to make this trade," he enthused.[18]

The next Indian to speak was a Quahada Comanche, White Eagle. Nearly twenty years earlier, then known as Eschiti (Coyote Droppings),[19] he had been a young and influential medicine man. Indeed, he is generally credited with helping inspire the predominantly Comanche and Cheyenne attack on the trading post for white buffalo hunters at Adobe Walls, in the Texas Panhandle. This was the opening engagement in the Red River War, 1874–75. That attack's failure had not seriously impaired his leadership position. The following spring he still headed the large Quahada band that included Quanah and was the last major Comanche group to surrender.

White Eagle prefaced his remarks with a comment about Quanah that helps explain Cynthia Ann's son's reputation as a middleman: "What he learns from the Government he writes on his tongue and we learn from him."[20] White Eagle then went on to ally himself with his fellow Comanches, who wanted to wait until the expiration of Medicine Lodge before making any decisions about allotment or sale of the surplus land.

A dialogue then ensued between Chairman Jerome and Chief Quanah, who had apparently reflected on Jerome's comments the previous day and concluded that overseeing construction of his porch could await another time. After Jerome had declared that the first thing to be done was that each Indian husband and wife should pick out allotments, Quanah interjected that he wanted to know how many acres they would get, observing that the 1867 treaty permitted heads of families to hold 320. He also wanted to know how much they would be paid per acre for the surplus.

Jerome brushed Quanah aside, "We will tell you in a minute,"[21] and went on to detail the process of selection that would be employed and the time that it would take to carry out the agreement. He estimated that it might take almost five years—the time remaining on the treaty. At that point Quanah interrupted him a second time: "You do not seem to understand; a good many are opposed to making any trade for four years and you seem trying to press a sale on them. We know that the Medicine Lodge Treaty will run out and the annuities will run out but the land will be good. The Medicine Lodge Treaty gives us 320 acres to the head of a family; you have not told us how much land you propose for one Indian to have nor how much for one acre."[22] Obviously annoyed, Jerome retorted, "I told you that we were ready to read the paper when you get through talking about Medicine Lodge. That has nothing to do with any trade."

After a few more remarks, Jerome called upon Warren Sayre to spell out the government's offer. He presented it, good attorney that he was, to the best interests of his client, the United States. That he was also dealing with a ward of his client never seemed to occur to him. Sayre dismissed Quanah's question regarding the 320 acres the treaty offered by noting that only the heads of families got that. Other members over eighteen were limited to 80 acres, and those younger got nothing. In contrast the government was offering 160 acres to each Indian, regardless of age. Sayre also argued that the recipient of 320 acres under the treaty was unable to rent any part of it, while the allottees could rent to tenants for fifty cents per acre and live a life of relative leisure.

In his usual thorough fashion, Sayre detailed the procedure by which the United States would pay for the land. Of the $2,000,000, each Indian's share would amount to $665. But having described what that would buy—twenty-five fat steers, or thirty good horses—he must have further confused them by stating that over a period of nearly three years each would actually receive three payments totalling $212, the remainder of the principal being held in the Treasury to draw 5 percent interest and provide an annuity of about $25 per Indian.

Quanah interrupted Sayre's presentation to ask again, "How much per acre?" And when Sayre could not tell him, the chief wanted to know how then he had arrived at the $2,000,000. Sayre replied lamely, "We just guess at it." Quanah then indicated why the Indians were so interested in learning the price per acre—they had heard that some tribes had received $1.25, while the Wichitas, their neighbors, were unhappy at being paid only fifty cents.[23]

To justify his guess Sayre listed factors that could only be estimated but would contribute to the amount of land the Indians would be selling, such as how many Indians would be getting allotments and how much land would be reserved for the military and education. Trying to end his presentation that day on a positive note, the commissioner promised that any grazing leases in force would be respected. He failed to note, however, that the current contracts were good for only one year and renewal was very problematic.

At the session the following day, the 28th, four Indians spoke—Lone Wolf, White Man, Tabananaka, and White Wolf. Jerome opened the discussion by assuring the Indians that the commission had nothing to conceal and wanted them to comprehend fully all that they were being told. Lone Wolf, who spoke first, carried the name of a celebrated Kiowa warrior chief who had adopted him when the chief's son was killed in a skirmish with Texas Rangers. Lone Wolf was now one of the leading chiefs of the Kiowas, had been to Washington, and ably represented the mass of the tribe who opposed the commission's offer. He observed that the three tribes had counseled twice since the previous session and that they were united in wanting to wait until the expiration of Medicine Lodge before further negotiations. He justified this on the grounds that, with the exception of a few educated young people, they were unable to "cope with the white man."[24] He described the tribesmen as having "made little progress from our forefathers, we are Indians today, wearing blankets and fond of painting our faces." Lone Wolf predicted that their getting allotments, "instead of . . . being a blessing it will be disastrous."[25] He was followed to the floor by White Man, an Apache, who insisted that his people still could not farm well enough to survive by agriculture. "[W]hen we plow we have to take our wives and children to manage the horses," he explained; "we are not ready for it."

Tabananaka, the Yamparika chief, went against the tide and expressed his willingness to accept an allotment. Possibly he did so because Quanah seemed to be opposing the commission, and Tabananaka was usually lined up against Quanah. Even he, however, insisted on knowing how much per acre they would receive for their surplus land. Tabananaka was followed by White Wolf, a Noconie chief who was also one of Quanah's rivals in tribal politics and an ally of Lone Wolf in reservation affairs. Like Lone Wolf, he opposed both pasture leasing and allotment. When he was in Washington in 1889 he had complained of Quanah, "a half-breed"[26] in the pay of the cattlemen and their spokesman. In addition White Wolf had declared that the Indians were not ready for severalty. Surprisingly, he now stated that "I am not inclined to refuse this proposition." He then offered a probable explanation for his change of heart; he had been listening to John T. Hill, who "is a friend of ours and can do something for us."[27]

This was the same John T. Hill who had insinuated himself into the confidence of the Tonkawas and then undercut their opposition to an agreement. For this the government had rewarded him with a fee of $5,000, deducted from the pay the Tonkawas received for their surplus land. That had worked so well for him that he got involved in the Kiowa, Comanche, and Apache situation. Shortly before the Cherokee Commission arrived on the reservation, Hill wrote Secretary Noble, informing him of the status of the tribes based on a ten-day visit there and also indicating that he had been in correspondence with the commission.[28] Once they had all arrived on the scene, Chairman Jerome permitted him to use a government interpreter on occasion, evidence that Hill was certainly not opposing the commission's agenda.

After White Wolf sat down, Jerome made his closing statement for that session. Addressing the pay-per-acre issue, about which he said that Quanah had "pushed Judge Sayre hard," the chairman came up with an estimate—somewhere between $1.00 and $1.10.[29] He maintained that the commission had already negotiated nine agreements and in each had specified only the total purchase price. He also told the Indians that they had to deal with Congress on other matters, meaning pasture leases and rations—a not-so-subtle reminder that they could not afford to alienate such a powerful institution in their lives. "Congress," he declared, "is pushed from the outside to have this work go on and sooner or later it will go on."[30] On that ominous note Jerome adjourned the council until the next day.

TAKING INDIAN LANDS

The first Indian speaker at the session the 29th was Iseeo, a Kiowa serving as a sergeant in the Army. He had been a respected warrior in his youth and an army scout after returning to the reservation late in the Red River War. Earlier in 1892, when the government authorized a troop of Indian cavalry, Iseeo enlisted. Despite being well over the maximum age permitted (his early forties), he was recruited by the commander of the troop, Lieutenant H. L. Scott, who signed him up as age twenty-nine.[31] The cavalry officer, who would rise to the rank of army chief of staff, had depended upon Iseeo's judgment and cooperation in two earlier crises, the Kiowa flurry of interest in the Ghost Dance in late 1890 and, the following year, the turmoil surrounding the death of three Kiowa schoolboys who fled a brutal teacher only to die in a blizzard.

Iseeo took the floor to describe the young men of his tribe as unready to fend for themselves, and he joined the other Indian speakers in urging a delay of several years in allotment and the sale of their land. He, too, spoke of the Cheyenne experience, describing how they had visited the Kiowas after their first payment, riding in new wagons and carriages and wearing handsome shawls and blankets. Nevertheless, they had come to the Kiowas to beg for cattle and horses, having spent all their money, and Iseeo predicted that they would be in worse shape soon. Because he was a government employee, he asked forgiveness for his stand. But he said he was an Indian also and had been asked by the chiefs to make a statement. Iseeo concluded dolefully, "Mother earth is something that we Indians love. . . . We do not know what to do about selling our mother to the Government. That makes us scared."[32] David Jerome then drew an admission from Iseeo that the Cheyennes had told him their rations were about to be cut off, whereas, the chairman maintained, they could be continued indefinitely. In short, said Jerome, "The sergeant sees trouble where there is none."[33] Jerome and Sayre blamed the Cheyennes' condition on their having squandered the money paid them.

The commissioners once again went over how much they were offering the Kiowas, Comanches, and Apaches, trying to put it in easily comprehensible terms. Thus the $2,000,000 became "two thousand boxes of money" that would require "26 six mule wagons to haul it from the fort over here." As always, the commissioners stressed the lump payments for families, "the more children . . . the richer,"[34] and the rosy estimates of rental income from their allotments. Sayre concluded with a warning that indeed the Treaty of

Medicine Lodge would soon expire, and the commission wanted to help the Indians prepare for that eventuality.

Three days elapsed before the next council on 3 October. Judge Wilson was the first commissioner to speak, and his presentation was most significant for his invocation of the Dawes Act, "that provides that the President may order that you must take allotments whether you want to or not."[35] Nor would the president be offering them any $2,000,000 for the land remaining after allotment—it would be up to Congress to decide what the government would pay. "It is dangerous business to go into the waiting business," Wilson warned.[36]

Poor Buffalo, a Kiowa, and Tabananaka, the Comanche, then spoke briefly. The Kiowa lined up with those wanting a delay of a few years. Tabananaka, who said that he was speaking for some Quahadas and Yamparikas, reiterated that he was ready to deal and that the allotments were "enough for us to be saved and live on." White Eagle, who was up next, identified himself with Quanah, who "stands just as I do in loving and wanting to keep the country."[37] He also stipulated a price of $1.50 per acre for the surplus land and then made a telling reference to John Hill, "my friend." The white man, White Eagle announced, had advised the Indians to deal with the commissioners, as "they are straight," but he added, "I do not know what kind of friend my friend is yet," indicating some reservations about that scoundrel.[38]

After White Eagle sat down, Quanah rose to offer a proposal that the commissioners could not have welcomed. Nor could they have enjoyed his preliminary remarks, which included a reference to their salary as being $15 a day. This was not quite accurate but close enough, and it must have sounded exorbitant to Indians who thought themselves fortunate to get that amount in a semiannual grass-money payment from the cattlemen. Quanah's idea was that each of the three tribes nominate someone to represent them and they in turn closet themselves with an attorney whom Quanah had already invited to advise them. To enable the three-Indian committee to prepare its recommendations, the Comanche proposed a recess of two months. He added that he did not expect the commissioners to decline his proposal, because their salary would continue even if they were not in session—a little dig. As he had indicated that the attorney would arrive the same evening, Jerome could only propose that the three Indians meet with him and then report to the council the following morning.

TAKING INDIAN LANDS

The initial speaker at the council of 5 October was the local Indian agent, George D. Day, a Maryland Republican politician and former sheriff. He had been in office less than a year when the Cherokee Commission arrived. Jerome announced that he had asked Day to address them, assuring the Indians that "he is not here specially to aid the commissioners so I suppose you will be glad to hear him."[39] The chance that Day would oppose the commission was virtually zero, however, as Jerome well knew. Certainly none of the other agents had been willing to sacrifice their standings with Washington to battle for their tribes.

Agent Day did have important news. Quanah's attorney—who turned out to be Henry E. Asp, an acquaintance of John Hill's from Guthrie—had concluded that there was nothing he could do and so departed. As could have been predicted, before leaving he advised the Indians that they had only two choices, the commission's offer and the Dawes Act, and that they should go with the offer of Jerome and his colleagues. Or, as Agent Day summarized it: "These gentlemen are your friends and can do anything that can be done for you here."[40]

Tabananaka, the first Indian to respond, continued to espouse acceptance of the government's offer. His only quibble concerned the size of the military reservation that the government would retain, and he set up David Jerome nicely by asking if the offer was made in good faith and would advance the interests of the Indians. That gave the chairman another opportunity to plug the offer. In doing so he enthusiastically described an overnight visit he had made to Quanah's new home. He spoke of how well it was furnished, the fine meal they had been served, and the Comanche chief's livestock holdings—five hundred to six hundred cattle, "a great drove of hogs and a great band of horses."[41] Moreover, Quanah had his one hundred acres under fence cultivated by a white sharecropper, who gave the chief one-third of all he produced. Jerome managed to leave the impression that any Indian who took allotment could have comparable success. He ignored the facts that Quanah derived additional income from the roughly 40,000 acres of reservation range that he had sequestered for his own use and that he received financial assistance from cattlemen grateful for the chief's help on pasture leases.

Two Kiowas, Big Tree and Komalty, then took the floor. Big Tree was a prominent chief and had earlier been notorious among the whites as a raider. In 1871 he had been arrested together with Satank and Satanta, noted Kiowa warriors, and had served time in a Texas penitentiary. By 1892 that was all behind him, and he was recognized as being an influential chief with ties to Lone Wolf. He spoke for the great majority of Kiowas, who wished to postpone negotiations. Responding to Jerome's statement that one reason the commissioners were unwilling to accept Quanah's proposal for a two-month recess was that the president would interrogate them about such a decision, Big Tree suggested that the president might listen to the chairman's explanation. "When I go away to trade and come home without the articles," the Kiowa declared, "my wife does not scold."[42] He also believed that the Indians should determine the price for the land that the United States wanted to buy.

Komalty, usually linked with fellow Kiowas Lone Wolf and Big Tree in reservation politics, declared their views to be "the sentiments of the tribe."[43] He expressed particular concern about the inadequacy of 160-acre allotments, predicting that within eighty years an Indian would be unable to find sufficient pasture for ten horses and fifty head of cattle. That was a safe prediction in a country where fifteen to twenty acres were required to support one head.

At that moment Quanah reentered the fray. "I want to take the part of the mockingbird," he announced; "I have several little songs to sing." First he made the point that he and Tabananaka were already doing the things that the government was urging Indians to do to become self-sufficient. He next referred to the quick exit of his attorney, Asp, saying "it looked like things were in such a shape that he could not do anything for us now."[44] And then the commissioners were pleasantly surprised to hear him say that he was willing to allow Congress to determine whether it wished to accept the Indians' demand for $500,000 more than the $2,000,000 the commission was offering. Although he did not indicate it, this decision seems to have been arrived at by a council of Quanah, Lone Wolf, and White Man, representing the three tribes, after talking to Asp.

Quanah went on to voice criticisms of other elements of the government's position. He could still see no reason why two sections of land should be reserved in every township for support of education—sections for which the Indians would not be paid. In addition he objected to the commission's claim that the Wichita Mountains were necessarily worthless. "I have noticed," the chief said, "that coal is burned in such localities, and that iron, silver and gold . . . are found in such places."[45] Indeed, prospectors had been infiltrating the reservation for many years, and at one time officers at Fort Sill dabbled in mining claims.

An Apache, Chewathlanie, then demonstrated the plight of being a member of the smallest tribe on the reservation. He claimed chieftain status, and for that reason was "not ashamed to get up before the rest of the chiefs and make a speech." Nevertheless, after assuring the commissioners that he was friendly to the whites, the most he could say was, "I am with the majority, if they are willing to sell all right, if not all right."[46]

Then it was the turn of three Comanches to comment. Cheevers (Goat), a Yamparika band chief, led off. He had been to Washington with a delegation in 1872 and had avoided fighting in the Red River War two years later. Like Quanah, although not on his scale, he had opened a farm and had cattle and was trying to set an example for his people. Cheevers indicated that he was willing to make a trade but would want more money. Like him, White Wolf, the Noconie Comanche who had spoken at an earlier council, was confident that a deal could be made if the commissioners sweetened their offer a little. And White Eagle, who had been holding out for a four-year delay, now appeared to be wavering.

Warren Sayre then rose to try to tidy up the loose ends and close the deal. First, he wanted to get Quanah to confirm his offer to let Congress decide if the Indians should get an additional $500,000.[47] The Comanche promptly complied, and then Sayre proposed another condition that Quanah had been advocating outside the regular councils—that the Indians be permitted to add several whites to the list of those who would be beneficiaries of the treaty. The commissioners were quite amenable, as this would provide additional people with an incentive to support the agreement. They only asked that the tribes specify whether the individuals listed be eligible for land only or for both land and money.

The following day, 6 October, the commissioners discovered that it was not a done deal. Tohauson (Little Mountain), a Kiowa chief and son of a chief of the same name, declared that he would not sign the agreement— and neither would at least half of his fellow tribesmen. He added that the white men who were being proposed as beneficiaries had married tribal members and were "bad characters" who should not be adopted. Jerome dismissed his criticism, saying that if Indians did not intend to sign, they should just keep quiet, not "weary us with their talk"[48]—a patent effort to stifle the opposition.

When the chairman offered to answer any specific questions, Tabananaka and Quanah responded. Tabananaka inquired about the possibility of the Indians' being taxed for land and personal property. Jerome assured him that the land could not be taxed, but as for personal property, "We do not know and do not want to deceive them."[49] That must have disturbed at least some of his audience, who had heard horror stories about tax collectors descending on newly allotted Indians.

Quanah made a long statement reflecting his concern about the possibility of the grass money's being cut off long before the Indians had begun to receive any payment for their surplus land. He also emphasized that he would not sign the agreement until he understood all the provisions. "I want to hear all the parts and various points," he declared; "I know that the law is a very particular thing." And he had no illusions about how he might be impacted by the agreement: "I do not expect myself to bring my condition in much better shape by this trade. Some of the Commissioners have been at my house and eaten with me and know how I live, but I am talking for my people who are not fixed yet."[50] Actually, Quanah stood to lose significantly, and he was well informed enough to comprehend this. Once the surplus land was opened to settlement he would no longer have his very large pasture, nor would the Texas cattlemen have any incentive to pay him retainers.

The chief again brought up the issue of the government's reserving two sections of each township for the support of schools. Jerome gave his complaint short shrift, stating that the government would not raise its offer even if those sections were not reserved. Quanah made one last effort to get more money per acre, arguing that while the commission might refer to the Wichita Mountains on the reservation as being worthless, the army used stone from them for building purposes, and they might contain gold. But the commissioners felt the tide was running in their favor and were in no mood to make concessions. Indeed, their instructions left them little room, as became apparent in a subsequent exchange between Jerome and Secretary Noble.

The day after the last session at Fort Sill, Jerome wrote Noble that they had already collected 193 signatures of the estimated 450 required to meet the Treaty of Medicine Lodge's stipulation that three-fourths of the adult male population must agree to any land cession. Jerome reported that the headmen of each tribe had signed and he was reasonably certain that the commission would be successful.[51] Noble's response was a telegram: "Close

TAKING INDIAN LANDS

on lowest terms possible in view of the claims of other Indians. There seems no other way. But Congress ought not to pay more than we shall get back. Congratulate you on prospect completing your part."[52] The claims he alluded to were ones the Choctaws and Chickasaws might make, as they had done successfully in the case of the Cheyennes and Arapahos. The Kiowa, Comanche, and Apache Reservation was also carved from the Leased District that the United States had obtained from the Choctaws and Chickasaws. The government was charging homesteaders $1.25 per acre, and so it tried to be sure that it paid the Indians no more. Obviously the government's cheap land policies were subsidized by the Indians, who did not get fair market value for their cessions.

Meanwhile, the commissioners held the last council at Fort Sill on 11 October, after a three-day interval during which they continued to solicit signatures for the agreement. The evening session was set up primarily to get members of Lieutenant Scott's Indian troop, mostly Kiowas, on board. After opening the meeting, Chairman Jerome remarked that the commissioners had talked enough about the terms and they now wanted to give the Indian soldiers a chance to sign. He added that the fact that they had enlisted was evidence of their desire "to enter upon this new life and the road that the white men travel." Jerome also denied the rumors circulating that the commission was attempting to "bull-doze" Indians into signing and to corrupt the interpreters.[53] When one Kiowa expressed his reluctance to sign because of his fear of fellow tribesmen around Anadarko, the chairman tried to assure him that every Indian had the right to vote his convictions.

Jerome alluded to Lieutenant Scott's presence as giving "countenance to this meeting" and further referred to the officer's being on the list of whites who would profit from the agreement. Scott hastened to disavow any idea that he might be trying to influence the course of negotiations: "I would rather that I never got a foot of land anywhere than that an Indian be induced to do anything . . . on account of any benefit it might bring to me."[54] Simply by permitting his name to remain on the list, however, he created an appearance of conflict of interest.

Wolf Bear, Iseeo, and Lucius Aitson were the last three Kiowas to speak. Wolf Bear declared that he would not sign until the rest of the Kiowas acted. Jerome chose to react to this positively, stating that the Kiowas who drew their rations at Anadarko had invited the commissioners to come there—an act he interpreted as indicating their desire to sign. Iseeo then comforted the commissioners by declaring that he has already signed and had no intention of asking that his name be removed: "I understand this matter fully and am on this road."[55] However, Aitson, a young man who had attended Carlisle boarding school in Pennsylvania, expressed apprehension about having "touched the pen," and the session closed on that discouraging note for the commissioners.[56]

Despite his brave talk, Jerome must have been worried about what awaited the commission at Anadarko. The three sessions there on 14, 15, and 17 October proved to be unpleasant experiences for the white men. At the first session all eight Kiowa speakers, half of whom had attended some of the meetings at Fort Sill, vigorously opposed the agreement. The first to take the floor was Apiatan (Wooden Lance), who was prominent in reservation affairs. A nephew of Chief Lone Wolf, he had been appointed by the agent to the Court of Indian Offenses—a sign of some willingness on his part to collaborate. He is best remembered for his role during the excitement that had been engendered by the Ghost Dance the previous year. Fellow tribesmen had collected funds to send Apiatan to contact Wovoka, who had inspired the Ghost Dance. Although he departed the reservation a devotee of the Ghost Dance, Apiatan returned disillusioned. His report was a major factor in the rapid decline of Kiowa interest in that religious movement.

That evening in the council at Anadarko, Apiatan addressed his initial remarks to the Great Spirit: "listen to me talk."[57] He asked that his words be recorded in a book in Heaven and appear unaltered in the commission's journal. He referred to his presence at Fort Sill sessions then declared that all of the Kiowas wanted to remain on the road that the Treaty of Medicine Lodge had laid out. At the end of his presentation, Apiatan asked all those who wanted to remain on the "old road" to stand. When they did, he proclaimed, "we . . . have voted solidly against the contract."[58]

Before Jerome regained the floor, Apiatan was followed by four other Kiowas. Three of them were undistinguished, but Chaddlekaungky had been present at the Medicine Lodge council, was a political ally of his brother Lone Wolf, and at one time had served briefly on the Court of Indian Offenses. Like the previous three speakers, he pled for a postponement of negotiations until Medicine Lodge had lapsed. He tried to avoid antagonizing the commissioners and stressed the dependence of the Indians on the government's generosity. He described them as "like a new born colt staggering along because of its tender feet."[59]

TAKING INDIAN LANDS

Chaddlekaungky also cited the opposition of some Kiowas to leasing pasture to the cattlemen, a position so strongly held that they had refused their shares of the grass money. He explained that they loved the land and "thought if they leased it, it would never come back to them again."[60] He also took the opportunity to voice Indian concern about what they regarded as efforts to subvert some Kiowas. "We are not desirous of seeing a few men taken upstairs by the Commissioners after each council," he warned, "wherever people do that they are liable to do crooked business."[61]

After Chaddlekaungky sat down, Jerome got in a few words before hearing the last Kiowas to speak at that session. The chairman did not respond to the Indian's apprehensions, only asked for any other objections the Kiowas might have so that the commissioners might consider them before the next meeting. Flying Crow, Big Bow, and Little Robe did take the floor, but their presentations differed little from those of their predecessors. Flying Crow did insist that the Kiowas had support among the Comanches and Apaches in their refusal to negotiate. He was followed by Big Bow, who was described in the early 1870s by Quaker teacher Thomas C. Battey as "the notorious Kiowa raider . . . who has, probably, killed and scalped more white people than any other living Kiowa."[62] Big Bow employed a metaphor that all the former warriors could appreciate, describing the message from the Great Father as "like an enemy coming to camp amongst the people and the people are disturbed." He assured the commissioners, however, that they need not fear being attacked, because "you came here to talk business and we are talking about it."[63]

The last Indian to speak at that session was Little Robe. He also relied on imagery to oppose the commission's proposition, comparing the Indians' plight to his situation if he had but a single horse: "while I am not using it to the best advantage yet I feel if I sell him I will regret it."[64] Moreover, Little Robe told the commissioners that he had been at the Fort Sill councils, so he already knew how they would respond to the Kiowas' questions. Jerome tried to close the session on a good note, assuring the Indians that the agent would issue beef that evening: "Now go and get your beef and go home and go to sleep and sleep good and dream happy dreams . . . because you know that the Government sent us here not to do you harm but to make one of the best contracts that the Government ever made with any Indians."[65]

There was nothing in Kiowa demeanor during the session the 15th to suggest that they had had happy dreams. Jerome first tried to respond to some of the grumbling about interpreters, especially Joshua Given. Although the son of the much feared raider Satank, who chose to die rather than be taken to Texas for trial, Joshua derived his surname from Dr. Obadiah G. Given, who had served as agency physician. Known around the reservation simply as Joshua, the young Kiowa had been educated in the East, where he was ordained as a Presbyterian minister. In the summer of 1889 he returned to the reservation as a missionary.

Joshua speedily discovered that it was much more difficult actually to live among his people and try to steer them down the white man's road than it was to advocate it in Philadelphia parlors. The local Indian agents certainly appreciated Joshua's efforts. Like all "returned students," however, he found most of his people resistant to his efforts and critical of his new lifestyle. Before long he was dubbed by fellow tribesmen "that Kiowa white man who wears glass eyes."[66] When the tribe was thrown into turmoil by the arrival of the Cherokee Commission, Joshua found himself charged with collaboration—selling out his fellow tribesmen.

Jerome tried to defend him by mentioning the problems faced by interpreters. On a reservation where three distinct languages were spoken, at any given time all three interpreters could be talking at the same time. He also made the point that the commissioners had accepted Joshua as an interpreter because it had seemed that was the wish of the Kiowas. If they were now dissatisfied with him, Jerome averred, they could have another who would sit in and correct any mistakes that Joshua might make. The Kiowas did nominate two backups—intermarried white men—and they were duly sworn in. Because of his greater familiarity with tribal members, however, Joshua would record the names of the Indians signing the agreement.

That did not end the dispute. Big Tree, who had spoken at sessions at Fort Sill, blamed Joshua for failing to have the Indians' wish to delay negotiations included in the agreement. Jerome tried to explain that it was the commission's stenographer, not the interpreters, who recorded what was said. He also briefly summarized the commission's version of how the deal had been reached. To that Big Tree responded sharply, "I do not want to hear, I want to see the writing."[67] Jerome replied with equal heat, "He will have to hear what I say or go away."[68]

The chairman, however, did calm down and elaborated on some of the key issues, while taking the opportunity to warn the Indians of the seriousness of their situation. The Congress, he declared, "had determined to buy up the surplus lands in the Indian Territory and open them for white settlement. . . . Congress has the power and will provide a way to do it."[69] He also cautioned the Indians against doing "ugly things" to those who supported the agreement. In such a situation, "the Government will stand by the Indians who stand by it."[70]

Jerome then asked Warren Sayre to read and explain the Treaty of Medicine Lodge to the Indians, whom he felt had some misconceptions as to its terms. Sayre read both the treaty with the Kiowas and Comanches and the supplementary one with the Apaches that applied the main treaty's provisions to them. He again spelled out the proposed agreement and once again offered his favorite hyperbole, "there is no community of so many people anywhere on earth that will have so much money and as much land."[71]

The Indians were not persuaded. Komalty (Friendship Tree), a Kiowa warrior who had made a name for himself raiding in Texas, insisted that the Medicine Lodge Treaty provided them immunity from allotment. In this he was wrong, as it actually stated that the president "may, at any time, order a survey of the reservation and. . . . Congress shall provide for protecting the rights of [Indians] in their improvements, and may fix the character of the title held by each."[72] Jerome chose to summarize it for Komalty: "Congress may make any rule about the land and you agreed to it in the Medicine Lodge Treaty."[73] It is highly unlikely, however, that any Indian present at the treaty really understood the import of that clause.

Apiatan came to Komalty's support, reminding Jerome that only the day before, and by a standing vote, the Kiowas had made clear their determination not to make an agreement, yet "now you say all these things that you said at Fort Sill."[74] The chairman fired back that the Kiowa had been "misinformed" about other features of the treaty, including provision for rations. He closed Saturday's session with the injunction: "As sensible men now that we have told you about the Medicine Lodge Treaty . . . go home and think about it and come back Monday noon and talk business. . . . you can make a better trade with this Commission than you can under the Dawes law."[75]

The council on Monday the 17th did not get off to a good start. David Jerome was launching into a review of the government's offer when he was interrupted by Big Tree, who objected that the Indians were not getting a chance to speak. He declared that he had already heard all that the commissioners had to say: "I listened and listened time and again until the words go through the other ear and still you talk and talk and talk. Now you sit down and let us talk a little time."[76]

During further exchanges both Jerome and Big Tree became more agitated. Big Tree finally told the chairman to sit down: "You told the Indians on Saturday that Monday would be the day to talk and now my ears are stuffed with the words of the Commission." Jerome flatly refused to yield the floor: "I will not be stopped by you or any other Indian."[77] He maintained that Agent Day, at the request of the Indians themselves, had asked the commissioners to come to Anadarko to explain their proposition. A few minutes later Apiatan spoke of "fraud" and of the commissioners' getting signatures "in a dishonest way." That led to a final heated exchange:

> JEROME: Let the council stop right here. I will not be talked to that way
>
> APIATAN: You have missed the road and cheated them.
>
> JEROME: You can go home all of you and do not come back here. Go on every one of you.

At that point his voice was lost in the tumult, as "the Indians rush out amid cries and shouts and a great disturbance."[78] Remaining were a very few Kiowas and Comanches.

Once quiet had been restored, Jerome and then Judge Wilson lectured those still in their seats about the advantages of the proposed agreement. Following this Agent Day stepped up to promise to "recognize as long as I am on the reservation" those who had remained in their seats. He singled out for particular censure an Indian policeman, "a man paid by the great father at Washington," for having urged others to abandon the meeting. The agent then promised, "if any of you are hungry, just say so and I will give you something to eat," demonstrating an agent's power to penalize those opposing the government and reward the cooperative.[79]

Jerome, as usual, had the last word. He justified his refusing Big Tree the floor on the grounds that the commissioners needed "ten times" the speaking time of the Indians, because the white men had the burden of explaining the government's offer.[80] As for Big Tree's peremptory demand that he give up the floor, Jerome said that the Kiowa would not have addressed the president in that fashion, nor should he so address the Great Father's representatives. "If they thought they were running this council," Jerome said of the Kiowas, "they were mistaken."[81] On that contentious note the formal deliberations between the commission and the Kiowas, Comanches, and Apaches concluded.

The commissioners continued to collect signatures for the agreement. Later their critics would denounce them for having employed Joshua to get the signatures under false pretenses and having at least one intermarried white sign under both his American and his Indian names. On 22 October Jerome and his colleagues reported to the president that of 562 adult males, 456 had signed on. They estimated that the Indians would take 453,000 acres of a total of 2,968,893 in the entire reservation. The Wichita Mountains area, which the commissioners dismissed as of limited value, comprised about 350,000 acres. The $2,000,000 price, if applied to the entire area, worked out to less than eighty cents per acre.[82] Clearly the commissioners did not expect Congress to give the Indians the $2,500,000 they wanted, though they did include for the president's consideration the Indians' wish to send a delegation and an attorney to Washington to make their case for the additional half million.

The commissioners also called the president's attention to Article X, which provided that "all the benefits of land and money conferred by the agreement" be granted to sixteen men and two women who had married into the three tribes, or had rendered them service.[83] Another seven who had also been supportive were provided allotments but no money. Three of the five interpreters for the councils, Horace P. Jones, Thomas F. Woodward, and Edward L. Clark, received both allotments and money, as did the wife of interpreter Joshua Given. Another interpreter, Emsy L. Smith, a white girl who had attended Indian schools on the reservation and become proficient in Comanche, received only the allotment. Also on the list of those to receive allotments but no money were current agent George D. Day and former Agent Charles E. Adams's infant daughter Zonee. Reverend J. J. Methvin, a Methodist missionary who had founded an Indian school on the reservation, Lieutenant Hugh L. Scott, and the infamous John T. Hill also made the list, as did David Grantham, Quanah's sharecropper.

Including people such as these who might be helpful in getting signatures on treaties and agreements was commonplace in government negotiations with the Indians. Nevertheless, the Kiowa, Comanche, and Apache agreement was a particularly egregious example. When the agreement was vetted by the commissioner of Indian affairs, he advised that the army officer and the current agent be dropped, with which Secretary Noble concurred.

Protests against the agreement were quickly heard, and not until 1900 would a modified version finally be ratified by Congress. By that time David Jerome was dead and the other two commissioners no longer had any federal government connections. But even before the commissioners had obtained the signatures of three-fourths of the adult males, serious objections were being raised. At a council on 17 October in Reverend Methvin's church, over four hundred Indians—many of whom, including Quanah and Lone Wolf, had signed the agreement—now backed a memorial opposing it. Methvin gave the document to Agent Day to be forwarded to Washington, but apparently Day suppressed it.[84]

In the aftermath of the negotiations, Joshua Givens's fellow Kiowas bitterly denounced him. Some of them charged that he had deliberately misled them about the length of time that would elapse before the agreement went into effect. Others claimed that Joshua had assured them they would receive $2.50 per acre for the surplus land—a charge that did not ring true given the extended debate over price and the absolute refusal of the commissioners to meet that figure. Regardless, when Joshua died a few months after the Cherokee Commission departed the reservation, some of his fellow tribesmen believed that it was a result of his having been placed under a curse by his enemies. The charges against Joshua lacked substantiation, but he proved a convenient scapegoat for the Kiowa failure to unite effectively against the agreement.[85]

Meanwhile, others were rallying to the support of the three tribes.

Lieutenant Scott organized another protest the following spring, this one endorsed by the Fort Sill commandant and General Nelson A. Miles and sent to Washington through military channels. Then a new agent replaced Day; at the direction of the commissioner of Indian affairs, he conducted an investigation and reported that virtually all members of the three tribes now opposed the agreement. The Indian Rights Association, which had been critical of other agreements, was urged by James Mooney of the Bureau of Ethnology to use its influence on behalf of the Kiowas, Comanches, and Apaches.[86] On their own, the Indians prepared still another protest signed by over three hundred of them, including Quanah and Lone Wolf. Indians also went to Washington to lobby, Quanah at least five times. On some of these occasions Quanah had his expenses paid by Texans who held grazing leases on the reservation and had a big stake in preserving the status quo.

TAKING INDIAN LANDS

Of course there were the customary vigorous proponents of the agreement, mainly business interests and white settlers seeking homesteads. The Chicago, Rock Island and Pacific Railroad, which had one line across the northern part of the reservation and another that ran close to its eastern boundary, was particularly active. Understandably, the railroad was eager to see the area open to development. Nevertheless, it would be eight years before the agreement would be ratified and the surplus land thrown open for settlement.

Each of the Congresses from 1893 to 1900 saw bills introduced to ratify the agreement, and they engendered support and opposition from the usual sources. The three tribes were even prepared to sell land to other Indians as a means of keeping the whites out. The Indian Rights Association argued that the Kiowas, Comanches, and Apaches should receive 640-acre allotments if they were to have any hope of surviving as ranchers. That, of course, was completely unacceptable to the business interests and the land-hungry whites.

The lobbyists for both sides, principally the Washington agent for the Indian Rights Association and an attorney for the railroad, finally framed a compromise bill, a version of which became law in June 1900.[87] The Indians were still restricted to 160 acres, but another 480,000 acres were set aside for the tribes to hold in common. Most of that land was leased to cattlemen and a much smaller portion to white farmers. The claims of the Choctaws and Chickasaws, who had their own lobbyists and support in Congress, were left to the disposition of the courts. Until they acted the Kiowas, Comanches, and Apaches were certain of recovering only $500,000 of the $2,000,000 government offer. Fortunately for the three tribes, in December 1900 the Supreme Court ruled against the Choctaws and Chickasaws.

The federal judiciary would also have the last word on a suit brought by Lone Wolf and several other Indians. Quanah, Apiatan, and Apache John, the government-recognized principal chiefs of the three tribes, and most of their followers were persuaded by Agent James F. Randlett that they had received as good a deal as was possible. But Lone Wolf and his supporters hired an attorney and filed suit. In January 1905, the Supreme Court in *Lone Wolf* v. *Hitchcock* ended the effort to nullify the agreement, incidentally reaffirming Congress's "plenary authority over the tribal relations of the Indian," a most unfortunate outcome of the case for all tribes.

Meanwhile, the Kiowas, Comanches, and Apaches had received their allotments, following which 164,416 people registered for the available thirteen thousand homesteads on their reservation and on that of the Wichitas, since the two were opened in a single operation.[88] As a lottery was employed to determine the order in which participants could select their claims, this opening lacked some of the frenzy of earlier ones. There still remained the 480,000 acres, which in 1906 Congress determined should be open to settlement at $1.50 per acre, the proceeds to go to the Indians.

President Theodore Roosevelt refused to sign that bill. He was listening to Commissioner of Indian Affairs Francis E. Leupp, his handpicked choice for the position. Leupp had been an agent for the Indian Rights Association, 1895–98, and had thoroughly investigated conditions on the Kiowa, Comanche, and Apache Reservation. He persuaded the president to refuse to sign until the payment to the Indians had been increased to $5 per acre and the 517 Indian children born since allotment were permitted to obtain homesteads from the 480,000 acres. Even then, settlers with leases in one section of the 480,000 acres were permitted to purchase their farms at appraised value rather than to engage in competitive bidding.[89] The entire 2,531 homesteads that the settlers did purchase put a respectable $4,015,785.25 in the tribes' Treasury account.[90] This was one of the rare instances when concern for tribal welfare motivated a president to force Congress to modify a bill before he would sign.

When the Indian Claims Commission came into existence in the late 1940s, the Kiowas, Comanches, and Apaches filed suit to secure additional compensation for the surplus land sold to the United States under the 1892 agreement. In 1951 the commission ruled that in 1900 Congress had made "substantial changes" in the agreement that were "never submitted to the Indians for their acceptance or approval, and never agreed to by them."[91] The commission then ruled that the case be continued until a determination could be made as to the difference between the value of the land on 6 June 1900 and what the United States actually paid. Not until December 1955 was the commission able to announce its finding. It held that the $1.25 per acre price dictated by Congress was "unconscionable" and that in 1900 the land actually had a market value of $2 per acre. Another year and a half was taken up with consideration of the government's efforts to reduce the judgment against the United States by calculating the value of government gratuities for the Indians. The final decision called for a payment to the Indians of $2,067,166, of which 10 percent would be used to compensate their attorneys.[92]

Attorneys for the three tribes next filed suit for compensation for 12,000 acres the government had acquired by the agreement, principally land retained for the agency, missions, and schools. In 1974 the Indian Claims Commission finally awarded the three tribes $60,000 in the case.[93] That judgment attracted little attention because it was a very minor part of the $35,060,000 the government was ordered to pay the Kiowas, Comanches, and Apaches for the government's "unconscionable" payment for huge areas in Oklahoma, Texas, Kansas, Colorado, and New Mexico that it had acquired under treaties negotiated in 1865 and 1867.

All of this would have come as a surprise to both the commissioners and the Indians who had participated in the 1892 negotiations. David Jerome and his colleagues had left the reservation confident that they had achieved their goals on their terms. Nor could Quanah, Lone Wolf, Apache John, and the other reservation leaders have been confident that ratification might be postponed until 1900—much less that it would be altered to their benefit. Certainly no one expected in 1892 that the Indians would someday be even partially compensated for land taken from them by the 1865 and 1867 treaties.

10

A Pawnee Agreement

WITH THE KIOWA, COMANCHE, AND APACHE NEGOTIATIONS behind it, the Cherokee Commission turned to the Pawnees, arriving at their reservation in late October 1892. Like the other tribes supervised by their agent—the Poncas, Otoe-Missouris, and Tonkawas—the Pawnees had been removed to Oklahoma as part of the government's consolidation policy after the Civil War. In the case of the Pawnees, many of them had wished to unite with their old allies the Wichitas in order to escape Sioux raiders. Indeed, some of them had moved to the Wichita Reservation before the official removal occurred. Those and the ones that had remained in Nebraska were all located on their new reservation by 1875.[1] The Pawnees' new home had been purchased from the Cherokees and the Creeks with funds from the sale of their Nebraska reservation. It consisted of 230,014 acres in the Outlet acquired from the Cherokees at seventy cents per acre and an adjoining area to the south, 53,006 acres, sold them by the Creeks for thirty cents per acre.[2] Although the new reservation had been purchased with Pawnee funds, the United States retained the title.

There was evidence of the popularity of the concept of land in severalty among non-Indians in the 1870s in the legislation authorizing the transaction. The law provided for allotment of 160 acres of land to each Pawnee head of family or single person over eighteen, should he or she "so elect."[3] If the allotment showed signs of cultivation for five successive years, the Indian could get a patent that would be inalienable for fifteen years. There is no evidence that any Pawnee took advantage of that clause.

When the negotiations opened, almost eight hundred Pawnees divided among four autonomous bands—the Chauis, Kitkahahkis, Pitahawiratas, and Skidis—occupied their reservation. Their chiefs continued to enjoy positions of power among their people. At the same time the Pawnees were sending their children to school and their agent estimated that a quarter of the Pawnees could understand English and a number of them were literate.

As a tribe the Pawnees had a history of cooperation with the United States, having rendered valuable service to the army as scouts during its campaigns against the Sioux and Cheyennes. In 1892 their agent described them as "known for their bravery and strict adherence to diligence in obeying laws and orders from the United States Government."[4] One would have expected that such exemplary conduct would have persuaded the government to be lenient with the Pawnees. Regrettably, the journal of 152 pages compiled in the thirteen meetings held by the Cherokee Commission reveals little sign of American gratitude for past Pawnee services.

The meetings between 31 October and 24 November can be roughly divided into three periods. During the initial six sessions, the contending parties established their bargaining positions. David Jerome as usual took the lead for the commissioners. He was supported only by Judge Wilson, as Warren Sayre was back in Indiana for the closing days of the 1892 presidential campaign.

At the opening session on 31 October, Jerome and Wilson encouraged the Pawnees to nominate an interpreter to assure them that the government interpreter was properly discharging his duties. The commissioners probably were reacting to the furor over Joshua Givens in their just completed negotiations with the Kiowas, Comanches, and Apaches. The result was that the councils got underway with Ralph C. Weeks, a Pawnee product of Indian schools who had traveled with Buffalo Bill Cody's Wild West Show, as the official interpreter, while Harry Coons, also a product of Indian schools, monitored Weeks's performance for the tribe.[5]

With the selection of interpreters out of the way, Jerome set the stage by sketching the developments that had led Congress to send the Cherokee Commission to Indian Territory, emphasizing the law that "good old Senator Dawes wrote."[6] He explained that the Dawes Act was responsible for the appearance of government employee Helen P. Clarke, herself a mixed-blood Sioux, to arrange for their being allotted. After that had been completed, the Pawnees could dispose of the remaining 200,000 acres. Jerome was careful to make clear that the United States would not permit them to lease the surplus land to cattlemen and that only the government could purchase it. Nor should the Indians be unduly concerned, he observed unctuously: "When

the Government thinks it is best for the Indians to sell their lands it is willing to buy them itself and see that they get full value for it."[7] Judge Wilson
also warned them against "outside folks" who would offer advice; "the Government is your best friend," he assured them.[8]

At the end of the first day's session, Brave Chief (Kitkahahki) observed
that few Pawnee headmen were present and requested that at the next meeting Jerome repeat what he had just told them. When they reconvened on 1
November, Jerome and Wilson therefore reviewed the steps leading to their
arrival at the Pawnee agency and the general proposition the government
was offering. As usual, the commissioners spoke in terms of all the land—
400 acres—that a family of five would be allotted and how the Indians could
derive "a very handsome income" from white tenants.[9] Curly Chief (also
Kitkahahki) was the first to respond to the commissioners. He informed
them that the Pawnees had purchased the land themselves and would "have
a good deal to say" about its disposition. He asked that the commissioners
first go to the Osages; meanwhile, "this land it is not running away, there is
no use for the Government to be in a hurry about it."[10] He then observed
that not all Pawnees had yet been allotted.

Curly Chief's stand was supported by four more Pawnees, each identified with one of the four bands: Sun Chief (Chaui), Baptese Bayhylle (Skidi),
Eagle Chief (Pitahawirata), and Brave Chief (Kitkahahki). Sun Chief, also
the ranking tribal chief, argued that he knew the value of the land and that
it belonged to them as they had purchased it. Moreover, they could do nothing until allotment had been completed. Bayhylle, a mixed blood who frequently served as an interpreter, endorsed what the chiefs had said, and then
Jerome took the floor.

The chairman proceeded to employ a favorite scare tactic, raising the
specter of white settlers crowding in upon the Indians: "they are pretty trou-
blesome." Referring to the previous "runs" by which the settlers had staked
out homesteads in the Sac and Fox and the Cheyenne and Arapaho reservations, he described the white people as being "in a dreadful hurry."[11] The
problem for the Indians, Jerome declared, was that Congress had authority
over their land, which they could escape only by taking allotments. Nor
would he accept the Pawnee suggestion that the Cherokee Commission first
deal with the Osages, who—he predicted—would only advise that the commissioners first go on to the Poncas, who in turn would suggest other tribes.

Eagle Chief (who was active in the Ghost Dance, recently arrived among the Pawnees) spoke to an additional issue, which the commissioners had heard much of from other tribes. He deplored the plight of those born after allotment, as "we are not decreasing and the surplus land could be used for that."[12] Brave Chief also complained of the councils' taking the Indians from their work: "There is not a day that I do not work for my living." And he made clear that he understood "this trading business. . . . when I let the land go I will do the pricing of it."[13] What the two chiefs had said was endorsed by Charley White. "We still recognize these head men," he declared, "and whatever they do we have to go by."[14] That degree of tribal unity was not something that the Cherokee Commission commonly encountered.

Then ensued a discussion about the Indians' being fed, as they argued that they could not subsist by themselves away from home. Jerome assured them that he and Judge Wilson sympathized, "but the Government can not afford to send steers here simply to have the Indians stand up and say that they won't do what the Government wants them to." Lest the Pawnees not get his point that they must cooperate to be fed, he went on to describe a hypothetical situation in which he wired Washington to get food for those attending council and received a query in response asking whether the Indians were "going to keep on the Indians' road or will they take the Government's road. . . . they close their eyes and want me to send them food."[15]

The following day Jerome began by having the proposed agreement read to the Indians clause by clause and commenting on each. The Pawnees learned that they were being offered $1.25 per acre for the surplus land, for a total of $250,000 for the approximately 83,000 acres. That was only an estimate, as the agreement offered the Indians 160 acres each if they took grazing land and 80 if they took arable land, and those choices could not be made until after the agreement was signed.

The tribes were always interested in money up front, so Jerome promised the Pawnees that they would divide a cash payment of $30,000 among them within three months after congressional ratification. The following year they would receive another $30,000, but the government would dictate how that would be spent. The balance of the $250,000 would be placed in the Treasury at 5 percent interest, which would be paid them annually. As always, Jerome broke the payment down to demonstrate how much a family of five would receive in cash that first payment. He also cited the amount—

$1,187.50—that each Indian would get in the unlikely circumstance that they chose to divide the tribe's estate.[16]

The first three Pawnees to respond were Curly Chief, Sun Chief, and Brave Chief, who united in demanding $2.50 per acre, the price they had received for their Nebraska reservation. In addition Curly Chief wanted 160-acre allotments, without reference to land quality. Judge Wilson attempted to convince the Indians of the error of their ways. He first predicted that if the commission agreed to the $2.50 per acre the Congress would reject the agreement. He also suggested that if it was worth that much the Pawnees should pay the Cherokees and Creeks more, because they had paid those tribes only seventy and thirty cents respectively. Wilson further maintained—as he commonly did in these bargaining sessions—that since the Indians had first choice of the tracts, "you are getting all the meat and you give us the bones." Then he had the temerity to ask that they be "fair with the government."[17]

Nine Pawnees responded to Judge Wilson, all supporting the chiefs' demands for $2.50 per acre. Among them, Young Chief stressed the contributions his tribe had made in helping to protect the newly constructed railroads and Lone Chief argued that given this service, "I think we are entitled to be pitied."[18]

Chairman Jerome, who was unpersuaded, must have been encouraged by the unanimous willingness of the Pawnees to sell—if they could get their price. Just getting the Indians to agree to sell at all had always been a breakthrough for the commission. His task was now to convince them that their land was not worth more than $1.25 per acre. Nevertheless, he pontificated, "It would be a very bad man and he would be a disgrace to himself and not worthy to be a Commissioner if he should try to drive a hard bargain with these Indians."[19] He would try, however, and he cited examples of other tribes that had ultimately capitulated, including the Cherokees, "who are virtually white men"; the Sac and Fox, who "have some of the smartest men that I have met in the territory"; and the Potawatomis, "so far advanced in civilization" that they needed no interpreter.[20]

Jerome concluded the day's session by maintaining that, with reference to price per acre, the commissioners had "gone to the extreme limit that our conscience will let us and that can not be changed." He did claim that he and his colleagues had taken cognizance of the Pawnees' having been "good Indians and kind to the Govt.," and that therefore they would receive the high-

TAKING INDIAN LANDS

est price offered any Indians in the territory.[21] In their report to the president, however, the commissioners defended their action on the grounds that before coming to the Pawnees they had been misled about the quality of their reservation, finding it actually to be "very much broken—a great deal of rocky and sterile land."[22]

At their next session on 3 November, Jerome came up with an unlikely explanation for offering the Pawnees a relatively high price for their land. He compared them to the Kiowas, Comanches, and Apaches, whom the Government had paid only two-thirds as much as the Pawnees would get: "Their poverty did not excite our sympathy as it did in your case."[23] He and Judge Wilson then went on to elaborate on the government's offer to the Pawnees and the impossibility of paying them the $2.50 per acre that they were asking.

The first Pawnee to respond was Curly Chief, and he was brief and to the point. He was not interested in taking an allotment. The Pawnees would sell at their price, and if the United States did not wish to pay it, "it would be no use to talk any farther for a while, just drop it there."[24]

That brought Jerome to his feet to expound on the Dawes Act, which the commissioners always unsheathed when confronted with recalcitrant Indians. He revealed that it only promised 3 percent on the balance of the purchase price held in the Treasury, not the 5 percent offered by the commission. What he did not reveal, however, was that the Dawes Act only authorized the Interior secretary to negotiate for the surplus acreage that a tribe might "consent to sell, on such terms and conditions as shall be considered just and equitable between the United States and said tribe of Indians."[25] Despite this, the chairman ridiculed Curly Chief's stance: "It is folly for the Indian to say he will not do this when the Government has said he must." Furthermore, he declared, "If it was not for the soldiers of the great father. . . . the whites would come in here in a week and you would not have any land left."[26]

Curly Chief was not intimidated. "I am not rebellious," he declared, "I am talking for my own good and interest." He was not acting, he said, like the Poncas who had demanded $10 per acre; if he had, "then you might take me for a fool." Above all, Curly Chief said, "I am speaking pretty strong because we bought the land with money that was our own"[27]—as indeed it was, although the United States had retained the title.

Initially, Sun Chief did not take as strong a stance as Curly Chief had: "I do not feel like saying anything that would conflict with the business that you are trying to do."[28] He recalled that he had been to Washington and en route had seen how white men could take poor land and improve it, so he was confident that the Pawnee land was worth $2.50 per acre in the hands of such men, and therefore the Indians should get their price.

The next Pawnee to take the floor, Knife Chief, spoke movingly about their connection with the land: "You can do anything with the land, it stays and is lasting. . . . The land is the cause we are living for."[29] He also mentioned having raised a potato crop on less than an acre that brought him $6 at the trading post. It obviously made no sense to him to sell, for $1.25, an acre that could produce $6 worth of potatoes. Although his land was not good bottomland, Knife Chief was able to raise wheat, and he always had the security of knowing that "The land will stay here, it will not go away."[30]

Eagle Chief, the last speaker that day, struck the same note. He refuted the commissioners' view that the surplus land was of no value to the Pawnees: "the Indians think the earth is good, it is our mother what we get our living from." He also asked that the commissioners give them time to reach a decision, saying they had been talking only three days, "and I think by the way you talk that you are tired already."[31]

If Eagle Chief thought that David Jerome was tired, the chairman disabused him of that idea at the session on the 4th. He gave his long lecture on American land policy, emphasizing that Congress mandated that public land should be sold only in 160-acre tracts. According to Jerome, that was because Americans had seen the ill effects of land monopoly in the British Isles, and he cited the emigration of millions of Irish as a tragic example. Therefore the Pawnees, who must have been bemused by the presentation, could not be permitted to hold thousands of acres idle. Jerome also spoke of the guardian-ward relationship and the concept of eminent domain. Finally, he summed it up: "I want to say to you as your friend, in all kindness, that the Government will never stop until it has acquired all your title to the surplus lands."[32] He might have added, and at a price that it would set.

After Judge Wilson briefly had the floor, Jerome proposed that they would postpone the next session for a few days to enable the Pawnees to deliberate on the government's offer. The chairman then observed coldly: "I wish our minds were together, but they will only get together on this matter of price by the Indians giving way."[33] To that, Sun Chief responded that Quanah Parker and the Comanches had been paid $1.50 per acre. Jerome denied it, citing 80¢ as the real figure. (That would have come as a shock to

Quanah Parker, who had been told that the government was paying $1 to $1.10.) Sun Chief had the last word. He announced that the Indians would get together to discuss the offer and asked, "Will you abide by what we decide?"[34] The record shows no response from the chairman, but we can imagine what he might have said.

It would be five days before the sessions resumed, and when they did so on 9 November, Jerome announced that Judge Wilson had left for Arkansas and that Warren Sayre would not be back until Saturday. The Pawnees, however, had conferred and were prepared to make a major concession. They now asked for only $1.50 per acre, but even that could not move Jerome. He would hold out for the $1.25 that Congress had authorized in the act creating the Cherokee Commission.

The impasse continued in the meeting the 10th. The Indians held that they had purchased the reservation with their money and should be able to set the price. Sun Chief summed up their position succinctly: "I have come down in my price and you come up on yours and we will split the difference."[35] Jerome was unmoved. Nor did he yield when Eagle Chief and War Chief added their support to Sun Chief's position. The chairman then closed the session with what amounted to an ultimatum: "Whenever these Indians make up their minds to agree about the price we are ready to talk about the other things, but there is no use talking when we do not agree about the price. In this case the Government can not change and the Indians can."[36]

At the next session, the 12th, the Pawnees sprang a surprise. Curly Chief announced that the Indians had held a council and Sun Chief had been selected to speak for the tribe. His message was that the chiefs would "rest for a while" and turn the negotiating over to Pawnees "that are educated and intelligent."[37] The new committee numbered eight, including the commission's interpreter, Ralph Weeks. Eagle Chief described them as those "in whom the Goverment has fulfilled its promise making men out of them."[38] This was indeed a departure from the tribe's normal submission to the authority of the traditional chiefs.

Before the meeting was adjourned the Pawnees mentioned another matter they wanted addressed—one they had raised earlier. This was the $15,000 that was half of their annuity, which the government had expended on clothing. The Indians were thoroughly dissatisfied with the quality of the government purchases. Jerome promised that they would take the complaint under consideration.

During the councils of 14, 15, and 16 November, three of the young men, Samuel Townshend, Harry Coons, and James Murie, initially carried the burden for the Pawnees. They did not, however, depart from the demand of the chiefs for $1.50 per acre, and they proved no more effective than their elders in convincing the commissioners.

The only new element was the request by James Murie that Helen Clarke, the alloting agent who was present, respond to Jerome's charge that the Indians were taking the best land while still demanding $1.50 for what remained. Between them, Murie and Clarke explained that because of malaria in the lowlands, the Pawnees had retreated to the less desirable uplands to open farms. Once having invested their labor in improvements at those sites, the Indians were reluctant to abandon them.[39] In short, they were not always selecting the best land for their allotments, vitiating the bone versus meat metaphor that Judge Wilson liked to employ.

On the 15th, Warren Sayre presented an option to the Indians that would put more money in their pockets, at no greater cost to the government. In response to their complaint regarding the half of their annuity spent on clothing, the commission offered to have that sum converted into cash, which would give them more money annually than the additional twenty-five cents per acre that they were demanding. The initial reaction of Sun Chief and Eagle Chief, again speaking for the tribe, was measured. They still held out for $1.50, but the seed had been sown.

The following day there was little new. David Jerome again cited his experience with the Utes and the Nez Percé. This the Indians recognized as a not-so-veiled threat, White Eagle objecting, "you should not try to scare us into it because the chiefs are working for the old women and children."[40] The Pawnees also reacted by invoking their war records as government scouts. Both Sergeant Peters and White Eagle claimed to have been among the first to enlist and complained that they were now in need, White Eagle noting that soldiers, but not the Indian scouts, got pensions.

Harry Coons then called for adjournment so that he and his fellow tribesmen could caucus to consider the commission's last offer. He felt impelled to protest, however: "it seems that you are trying to scare us into making this trade."[41] Jerome promptly denied it: "it is the act of a friend and the duty of a friend if they see trouble coming to the Indians to tell them what they see."[42] On that conciliatory if insincere note, the chairman closed the session.

It would be 23 November before Jerome opened the next council. In the interim the Pawnees were issued their annuity, a two-day project. They were paid in checks, not coin, and Curly Chief complained about that. Warren Sayre could only reply that their treaty did not specify coin and that whites actually preferred paper money. Then Brave Chief raised another issue that the commissioners regarded as irrelevant, their agent's practice of discriminating in issuing annuity goods. "When I ask the agent for a thing," Brave Chief grumbled, "he says do a certain thing and I will give you such a thing."[43] That was a technique widely employed by agents to reward the cooperative and punish the uncooperative.

Brave Chief next brought up another matter the commissioners were not qualified to deal with—the dances that "the Great Spirit handed down."[44] Despite government policy discouraging such activities, the commissioners hastened to endorse dancing. "In regard to the dances," Sayre proclaimed, "we do not want to put anything in the paper at all that forbids the Indians dancing all they want to. Any Indian can have a dance house on his farm and invite all the Indians to dance there all he pleases."[45]

The commissioners got past this diversion only to be confronted with others. Curly Chief wanted the first payment to be $100 instead of the $37.50 promised. Since that implied that he was willing to sell for the $1.25 per acre offered for the surplus land, Jerome did not dismiss it offhand. Eagle Chief proceeded to further irritate Jerome and Sayre by observing that while the commissioners could stay all winter and earn $16 a day, "I am here too but I do not get one cent. . . . the longer the councils go on the more money you make."[46] Jerome could not let that pass without comment, rebutting that the commissioners would draw their pay whether or not the Pawnee agreement was accomplished. He also declared that "every day I stay and work . . . in the Indian Territory I lose more money than he says I am getting."[47] That was possible, but unlikely.

At last things were beginning to move in the Cherokee Commission's direction. Knife Chief affirmed that "there is nothing in this that would injure us, I see you are working for our good as well as for the Government."[48] To the further relief of the commissioners, Good Chief added that the chiefs "are making up their minds to come to you and make the trade." However, he reminded Jerome that the commission had given other tribes a feast at the conclusion of the negotiations and that, "I did not hear that you had killed any beef for these Indians."[49] Sun Chief then closed the session with a statement Jerome and Sayre had been waiting to hear: "I want you to know that I have given my consent, but I do not want to sign the paper tonight; we will get the Young Men in here tomorrow and then vote and read the paper over and commence signing."[50] The Pawnee principal chief had spoken.

The meeting on 24 November began late, leading an ebullient David Jerome to open the council with a jocular comment equating Indian and congressional ideas of punctuality. When the session got underway, Ralph Weeks, the Pawnee interpreter, spoke first. He expressed appreciation for the patience the commissioners had displayed in dealing with his people and spoke poignantly of the inevitability of change: "We are but a remnant of what was once a strong tribe; it seems but yesterday that we were boasting of our strength, today we are a fast disappearing people. We are here in the midst of civilization and we owe it to ourselves that we protect our children. We as Pawnees can not afford to be left behind in the race of civilization: we must put on the garb of the civilized world and adopt its manners and push forward to the highest type of American civilization."[51] That declaration would have inspired applause at the annual meeting of the Lake Mohonk Conference of Friends of the Indian, whose members had been urging acculturation of the Native Americans for a decade.

The Pawnee chiefs had closed ranks in a way that enabled them to continue to be a power in tribal affairs. Eagle Chief, who had persisted the longest in his opposition to the agreement, testified that his relatives had persuaded him to "fall in line with Sun Chief and Curly Chief so I fall in with them and whatever they do I will follow."[52] Sun Chief then graciously deferred to Curly Chief, the oldest, to speak for the tribe.

Addressing the Cherokee Commission, Curly Chief announced: "You know yesterday evening that I was coming towards you and I was about to reach you."[53] He then asked those Pawnees willing to accept the agreement to stand, and all did. But Curly Chief had one last caveat—the commissioners had to agree to making the first payment $100. As that did not alter the total price and therefore cost the government nothing, Jerome agreed, and Curly Chief, followed by Sun Chief, Eagle Chief, and 135 more of the 203 adult Pawnee males, affixed their Xs or signatures to the agreement. The Pawnee leadership had demonstrated a remarkable degree of unity, but the inequity in the power relationships had nullified their opposition.

Congress ratified the Pawnee Agreement 3 March 1893. The allotments had totalled 111,932 acres, with 171,088 declared surplus. The government opened the latter to settlement in September 1893 as part of the run that also included the Cherokee Outlet and the Tonkawa surplus land. In reporting their success with the Pawnees, the commissioners complained about the extraneous issues that the Indians had brought before the councils. This was not the first tribe, however, to look upon the negotiations as their opportunity, while they still had some leverage, to get old grievances addressed and to try—usually unsuccessfully—to extract concessions from the United States.

Specifically, Jerome and his colleagues listed Pawnee concern regarding such issues as their earlier cessions of land in Nebraska, agents' cavalier handling of annuity distributions, the lack of pensions for army scouts, their right to hold social dances on their reservation, and "a demand for twenty-eight beeves" for a feast.[54] Although the Cherokee Commission did nothing about Pawnee charges that they had been underpaid for their Nebraska reservation, in 1950 the Indian Claims Commission awarded the Pawnees more than $7,000,000.

In their report the commissioners made note of the contributions of young, educated Pawnees. Harry Coons, James Murie, and Ralph Weeks were singled out as "progressive and patriotic" and meriting the gratitude of both their tribe and the United States. Obviously aware that they were on the home stretch, Jerome and his colleagues also summarized their achievements to date, eleven agreements that added 15,100,538 acres to the public domain.[55]

11

Running Out the Clock with the Poncas, Osages, Choctaws, and Chickasaws

IN NOVEMBER 1892, before they had assurances that the Pawnees would accept an agreement, the members of the Cherokee Commission were sufficiently optimistic to be looking ahead. A primary concern, however, was that their funds were again nearing exhaustion, and they so reminded Secretary Noble. At the same time they apprised him that there still remained much work assigned them by Congress in 1889. Agreements were yet to be negotiated with four of the "uncivilized" tribes, the Osages, Kaws, Otoe-Missouris, and Poncas. Moreover, Congress had also mandated that they treat with four of the "civilized" tribes, the Seminoles, Creeks, Chickasaws, and Choctaws, for the portions of those nations west of 96° longitude. David Jerome, however, was convinced that attempts to negotiate with them "would be fruitless."[1]

Nevertheless, the Choctaws and Chickasaws had signalled that they would be receptive to negotiations in Washington relative to the portions of the Leased District that involved the Wichita, and the Kiowa, Comanche, and Apache Reservations. The two tribes were eager to negotiate, as they had already been paid almost three million dollars for relinquishing their claims to the Cheyenne and Arapaho Reservation. The Cherokee Commission was willing to take on the task of dealing with the Choctaws and Chickasaws, Jerome arguing that they could do it at less cost to the government than if Congress did the job. For this assignment, however, they would need an appropriation to extend the life of the commission, and Jerome cautioned that the proposed negotiations might be a lengthy process. Obviously the commissioners were savoring the prospect of an extension of their lucrative assignments.

Secretary Noble did not encourage them, wiring: "Your best course will be to adjourn by time appropriation is exhausted." Noble did brief them about his having defended their record against the claims of Commissioner of Indian Affairs T. J. Morgan. In his annual report for inclusion in the secretary's report, Morgan had taken credit for proposing to Warren Sayre the tactics the Cherokee Commission had employed in its successful negotiations with the Cherokees. This the commissioners had hotly denied, and Noble forced Morgan to delete that portion of his report.[2]

Meanwhile the commissioners conferred with the Poncas on 29 and 30 November. They accomplished nothing, as the journal of thirty pages makes clear. David Jerome announced to the Indians that they were there to try to discover why the Poncas refused to turn out in sufficient numbers for councils with the commission and why so many had refused their allotments. He made his usual speech about the Congress and the Great Father's having decided that the Indians should select their homesteads and sell the surplus acres to the United States. Jerome singled out Standing Buffalo and Hairy Bear for criticism for their not taking their allotments and fronting for the other Poncas who had refused theirs. Each chief, he held, could do a better job of selecting his own allotment than the allotting agent could. He then asked Standing Buffalo to explain his opposition.

Standing Buffalo held forth at length. He said that he was over sixty and did not expect to live much longer, nor did he think that his people would listen to him. He suggested that the commissioners talk to the young men, as he no longer had influence: "I am like an old woman and not do anything."[3] This Jerome refused to accept, declaring that the commissioners still recognized Standing Buffalo as a chief and expected him to come to every council. Jerome also reviewed the disagreement that he and his colleagues had with Standing Buffalo and Frank LaFlesche as to what had occurred in their audience with Acting Commissioner of Indian Affairs R. V. Bolt early in the year.

Over the two days, six Poncas made their tribe's case against the commission's proposition. Rushing In Battle, also over sixty, declared that looking to the future had no attraction for him, as "I am only looking into the grave."[4] Hairy Bear reminded the commissioners that "In this tribe we are as one person."[5] Thick Nail rudely dismissed the chiefs, whom Jerome was courting, as "fools, you talk to them as chiefs but we do not recognize them as chiefs, they are fools."[6] For his part, Horse Chief described himself as "a man but not old enough to make a long talk."[7] Nevertheless, he insisted that they had purchased the reservation and it was theirs to do with as they wished. Samuel Hinman, son of White Eagle, stated that although they were the poorest of the Indians and received no government rations or other supplies, they would not sell their land even if the United States offered them seven dollars per acre. Finally, Harry King complained that the Poncas who had taken allotments had done it secretly and blamed White Eagle for leading them astray.

After Harry King gave up the floor, Chairman Jerome called on White Eagle to respond to the Poncas who had indicated that they were waiting for word from their principal chief as to what course to take. White Eagle first declared that he still held that office, regardless of what other Poncas might have said. Furthermore, he said, he had taken his allotment, and if every tribal member did so, he would be willing to sell the surplus land. The chief dismissed his critics as "three small boys," declaring, "chieftainship is a hard thing to break up."[8]

Jerome then announced that the commissioners would be leaving the next day, as the Great Father had sent them a telegram to report to Washington. He also referred to the Ponca inability to "get all the Indians in one row." However, he advised them, these commissioners or some others would be back "bye and bye."[9] Before that could take place, a Ponca delegation visited Tahlequah seeking support from the Cherokees. Overland, Rushing In Battle, Black Buffalo Bull, and Samuel Himman were accompanied by an interpreter. The Poncas were "elegantly dressed in fine beaded moccasins, silk fringed leggins, with their faces painted, and an eagle feather in their hair."[10] They carried a letter from Chief Standing Buffalo protesting the pressure tactics of the commissioners. The *Advocate*'s comment was scathing: "We cannot believe that the Commission would resort to intimidation in dealing with these simple minded savages to obtain their consent."[11] Nevertheless, the Cherokee Nation was in no position to provide the Poncas any meaningful support.

Meanwhile, Secretary Noble had reconsidered his earlier directive that the commissioners wind down their operation and now urged them to come to Washington to negotiate with the Choctaws and Chickasaws. But Jerome was reluctant to continue without some assurance that they would be compensated for their expenses. He did inform Noble that the conniving John T. Hill had obtained an attorney contract with the two tribes and was anxious for the Cherokee Commission to meet him and a delegation of Choctaws and Chickasaws in Washington. Robert Owen, the mixed-blood Cherokee attorney, also had a contract with these Indians; the jackals were gathering. Warren Sayre did visit the capital in search of patronage, taking the opportunity to confer with Secretary Noble, who had cooled again about the prospects of negotiations with the Choctaws and Chickasaws.

In early March 1893 in the closing days of the 52nd Congress, the Cherokee Commission got a reprieve—a fifteen-thousand-dollar appropriation to try to complete its work. Jerome promptly made plans to make another effort with the Poncas, abruptly informing authorities in Washington by wire of his impending departure for Indian Territory. But now he was dealing with a Democrat administration and a new Interior secretary, Hoke Smith. Between finding jobs for fellow North Carolina Democrats, Smith was trying to master the complexities of one of the most diverse departments in the national government.[12]

Secretary Smith's first reaction to Jerome's telegram was clearly one of annoyance. He had already concluded that Secretary Noble had been lax in his supervision of his subordinates, and when he received Jerome's peremptory telegram, he rebuked him sharply. For Jerome to announce a course of action, Smith observed acidly in a return telegram, "without giving time here to consider its propriety, was practically to determine the matter for yourselves."[13] Under Secretary Noble's casual oversight the commission had indeed become semiautonomous, going for weeks or even months without reporting its activities. But even the new secretary quickly realized that he could not interfere with their immediate mission given their congressional mandate, and the commissioners headed for Ponca country as planned.

Early in April they arrived at the Ponca Agency, and by early June they would have concluded twenty-one sessions, recorded in a journal of 237 pages. The negotiations were carried on at a relatively leisurely pace, with half-day sessions no more than three times a week. Presumably this was to permit the Poncas to get in their spring planting and the necessary follow-up cultivation.

Jerome and his colleagues realized that their prospects of securing an agreement were not good. Although the reservation had been surveyed for allotment, only a few Poncas had made their selections. The remainder were in the process of having their choices made for them by the allotting agent. With rare exceptions the Poncas were as intransigent as they had been during the negotiations the previous spring, something the commissioners became aware of from the first sessions.

Chairman Jerome opened the negotiations 6 April. Judge Wilson was ill and would not put in an appearance until late May, and Warren Sayre had been delayed, having lost his baggage in the Kansas City depot. Alone, Jerome tried to make the case that the Poncas inevitably would have to accept their allotments and sell the surplus land to the United States. Even the Five Civilized Tribes faced allotment, he informed them, as Congress had created what would become known as the Dawes Commission to bring those tribes the blessings of severalty.

Big Goose, who had opened for the Poncas in March 1892, was again the first Indian to respond. In a brief statement he reminded the chairman that their chiefs no longer spoke for them and that he still opposed a cession. Moreover, as he had to get his planting done, he did not expect to have much time for councils. When Jerome asked how he proposed to stop the government from achieving its ends, Big Goose admitted that he did not know but said he would ask other Poncas to respond, and five of them did.

Fire Shaker was the first to speak. While he had actually selected allotments for his family, he denied that the government could force the Indians to sell the surplus acres and declared that he would never sign an agreement. Principal Chief White Eagle took essentially the same tack. He had also taken allotments for his family but now referred to the women "with big stomachs" and the need to hold the surplus after allotment for children yet to be born. "When animals come out there is grass for them to eat," said the chief, "and we would like to have land for the children as they come."[14]

The second chief, Standing Buffalo, who had been prominent in opposing the Cherokee Commission in 1892, again denounced allotment and sale of the surplus land. Referring to the previously large Ponca country in the North, he blamed the Sioux and the United States for his people's losing out there, "and now I am down here like a fox that has no hole."[15] He was supported by Rushing In Battle and Hairy Bear. Rushing In Battle argued that since the Poncas had bought the reservation in the Outlet, it was theirs to sell or keep. He said that he had told the commissioners this when they last met and he had not changed his mind.

Hairy Bear had also been a sharp critic of the commissioners the year before, reminding Jerome then of his generous salary and dismissing the chairman's oratory as "like the wind that is blowing real loud." Now he reaffirmed his opposition and cited the threat of taxes accompanying allotment. He concluded by defiantly stressing his ties to the traditional life: "if I die of starvation I will die in my way."[16]

Jerome responded by maintaining that the government had retained title to the Ponca Reservation and could do with it what it chose. Despite the opposition the government would continue to allot the Indians, and it could also refuse to permit them to lease pasture to the cattlemen. Comparing the Poncas to a recalcitrant child whom his father whips to force him to attend school, the chairman observed ominously, "the Government may do strange things if it is forced to."[17] The Shawnees and Potawatomis had also talked tough like the Poncas, said Jerome, but in time they were forced to take allotments. He then sought to close the session, but McDonald, who despite his good reputation as a farmer had been highly critical of the commission the previous year, had the last word. He stated that his plowing had to be done and he would not be with them if they met the following day.

The next council was four days later, however, and McDonald was among the participants. Jerome began by announcing that the commission intended to remain on the reservation until the Poncas accepted an agreement—and then listened while fifteen Poncas told him why they would not do so. McDonald and Standing Buffalo compared the plight of children who would be born after allotment to those infants that King Herod had killed in biblical times. Little Soldier, a policeman for ten years, was of the same opinion. It was as if, he declared, the Great Father "intends to kill all the children that come hereafter."[18] There was little doubt that, as had been the case with other tribes, the Poncas were deeply concerned about the future of their children born after the land had been allotted and the surplus sold.

Thick Nail and White Feather at least briefly held the attention of Chairman Jerome. The previous year Jerome had criticized Thick Nail for delivering the same lecture repeatedly, and he would continue to irritate. The Ponca reminded the chairman that "You are getting paid . . . and when I am talking I am making money for you."[19] For his part, White Feather had to be censored by the stenographer when he became a little too graphic in depicting the slit pants of an impoverished Indian: "you could see his xxxxx hanging down."[20]

Jerome must have been relieved at the presence of Warren Sayre for the next session on 13 April. He told the Indians of having been in Washington and talking to Secretary Hoke Smith, who—like his predecessor John Noble—had insisted that the Cherokee Commission get the Poncas to accept an agreement. Sayre also warned that the annual grass-money payment from the cattlemen leasing sixty thousand acres of their reservation, about seven dollars per capita, could be terminated any time the government chose to do so. Moreover, when the Cherokee Outlet and the Pawnee and Tonkawa Reservations were opened to settlers, predicted Sayre, the Poncas' new neighbors were likely to cut the cattlemen's fences, forcing them from the area. But the attorney could also offer a carrot. He painted his now-familiar picture of the Indian with an allotment who was able to rent a portion of it, enabling him to live comfortably, "go when and where you please," have visitors, and "they can sing and dance all they want."[21]

There was no evidence, however, that Sayre's rosy scenario was having much impact. Five Indians followed him to the floor, and none showed any sign of having heard the commissioner. Fire Shaker resorted to the old argument that the tribe had purchased their reservation and could refuse to sell. Buffalo Head announced that he needed to hurry home to work his land and complained that because the agent hoarded their lumber, he had nearly broken a foot crashing through the flimsy floor of a fellow Ponca's house.[22] This was typical of the innumerable digressions into what the commissioners believed to be unrelated matters. Probably the one that annoyed them the most related to Ponca complaints about earlier land transactions in Dakota, something Sayre had once moaned about having been forced to listen to a hundred times.

The third Indian speaker, Standing Elk, protested that several of his horses had died in 1892 because attendance at the commission's councils had forced him to neglect them. Harry King then took the floor with the frequently expressed entreaty that the commissioners first approach the Osages and then, only if they succeeded there, come back to the Poncas. The last of the five was Stands Yellow, who offered yet another familiar refrain: "you are getting pay and when we are sitting around we do not get any pay."[23]

In response David Jerome could only complain that every council was attended by Indians who had missed other sessions, forcing him and his colleagues to reiterate and reiterate their proposals and the arguments for them. Having said this, he then proceeded to discuss, at length, the government's view of the Ponca land title, namely that it was insufficient to permit them to sell or lease their land without government consent. If the Indians were dissatisfied with allotments arbitrarily assigned them when they declined to make their own choices, Jerome said that changes could be made, but only if they accepted an agreement with the United States.

The exchanges during those first three councils were typical of what recurred in the last eighteen sessions. The commissioners became increasingly strident in their demands that the Poncas engage in serious negotiations. They continuously reminded the Indians that the United States held title to their reservation and was intent on having it allotted and purchasing the surplus acres. Using arguments honed during three years of negotiations, the commissioners tried to cultivate an aura of inevitability. White pressure for land was "such a great power that it can not be stopped."[24] "The Congress and the Great Father . . . have both said that every Indian reservation is going to be broken up."[25] "If you do not sell the land to us the Congress can make a law and pay you and take it."[26]

The more frustrated they became by Ponca intransigence, the more the commissioners tried to control council debate. They became particularly agitated when Thick Nail tried physically to remove another Indian from the floor. "If he ever does that again," stormed Jerome, "we will put him in jail."[27] Aware that the rank-and-file Poncas had agreed to oppose the government, the chairman sought to use the chiefs to accomplish its goals. This proved impractical, because Standing Buffalo kept saying that the young Indians would no longer accept his leadership, while White Eagle was unwilling to assert himself. Jerome and Sayre could do little except try to encourage the chiefs by flattery, describing them as talking like businessmen while disparaging the opposition as conducting themselves like boys.

For their part the Indians complained that the white men ran the meetings, Big Goose charging Warren Sayre with monopolizing the floor. Toward the end of the negotiations Thick Nail, while admitting that he was speaking for the fourteenth time, accused the government of treating the Poncas like they were Texas steers—a comparison he had also made the previous April.

Perhaps even more telling were the statements of some Indians that the commissioners were devious in their presentations. Little Soldier regretted that they could not write, because had he been able he would have confronted the white men with the evidence when "they got up and changed their words." "When a white man says anything once the next time he will change it," he charged.[28] Harry King maintained that "the white men have many words to cheat a man with," while the Indians "can not put up any words to cheat a man with but use plain words and say what is right." More to the point, King observed that the Indians "do not listen when you talk so earnest, and . . . when we think we have got you—you do not pay any attention."[29] That trenchant observation came late in the negotiations, when the parties were principally talking past each other.

As they had in the previous Ponca negotiations as well as in those with other tribes, the commissioners sought to frighten the Indians with the loss of their government services and protection. Warren Sayre informed them that currently the United States was providing the tribe with an eighteen-thousand-dollar subsidy for their schools, mills, and shops, but "If the Poncas say they refuse to do what the Great Father wants, the Great Father then can say the Poncas can take care of themselves."[30] On 20 May David Jerome brought up a recent robbery at a local railroad depot that was the talk of the reservation, using it to make the point that the government must open the country to settlement to deny criminals sanctuary in undeveloped areas. The chairman even used the recent spate of "High Twist Winds" (tornadoes) that had led Indians to dig storm cellars as an argument for their reaching an agreement with the United States. Allotment would occur, he stated, and the Indians "must have a cyclone cellar or you will get hurt."[31]

The Poncas, however, were genuinely frightened of changes that could accompany allotment, such as county governments levying taxes on personal property and the white tenants whom the commissioners were always recommending as being able to ensure the allotted Indian a life of leisure. Buffalo Head summed up the apprehension by envisioning a situation in which he had to pay workers on the family's properties. That could result, he predicted, in his inability to pay the local taxes without borrowing money, on which he then could not pay the interest.[32] He was somewhat confused about the financial aspects but, like many Poncas, had a real fear of ultimately losing his land to the white man if the tribe ceased to hold the property in common.

On 3 May Sayre finally addressed the issue head-on, trying to quiet their fears by arguing that local taxes would probably be levied but would be insignificant, no more than the equivalent of a few bushels of wheat or corn or the price of a pair of moccasins. At the same time he went into greater detail about the arrangements the allotted Indian could make with his share-cropper. For the first two years the Ponca would receive only one-fifth of the crop, but during that period the tenant would clear the land and break and fence it. By the third year the owner would be receiving one-third of the crop and, Sayre maintained, their agent was even then making such leases for the Tonkawa allottees.

Two weeks later, when Sayre returned to the topic, he belittled the tax as "not enough to make a little child afraid, let alone big men like you are."[33] When McDonald expressed his fear that white renters "always cheat the Indians," Sayre responded that thousands and thousands of white farmers had tenants, "and the renter does just exactly as he agrees to do."[34] Moreover, the Indian agent would supervise the leasing arrangement and would require the prospective tenant to have two cosigners to guarantee that the Indian would be compensated as provided by the lease.

On several occasions the Poncas articulated a basic fear that they shared with other tribes—that Indians were not equipped to survive in a white-dominated environment. This they attributed to the Great Spirit's having endowed white people differently or as Overland phrased it: "made them to know how to write and showed them how to make things. . . . The Great Spirit made me but did not give me anything to make a living on except the wild beasts and the Indian is just as wild as the wild beast and he kills them and makes clothes and food. The Great Spirit knows that the white people would not treat the red brothers right so he put the Indians and the white people with a great water between, but the white people came over somehow."[35]

Overland returned to this same theme a month later. By that time Judge Wilson had made his first appearance during these negotiations. He reported that he had been to Washington and had talked to the president, the Interior secretary, and the commissioner of Indian affairs. Apparently David Jerome had concluded that the Cherokee Commission needed to use its only Democrat to establish a relationship with Grover Cleveland's new administration. But the message from the Democrats was essentially what had been heard from the Republicans—the Indians did not need all of their reservation and should sell the United States the surplus after allotment.

At the brief session 31 May, the commissioners made a halfhearted effort to persuade the Poncas to consider selling. Sayre's ploy was to implore them again at least to talk about price. If $1.25 per acre was insufficient, what did they want? "[I]t is much better to tell the Great Father that we could not agree on the price," he declared, "than to tell him that you did not want to do anything." Overland replied that he could only say what he had said before: "When the Great Spirit made me he gave me less things to do with than he gave the whites. He made me an Indian and I could not make a white man out of myself. I am afraid of the white man's ways. I do not want any allotment, this land is too small now."[36]

In desperation Sayre turned to Standing Buffalo, but he must have regretted it. The chief was as obdurate as Overland, would accept no allotment less than 160 acres, feared that no land would be available for children yet to come, and was convinced that their white tenants would cheat them. Overland had the last word that day, justifying his refusal to sell land: "Money is like the wind . . . it goes every way but the land stays where it is. . . . It is not the money but the land that the Indians want."[37]

The last session, on 6 June, was anticlimactic. Chairman Jerome had already left, and few Indians attended. Warren Sayre and Judge Wilson maintained that they still hoped for a deal and denied that they were threatening to use force. The only Ponca to speak was Standing Buffalo. The chief reiterated his belief that the white ways might be superior, but the Indians could not adopt them. When they sent their children to school, he said, they either became ill and died or returned to the reservation and resumed the old ways. He reminded the commissioners that the Poncas had no blood of white men on their hands and asked "what we have done that the Great Father should treat us this way."[38] Sayre did not answer the question, concluding lamely that he and his colleagues had only taken three and one-half days out of each week for their councils, so they should not be blamed for the young men not getting their corn planted. Thus ended more than two months of fruitless wrangling.

For the Poncas, however, it was a victory. In no other tribe had the Cherokee Commission invested so much time with so little to show for it. A significant factor in the Indians' triumph had been their rejection of the authority of the chiefs. The rank and file had been able to unite and devise effective strategy—keep attendance at the councils at a minimum while making certain that those who did attend would hew to the Ponca line. Thus they denied the commissioners the opportunity to work through recognized chiefs in order to win over the younger men. Their Indian agent, a close observer of the process, described Jerome and his colleagues as finally abandoning the effort after "failing to procure a quorum." The agent believed that if they had not aborted the negotiations the previous year they might have obtained an agreement, "but when an Indian succeeds once in baffling what he calls his enemy he then thinks he can always do so."[39]

The commissioners justified their expending so much time and energy on the Poncas on the grounds that success with them would have facilitated negotiations with their neighbors, the Kaws, Otoe-Missouris, and Osages. The Poncas were in effect a test case, as the other three tribes closely monitored the commission's work with the Poncas, so "failure with them was, at least, a vigorous promise of failure with the other tribes named."[40]

In 1904 Congress finally recognized the Ponca victory over the Cherokee Commission by authorizing their children born since 1894 and still alive to have homesteads from the surplus after the original allotment. By that time, however, other Ponca land was slipping from the tribal grasp. This was the result of another congressional action, the so-called Dead Indian Act of 1902, which permitted Indians to sell trust land that they had inherited. By 1905 Poncas had sold 12,639 acres at an average of about $20 per acre.[41] That amounted to a loss of nearly 10 percent of their original reservation holdings, and the sales would continue.

The temporary increase in Ponca income, together with roughly $50,000 the Indians received annually from their tenants, permitted them to live with as little personal labor as the commissioners had predicted. Even before the passage of the Dead Indian Act, their agent described them as "not compelled to labor for a living."[42] Their prosperity, however, would prove temporary as other legislation, the 1906 Burke Act and the 1907 Noncompetent Indian Act, contributed to a further erosion of their land base. With less land to rent or sell, Ponca prosperity quickly dissipated.

During the frequent intervals between their bargaining sessions with the Poncas, the commissioners took the opportunity to contact the principal chief of the Otoe-Missouri Tribe. But those Indians were encouraged by the successful resistance of the Poncas and simply declined to agree even to parley. Their resistance paid off in 1904 when the same law, which provided final distribution of the surplus land of the Poncas among members of that tribe, permitted the Otoe-Missouris to divide their entire holdings among themselves.

Following the final session with the Poncas, 6 June, the commissioners moved on to the Osages. Still another tribe that had been removed to land in the Outlet purchased from the Cherokees, these Indians were on their new reservation by 1872. When the Cherokee Commission came calling in late June 1893, there were roughly 1,650 Osages, about two-thirds of them full bloods, on a 1,500,195-acre reservation.[43] Although many of the tribal members had staked out homesteads, they had been exempted from allotment under the Dawes Severalty Act and evidenced no interest in it in their negotiations with the commissioners, which got underway 22 June and lasted until the first week of August.

No journal of the councils has been uncovered, and for what occurred investigators have been forced to rely on a mere three pages in the final report the Cherokee Commission submitted to the president. Apparently Jerome and his colleagues quickly learned that they had little chance of success with the Osages. Although they had a "crude sort of Government with a written constitution and laws,"[44] they flatly refused to negotiate on a government-to-government basis, preferring that they meet only in general councils that any Osage could attend. Nevertheless, the Osage National Council appointed a five-man committee to speak for the nation. The members of the committee were solidly opposed to allotment and sale of their surplus land, hardly surprising as their constitution prescribed that only the National Council could authorize allotment. Although most of the mixed bloods were ready to deal, at the general meetings the full bloods, who opposed any change easily dominated.

The commissioners were annoyed, as usual, with the peripheral issues raised by the Osages. The Indians suggested that if their tribe could get satisfaction on these matters, including three old claims against the United States, they would be more receptive to the commission's proposals. But due to what the commissioners described as "an ill feeling" between the full bloods and mixed bloods, Jerome and his colleagues concluded that "there was not even a hope of reaching an agreement at this time."[45] They also believed that the Cherokees had encouraged the Osages to resist the government, holding forth the possibility that they might become the "Sixth Civilized Tribe" and part of a proposed state for the Native Americans of eastern Oklahoma.

While they were with the Osages, the commissioners also spoke to a Kaw delegation. That tiny tribe of slightly over a hundred members had a 100,000-acre reservation adjoining the northwest corner of the Osage country that they had also obtained from the Cherokees, and on the same terms.

As the members of the delegation declared that they would not conclude an agreement with the Cherokee Commission unless their more numerous Osage neighbors did, Jerome and his colleagues did not even trouble themselves to go to the Kaw Reservation.

The commission's leisurely negotiations with the Osages also gave them time to approach the Choctaw and Chickasaw nations about a meeting to discuss a familiar topic, those Indians' claims to lands the United States had already purchased from the Wichitas and from the Kiowas, Comanches, and Apaches. Their only instructions from Secretary Noble had been to keep any payment to the Choctaws and Chickasaws to a level that, together with what was paid other tribes with reservations in the Leased District, would keep the total price at no more than what the government could expect to get from settlers for the land. A meeting did take place in August 1893, in St. Louis, but the delegates of the two tribes refused an offer of $1,750,000, ending those discussions.[46]

The Cherokee Commission had gone out in style, negotiating in a hotel and in the process spending the remainder of its appropriation. In reporting this to President Cleveland the commissioners observed that having once again exhausted their funds, they were adjourning. They claimed success in their mission and admitted only to "having temporarily failed" with the Osages, Poncas, Otoe-Missouris, and Kaws. Expressing confidence in their ability to reach agreements with those tribes "in a few months," the commissioners volunteered to continue if the president wished.[47] Secretary Hoke Smith passed the offer on to Indian Commissioner Daniel M. Browning, T. J. Morgan's successor, for his recommendation. Browning advised that the Cherokee Commission not be continued, and Secretary Smith concurred.

Nevertheless, early in 1894 Senator James K. Jones of Arkansas, who had recommended Judge Wilson for his place on the commission, asked if the commissioners could be paid for the period of late August to early November, when he said they had finally ceased to serve. Just what they might have done for that period was unspecified, but since they had been given unusual latitude in their pay arrangements, the commissioners possibly thought that there was yet another opportunity to tap the Treasury. Indian Commissioner Browning, who had already recommended against their continuance, reported that he had no evidence of any work that they had performed, and the Cherokee Commission was not resuscitated.[48] For David Jerome, Warren Sayre, and Judge Wilson it had been a long and profitable relationship.

For its part the United States had obtained most of the area that Congress had targeted when creating the commission, the extension of its public domain by about fifteen million acres. For the Indians that accepted agreements, it had been a disaster.

Epilogue

IN AUGUST 1893 THE LAST OF FIVE APPROPRIATIONS for the Cherokee Commission, totaling ninety thousand dollars, was exhausted and the commission ceased to function. David Jerome returned to Saginaw and died less than three years later. Judge Wilson, despite his ill health, survived until 1907. A younger man, Warren Sayre resumed his law practice and later served another term in the Indiana Legislature, dying in 1931.

By their own computations, during their fifty-two months of existence the commissioners had acquired from the Indians 23,595 square miles, the equivalent of "nearly two-thirds of the State of Indiana or nine times the size of original Oklahoma [the Unassigned Lands]."[1] Only with the Poncas, Kaws, Otoe-Missouris, and Osages had they failed to secure agreements; they were also unable to quiet the claims of the Choctaws and Chickasaws to all of the Leased District.

The commissioners had driven hard bargains with the tribes, although they had had little leeway in their negotiations. In its enabling legislation Congress essentially set the maximum to be paid at $1.25 per acre, and Secretary of the Interior John Noble had insisted that they obtain the land as cheaply as possible. Throughout most of the commission's existence Noble was the official to whom they reported, and he set the tone for their operations. The secretary had entered office with no Indian expertise and displayed no particular sympathy for the Indians as an administrator. Commissioner of Indian Affairs T. J. Morgan was more supportive of the tribes, but he was clearly the subordinate; some knowledgeable friends of the Indian described his post as less important than that of the clerk who headed the Indian Division of the secretary's office.

The members of the Cherokee Commission represented a considerable range of experience with Native Americans. Lucius Fairchild, the first chairman, had been governor of a state with a significant indigenous population and had had contact with California tribes during his gold-rush period. There is no evidence, however, that he had any particular interest in Indians or views of them different than those typical of the westerners of his day. Moreover, he had accepted appointment on the basis of unrealistic estimates by Secretary Noble as to how long the assignment would take. The anticipated several weeks stretched into months of frustration with no discernible progress, a development for which he blamed the Cherokees, impugning their honesty and sincerity.

David Jerome, Fairchild's replacement as chairman, was as well qualified as an appointee was likely to be. He had a genuine interest in and knowledge of Indian affairs, as demonstrated by his four years on the Board of Indian Commissioners. He was very well acquainted with the general thrust of government policy and had had actual negotiating experience with western tribes. Jerome's general views on Indians were considered enlightened by the conventional wisdom in the 1890s. He honestly believed that salvation for the Indians required their making the necessary adaptations to the ways of the dominant population. This meant accepting allotment in severalty, Christianity, and the education of their children. A concomitant was the sale to the United States of land in excess of what would be required as homesteads of up to 160 acres for each Indian.

Alfred M. Wilson, the first commissioner appointed, was well acquainted with the Cherokees as a result of his practice of law in western Arkansas. There is no evidence that he held any other than the standard western view—that the Indians would have to accept a reduction of their landholdings to individual homesteads. As the Democrat minority member of the commission, he was content to follow the lead of the Republican chairmen. Unfortunately, ill health limited his attendance at some negotiations, but he clung to his sinecure.

In contrast Warren Sayre, the other Republican commissioner, played a major role. He was an able lawyer, Chairman Jerome relied on him to argue the legal points, and he did so effectively, although he came to the post with no special knowledge of Indians or government policy. He was the stereotypical attorney, the hired gun intent only on representing his client's interest. For Chairman Jerome he had an additional value; because of his close political ties to his fellow Indianan, President Harrison, Sayre could speak to power in Washington.

All of the commissioners, even Judge Wilson, rather quickly appeared to become caught up in a real effort to coerce the tribes into accepting agreements on the government's terms. Undoubtedly they did believe that the Indians could not be permitted to remain indefinitely in their current situation, for their own good as well as for the benefit of the multitude of whites who were seeking homesteads. The commissioners' willingness to use any tactic to achieve the government's ends, however, suggests that as time wore on they came to view the negotiations as some kind of competition that they must win. This possibly explains—but does not justify—their resort to unethical tactics in the struggle to prevail. Eventually the Indian Claims Commission would denounce Lucian Fairchild's "petulance," but certainly Jerome, Sayre, and Wilson also revealed their annoyance and frustration and reacted with questionable practices.

If a tribe failed to be persuaded of the beneficence of the Great Father, the commissioners could quickly became heavy-handed. They routinely warned the Indians that their titles were not the equivalent of those of white landowners, although they could become so if they accepted allotment. The white men also drew confusing and disturbing distinctions between titles originating in treaties and presidential proclamations and those in fee simple acquired by purchase. Regardless of the nature of their title, however, the tribes were always quickly informed that they would not be permitted to retain great undeveloped expanses while thousands of white families were desperate for land and bringing pressure to bear upon Congress and the executive branch.

Furthermore, under no circumstances could the tribes sell to anyone other than the United States, and the president could terminate any leases of reservation land at will, thus cutting off that source of tribal income. Indians still receiving rations were reminded that these were not called for by treaty and that even actual treaty provisions for schools, grist and sawmills, farm implements, and clothing all had time limits. Whether or not they were extended after expiration of the treaty, the Indians were told, could depend upon how they now responded to the government's offer to buy their land.

The tribes learned early on that they would not be permitted to determine the price at which they would sell. On a few occasions the commissioners finally paid a few cents more per acre than their original offer.

Usually, however, any concessions involved altering the method of compensation, such as increasing the size of the initial payment, which did not cost the government a cent. Indeed, that could save the United States money, because it reduced the amount of the principal held in the Treasury and earning 5 percent interest. Another favorite tactic of the commissioners was to brandish the Dawes Severalty Act as the only alternative to the agreement being offered. That law authorized less land than the commissioners were offering and provided for only a 3 percent return on tribal funds held in the Treasury.

Nor should it be forgotten that the commissioners did not cavil at tactics involving attorneys who were presumably representing Indian interests. Those individuals were normally operating with contracts specifying that their fees be a percentage of what the Indians received for the land—therefore, no sale, no fee. Not surprisingly, the attorneys appeared more allies of the government than advocates of tribal interests. Equally improper was the commission's willingness to work with various unsavory characters who showed up at negotiations. Serving as unofficial advisors to the tribes, they helped to undercut Indian resistance and to collect sufficient signatures to authenticate the agreements. These documents could then include clauses that provided compensation in land and/or money for the influence peddlers. They could also receive payments under the table from attorneys trying to ensure their own compensation.

The nature of negotiations varied greatly among the tribes, which is not surprising given the pronounced differences among them. At one extreme was the 25,000-member Cherokee Nation, with a constitution-based government led by men as educated and articulate as the commissioners. At the other extreme were the tiny bands of less than a hundred Iowas and Tonkawas, led by chiefs and headmen unable to speak English and regarded by the commissioners as primitive. Despite the great variations among the tribes, some arguments they employed resonated throughout the negotiations. Indian speakers made references to the Great Spirit's having given the tribes the portion of Mother Earth that the United States was trying to acquire, and they alluded movingly to their attachment to Mother Earth. As people who lived close to nature, their physical environments had shaped all aspects of their lives, from their modes of subsistence and housing to their religious and worldviews. For them to give up access to large tracts that they had owned in common and abandon village or band encampment life for isolated farms was to suffer traumatic disruption of their lives.

These tribes had already been forced to relocate at least once and to give up substantial areas of land. Now they were threatened with the loss of their burial sites and their last common land. These were the tracts open to the livestock of all tribal members, to the hunters, the berry pickers, the nut gatherers, and those seeking therapeutic roots and herbs. Particularly unnerving was the knowledge that sale of the land left after allotment would deny to all succeeding generations a guaranteed access to their share of Mother Earth. Speaker after speaker raised the issue of land for the children yet to be born.

Among the Plains tribes there was, in addition, a justified fear that 160-acre tracts that far west were insufficient to support a family, particularly if at least 80 acres of that had to be grazing land as the government insisted. Commissioners might point to Indians such as Quanah Parker as examples of self-sufficiency, but he—like entrepreneurs in other tribes—had managed to monopolize thousand of acres of tribal land for his own use besides being in the pay of cattlemen who wanted access to tribal pasture. Other concerns were repeatedly expressed by the Indians. Fear that allotment would be accompanied by taxes on personal property was one deterrent to their accepting homesteads. Ample reason for alarm existed, and the commissioners could not allay those fears. Nor did the white men effectively counter the argument—of Cherokees in particular—that the tracts neighboring Indian land were selling for substantially more than the $1.25 or less per acre that the government was offering the Indians.

During the actual negotiations conducted by the Cherokee Commission, Indians had loudly criticized the way the white men conducted the councils, determining the agendas and controlling access to the floor. The tribesmen frequently complained of being denied opportunities to talk about issues they wanted to raise and being threatened with expulsion if they did so. Another objection often raised by farming Indians was that since the commissioners tried to avoid camping in the severe winter and summer weather, the negotiations tended to come during the spring and the fall when the Indians needed to be working in their fields. That led tribesmen to make sarcastic remarks about the commissioners' continuing to enjoy their generous stipends while the Indians were being asked to neglect the crops upon which their families depended.

Only the Cherokees, the best equipped for genuine negotiations, raised the issue of the ward-guardian relationship. It is sad that the commissioners, as agents of the government that the Supreme Court in the early 1830s had declared to be the guardian of its Indian wards, should have completely ignored this obligation in the face of unrelenting pressure from white land seekers and businessmen. Warren Sayre even denied that such a guardian-ward relationship existed.

Probably it is too much to expect that, however well intentioned, any government responsive to its constituents could have long ensured tribal control of so much—by the white man's standards—undeveloped land. Certainly, throughout history, their better utilization of the land has been a rationalization used by the strong to justify their eviction of the weak. That the tribes, given the relative strength of the contestants, would be forced into allotment and the sale of their remaining land was inevitable; it is difficult to envision any other logical outcome. Nevertheless, at the very least the government should have offered market value for land essentially being taken by the condemnation process. That would have increased the payments for the land, some of them so inadequate as later to be labeled "unconscionable" or "very gross"—terms that the Indian Claims Commission employed to describe payments "so much less than the actual value of the property sold that the disparity shocks the conscience."[2]

In time, the Indian Claims Commission rendered judgments totaling about forty-one-million dollars on behalf of tribes that had suffered at the hands of the Cherokee Commission. The records of the Indian Claims Commission, together with the journals recording the negotiations of the Cherokee Commission document the cavalier manner—unbecoming to a great nation—by which the United States acquired fifteen million acres from its wards in Oklahoma between 1889 and 1893.

Abbreviations

AR	Annual Report
CAJ	Cheyenne and Arapaho Journal
CIA	Commissioner of Indian Affairs
CJ	Cherokee Journal
CNP	Cherokee Nation Papers
FP	Fairchild Papers
HD	House Document
HED	House Executive Document
HMD	House Miscellaneous Document
HR	House Resolution
ICC	Indian Claims Commission
IJ	Iowa Journal
KCAJ	Kiowa, Comanche and Apache Journal
KJ	Kickapoo Journal
LR	Letters Received
NAM	National Archives Microfilm
NAR	National Archives Record Group
PAJ	Pawnee Journal
PJ	Ponca Journal
SD	Senate Document
SED	Senate Executive Document
SMD	Senate Miscellaneous Document
SR	Senate Report
WJ	Wichita Journal

Notes

CHAPTER 1   *The Origins of the Cherokee Commission*

1. Francis Paul Prucha, *The Great Father* 2: 896.
2. Knox to President Washington, 7 July 1789, *American State Papers: Indian Affairs* 1: 52–54.
3. AR of CIA for 1862, 347.
4. AR of CIA for 1864, 33–34.
5. AR of CIA for 1865, 34.
6. Charles J. Kappler, *Indian Treaties 1778–1883*, 919.
7. Ibid., 933.
8. Ibid., 911.
9. Ibid.
10. HR 3786, 51st Congress, 2d Session, serial 2888: 22–24.
11. The best account of leasing on the Outlet is William W. Savage, Jr., *The Cherokee Strip Live Stock Association*.
12. Ibid., 62–65.
13. *U.S. Statutes at Large* 23: 384.
14. Roy Gittinger, *The Formation of the State of Oklahoma*, 176.
15. Herbert Welsh to Mrs. E. F. James, 19 January 1889, in Indian Rights Association Papers, R69.
16. *Cherokee Advocate*, 9 October 1892, 2.
17. Ibid., 4 January 1888, 2.
18. Ibid., 1 March 1888, 2.
19. Ibid., 13 February 1888, 2.
20. Ibid.
21. Ibid.
22. "Chief Joel B. Mayes of the Cherokee Nation," *Chronicles of Oklahoma* 44 (Autumn 1966), 325–27. See also Stanley W. Hoig, *The Cherokees and Their Chiefs*, 250–52.
23. Savage, *The Cherokee Strip Livestock Association*, 110–11.

24. *Cherokee Advocate*, 11 January 1888, 1.

25. HR 263, 50th Congress, 1st Session, serial 2599: 9.

26. Ibid., 10.

27. Ibid., pt. 2: 13.

28. Ibid., 14.

29. *Congressional Record* (2 March 1889), vol. 20, pt. 3: 2593.

30. Ibid., 2592.

31. Ibid., 2608.

32. Ibid., 2601.

33. SMD 80, 50th Congress, 2d Session, serial 2615: 1.

34. Ibid., 19.

35. Ibid., 24.

36. *Washington Post*, 25 February 1889, 4.

37. Ibid., 27 February 1889, 4.

38. Ibid., 28 February 1889, 4.

39. *Congressional Record* (2 March 1889), vol. 20, pt. 3: 2592.

CHAPTER **2** *Initial Contacts with the Cherokees, Iowas, Sac and Fox, and Kickapoos*

1. Boudinot to Secretary Noble, 25 March 1889, NAR 48, box 612.

2. Parker to Secretary Noble, 25 March 1889, NAR 48, box 612.

3. Sam Ross, *The Empty Sleeve*, 160–76. This is the only biography of Fairchild, and a good one.

4. Noble to Fairchild, 14 June 1889, FP.

5. *Washington Post*, 4 March 1889, 1.

6. Fairchild to Frank [his wife], 24 June 1889, FP.

7. Noble to Fairchild, 28 June 1889, FP.

8. SED 78, 51st Congress, 1st Session, serial 2688; Berlin B. Chapman, "Secret 'Instructions and Suggestions' to the Cherokee Commission," 449–58.

9. *Cherokee Advocate*, 17 April 1889, 2.

10. Ibid.

11. *Cherokee Advocate*, 5 June 1889, 2.

12. For a thorough discussion of the Watts Association, see Nancy Hope Sober, *The Intruders*, ch. 4.

13. *Cherokee Advocate*, 12 June 1889, 2.

14. Mayes to Wilson, 9 May 1889, NAR 48, LR 1889: 2978.

15. Wilson to Noble, 15 June 1889, NAR 48, box 612.

16. *Cherokee Advocate*, 19 June 1889, 2.

17. Noble to Mayes, 2 July 1889, NAM M606, R60; Mayes to Noble, 8 July 1889, NAR 48, LR 1889: 4144; Noble to Mayes, 17 July 1889, NAM M606, R60.

18. Norman *Transcript*, 19 July 1889, 1.

19. Wilson to Fairchild, 6 March 1890, FP.

20. Fairchild to Frank, 22 July 1889, FP.

21. Fairchild to Frank, 27 July 1889, FP.

22. The best source for Robert L. Owen is Kenny Lee Brown, "Robert Latham Owen."

23. Fairchild to Frank, 29 July 1889, FP.

24. Fairchild to Frank, 31 July 1889, FP.

25. Ibid.

26. Mayes to Cherokee Commission, 12 August 1889, in *Cherokee Advocate*, 14 August 1889, 2.

27. Fairchild to Frank, 12 August 1889, FP.

28. Mayes to Cherokee Commission, 12 August 1889, in *Cherokee Advocate*, 14 August 1889, 2.

29. *Cherokee Advocate*, 21 August 1889, 1.

30. Hartranft to Noble, [illegible] August 1889, FP.

31. Noble to Wilson, 9 August 1889, NAM M26, R61.

32. Speed to Fairchild, 6 September 1889, FP.

33. Wilson to Fairchild, 6 September 1889, FP.

34. Speed to Fairchild, 14 September 1889, FP.

35. *Cherokee Advocate*, 25 September 1889, 2.

36. Noble to Fairchild, 4 October 1889, NAM M606, R61.

37. Hartranft to Fairchild, 7 October 1889, FP.

38. Fairchild to Frank, 24 October 1889, FP; Noble to Speed, 7 December 1892, NAM M606, R77.

39. For background on the Iowas, the best source is Martha Royce Blaine, *The Ioway Indians*.

40. AR of Agent Moses Neal, in AR of CIA for 1889, 199.

41. Synopsis of Cherokee Commission, NAR 48, LR, 1890:7001, 29.

42. Fairchild to Frank, 20 October 1889, FP.

43. For early history of the Sac and Fox, see William T. Hagan, *The Sac and Fox Indians*.

44. AR of Agent Moses Neal, in AR of CIA for 1889, 199.

45. Synopsis of Cherokee Commission, NAR 48, LR 1890:7001; Fairchild to Frank, 22 October 1889, FP.

46. For background on the Kickapoos, see A. M. Gibson, *The Kickapoos*.

47. Fairchild to Frank, 22 October 1889, FP.

48. Fairchild to Frank, 27 October 1889, FP.

49. Ibid.

50. Fairchild to Frank, 31 October, 1889, FP.

51. Noble to Fairchild, 26 October, 1889, in HR 3768, 51st Congress, 2d Session, serial 2788: 15–16.

52. Mayes to Fairchild, *Cherokee Advocate*, Supplement, 7 November 1889.

53. *Cherokee Advocate*, 6 November 1889, 1.

54. Fairchild to Frank, 6 November 1889, FP.

55. Fairchild to Frank, 10 November 1889, FP.

56. AR of Noble for 1889, vi.

57. Ibid., xiv–xv.

58. J. D. Richardson, compiler and editor, *Messages and Papers of the Presidents* 12: 52.

59. Synopsis of Cherokee Commission, NAR 48, LR 1890: 7001, 7.

60. Harry J. Sievers, *Benjamin Harrison* 2: 270–71.

61. *Wabash Times*, 15 November 1889, 1.

62. Sayre to Harrison, 26 November 1889, Harrison Papers, R23.

63. Commissioners to Mayes, 16 December 1889, CNP, folder 166.

64. Mayes to Cherokee Commission, 16 December 1889, *Cherokee Advocate*, 18 December 1889, 2.

65. Sievers, *Benjamin Harrison* 3: 2.

66. Fairchild to Frank, 23 November 1889, FP; clipping in Sayre File, M98, box 70, folder 6, Indiana Historical Society.

67. Fairchild to Frank, 22 December 1889, FP.

68. Fairchild to Frank, 25 December 1889, FP.

69. Fairchild to Frank, 5 December 1889, FP.

70. Fairchild to Frank, 9 December 1889, FP.

71. Fairchild to Frank, 13 December 1889, FP.

72. Mayes to Cherokee Commission, 28 December 1889, *Cherokee Advocate*, 1 January 1890, 2.

73. Fairchild to Harrison, 1 January 1890, FP.

74. Clearly Fairchild had not exhausted his political capital. Six months later he complained to Secretary Noble about discourtesies suffered at the hands of an ex–Confederate postmaster at Vinita. Noble forwarded his complaint to the president's private secretary. Later, Noble reported to Fairchild that "your Minnie [*sic*] ball . . . reached its mark, and . . . the gentleman who abused you old veterans down in the Indian Territory got his walking papers." Noble to Fairchild, 21 August 1890, FP.

75. Speed to Fairchild, 26 March 1890, FP.

76. Speed to Fairchild, 20 January 1890; Sayre to Fairchild, 27 January 1890, both in FP.

77. Adair to Watie, 12 June 1866, in CNP, folder 4245, R39.

78. *Cherokee Advocate*, 22 January 1890, 2.

79. *Cherokee Advocate*, 12 February 1890, 2.

80. Mayes to Harrison, 24 February 1890, *Cherokee Advocate*, 5 March 1890, 2.

81. Sayre to Harrison, 15 February 1890, Harrison Papers, R25.

82. Sayre to Jerome, 14 March 1890, FP.

83. *Congressional Record* (11 February 1890) vol. 21, pt. 2, 1197.

84. Ibid., 1198.

85. *Cherokee Advocate*, 30 April 1890, 2.

CHAPTER **3**   *Agreements with the Iowas, Sac and Fox, Potawatomis, and Shawnees—Failure with the Kickapoos*

1. Sayre to Halford, 24 April 1890, Harrison Papers, R26.

2. *Eleventh Annual Report of the Board of Indian Commissioners,* 50.

3. Jerome to Noble, 1 May 1890, NAR 48, LR 1890: 3593.

4. IJ, 1.

5. IJ, 4.

6. Ibid. Hogarshe's name has also been spelled Hogarache, Hogarashee, and Hogarachee.

7. IJ, 7.

8. IJ, 8.

9. IJ, 9.

10. SED 171, 51st Congress, 1st Session, serial 2688: 6.

11. *Cherokee Advocate,* 28 May 1890, 2.

12. IJ, 10.

13. IJ, 12.

14. Ibid.

15. IJ, 13.

16. IJ, 15.

17. IJ, 16.

18. IJ, 17.

19. IJ, 19.

20. IJ, 20.

21. IJ, 21.

22. IJ, 22.

23. IJ, 32.

24. Commissioners to the President, 28 May 1890, SED 171, 51st Congress, 1st Session, serial 2688: 6.

25. Ibid.

26. Berlin B. Chapman, "Dissolution of the Iowa Reservation," 477.

27. SED 171, 51st Congress, 1st Session, serial 2688: 13–14.

28. Ibid., 18–23.

29. IJ, 27.

30. IJ, 29.

31. Commissioners to the President, 12 June 1890, NAR 48, LR 1890: 3880.

32. SFJ, 1.

33. SFJ, 2.

34. SFJ, 3.

35. Commissioners to the President, 12 June 1890, NAR 48, LR 1890: 3880.

36. Ibid.

37. SFJ, 5.

38. SFJ, 8.

39. SFJ, 9.

40. SFJ, 11.

41. SFJ, 12.

42. SFJ, 15.

43. SFJ, 17.

44. Saginaw *Evening News*, 13 June 1990, 1.

45. Commissioners to the President, 12 June 1890, NAR 48, LR 1890: 3880.

46. Sayre to Halford, 13 June 1890, Harrison Papers, R27.

47. ICC, Docket 220, vol. 11, 724.

48. *Court of Claims Reporter*, 167: 724.

49. *Cherokee Advocate*, 18 June 1890, 2.

50. Kappler, *Indian Treaties*, 971.

51. *Ibid.*, 825.

52. Noble to Jerome, 23 June 1890, NAM, M606, R65.

53. Synopsis of Cherokee Commission, NAR 48, LR 1890: 7001; Commissioners to the President, 25 June 1890, NAR 48, LR 1890: 3916.

54. Actg. CIA Belt to Secretary Noble, 18 June 1890, NAR 48, LR 1890: 3916.

55. Commissioners to the President, 25 June 1890, NAR 48, LR 1890: 4195.

56. Ibid.

57. Commissioners to the President, 26 June 1890, NAR 48, LR 1890: 4197.

58. HR 3481, 51st Congress, 2d Session, serial 2887: 3.

59. ICC, Docket 96, vol. 19, 384.

60. *Indian Country Today*, 11 January 1999, A8.

61. Sayre to Harrison, 18 June 1890, Harrison Papers, R72.

62. Harrison to Sayre, 23 June 1890, Harrison Papers, R72.

63. Norman *Transcript*, 27 June 1890, 2.

64. Commissioners to the President, 1 July 1890. This entire letter is reproduced in Berlin B. Chapman, "The Cherokee Commissioners at Kickapoo Village."

65. Ibid.

CHAPTER 4   *The Cheyennes and Arapahos Brought to Terms*

1. Jerome to Noble, July 2, 1890, in Synopsis of Cherokee Commission, NAR 48, LR 1890: 7001; Noble to Jerome, 8 July 1890, (copy), NAR 48, LR 1890: 3573.

2. For background on the Cheyennes and Arapahos, consult Donald J. Berthrong, *The Cheyenne and Arapaho Ordeal*; Loretta Fowler, *Arapahoe Politics, 1851–1978*; Virginia Cole Trenholm, *The Arapahos, Our People*.

3. AR of Agent Charles F. Ashley, in AR of CIA for 1890, 177.

4. Ibid.

5. Kappler, *Indian Treaties*, 887–91.

6. Ibid., 984–89.

7. HR 3441, 51st Congress, 2d Session, serial 2885: 1.

8. Jerome to the President, 21 July 1890, NAR 48, LR 1890: 5649.

9. Noble to Jerome, 8 July 1890, (copy), NAR 48, LR 1890: 3573.

10. CAJ, 2.

11. CAJ, 4.

12. CAJ, 5.

13. Ibid.

14. CAJ, 6.

15. Jerome to Noble, 7 July 1890, NAR 48, LR 1890: 4387.

16. Both contracts appear in C. C. Painter, *Cheyennes and Arapahoes Revisited and a Statement of Their Agreement and Contract with Attorneys*, 52–62.

17. CAJ, 12.

18. Ibid.

19. CAJ, 13.

20. Ibid.

21. CAJ, 14.

22. CAJ, 15.

23. CAJ, 17.

24. CAJ, 18.

25. CAJ, 19.

26. CAJ, 21.

27. CAJ, 22.

28. Ibid.

29. Ibid.

30. Jerome to Noble, 12 July, 1890; Noble to Agent Ashley, 13 July 1890, both in NAR 48, LR 1890: 3573.

31. CAJ, 27.

32. CAJ, 28–29.

33. *Wabash Times*, 29 October 1890, 5.

34. CAJ, 39.

35. CAJ, 40.

36. CAJ, 47.

37. CAJ, 49.

38. CAJ, 53.

39. CAJ, 58.

40. Jerome to Noble, July 17, 1890, NAR 48, LR 1890, 4631.

41. Noble to Jerome, 17 July 1890, (copy), NAR 48, LR 1890: 3573.

42. CAJ, 67.

43. CAJ. 69.

44. CAJ, 75.

45. Ibid.

46. Jerome to the President, 21 July 1890, NAR 48, LR 1890: 5649.

47. Jerome to Noble, 21 July 1890, NAR 48, LR 1890: 4810.

48. Saginaw *Evening News,* 26 July 1890, 3.

49. *U.S. Statutes at Large,* 26: 356.

50. Jerome to Noble, 23 August 1890, NAR 48, LR 1890: 5515.

51. Jerome and Sayre to Noble, 4 September 1890, NAR 48, LR 1890: 6075.

52. Jerome and Sayre to Noble, 4 September 1890, NAR 48, LR 1890: 3585.

53. Noble to Reynolds, 23 September 1890, NAM M606, R67.

54. Noble to Jerome, 30 September 1890, (copy), NAR 48, LR 1890: 3573; AR of Noble for 1892, lxxi–lxxviii.

55. CAJ, 5.

56. CAJ, 12.

57. CAJ, 15.

58. CAJ, 16.

59. CAJ, 22.

60. CAJ, 23.

61. CAJ, 24.

62. CAJ, 32.

63. CAJ, 42.

64. 1892 AR of Secretary Noble, lxxvii; Sayre to Noble, 13 March 1891, NAR 48, LR 1891: 2156.

65. Painter, *Cheyennes and Arapahoes Revisited,* 48–49.

66. Ibid.

67. Berthrong, *The Cheyenne and Arapaho Ordeal,* 166.

68. Painter, *Cheyennes and Arapahoes Revisited,* 49.

69. Jerome to Noble, 22 October 1890, NAR 48, LR 1890: 6843.

70. Jerome to Noble, 25 October 1890, NAR 48, LR 1890: 7001.

71. CAJ, 6.

72. Jerome to Noble, 30 October 1890, NAR 48, LR 1890: 7103; Noble to Jerome, 31 October 1890, (copy), NAR 48, LR 1890: 3573.

73. Reynolds to Noble, 4 June 1891, NAR 48, LR 1891: 7103; Noble to George Chandler, 6 June 1891, NAR 48, LR 1891: 4695.

74. Painter, *Cheyennes and Arapahoes Revisited,* 52.

75. Ibid., 49.

76. ICC, Dockets 329 and 348, vol. 10: 1.

77. ICC, Dockets 329–A and 329–B, vol. 16: 162.

78. Oklahoma City *Daily Oklahoman,* 30 October 1966, 18, and 1 November 1966, 18.

CHAPTER **5**   *The Cherokees Revisited*

1. Jerome to Mayes, 10 November 1890, (copy), CNP, R3, folder 172.

2. Vinita, *Indian Chieftain,* 27 November 1890, 2.

3. Ibid.

4. Mayes to the President, 24 November 1890, (copy), in Joel Bryan Mayes Papers, box M48.

5. *Cherokee Advocate*, 28 November 1890, 2.

6. Stanley W. Hoig, *The Cherokees and Their Chiefs*, 229.

7. H. Craig Miner, *The Corporation and the Indian*, 121.

8. *Cherokee Advocate*, 3 December 1890, 2.

9. CJ, 17.

10. Kappler, *Indian Treaties*, 946.

11. CJ, 20.

12. CJ, 28.

13. Commissioners to Noble, 9 December 1890, NAR 48, LR 1890: 1695.

14. CJ, 30.

15. CJ, 44.

16. CJ, 48.

17. CJ, 51–53.

18. CJ, 53.

19. CJ, 58.

20. CJ, 62.

21. CJ, 63.

22. CJ, 64.

23. CJ, 66.

24. CJ, 68.

25. CJ, 69.

26. CJ, 70.

27. CJ, 71.

28. CJ, 73.

29. CJ, 76.

30. CJ, 82.

31. CJ, 86.

32. CJ, 94.

33. CJ, 106.

34. CJ, 109.

35. CJ, 109–10.

36. CJ, 127.

37. CJ, 139.

38. CJ, 142.

39. CJ, 143.

40. CJ, 156.

41. CJ, 164–65.

42. CJ, 170.

43. CJ, 211.

44. CJ, 225.

45. The final positions taken by both sides appear in the *Cherokee Advocate*, 7 January 1891, 2.

46. CJ, p253–54.

47. CJ, 258.

48. Ibid.

49. CJ, 279.

50. Morgan to Noble, 30 January 1891, NAR 48, LR 1891: 406.

51. Wolfe and Rowe to Commissioners, 9 February 1891, NAR 18, LR 1891: 406.

CHAPTER **6** *Agreements with the Wichitas, Kickapoos, and Tonkawas*

1. AR of Agent Charles E. Adams, in AR of CIA for 1891, 352.

2. For the Caddos and Wichitas, a useful reference is F. Todd Smith, *The Caddos, the Wichitas, and the United States, 1846–1901*.

3. Neighbors to CIA, 2 July 1859, in AR of CIA for 1859, 310.

4. Agreement with the Wichita and Affiliated Tribes, 18 October 1872, in Vine Deloria, Jr., and Raymond J. DeMallie, *Documents of American Indian Diplomacy* 2: 1394.

5. Berlin B. Chapman, "Secret 'Instructions and Suggestions' to the Cherokee Commission," 456.

6. WJ, 9.

7. Ibid.

8. WJ, 14.

9. WJ, 18.

10. WJ, 20.

11. WJ, 26.

12. WJ, 29.

13. WJ, 32.

14. WJ, 36.

15. WJ, 37.

16. WJ, 39.

17. WJ, 41.

18. WJ, 44.

19. WJ, 46.

20. WJ, 49.

21. WJ, 50.

22. WJ, 59.

23. Ibid.

24. Ibid.

25. WJ, 93.

26. WJ, 106.

27. Ibid.

28. WJ, 113.

29. WJ, 117.

30. WJ, 125.

31. WJ, 127.

32. WJ, 133–35.

33. WJ, 136.

34. WJ, 148.

35. WJ, 151.

36. WJ, 152.

37. WJ, 155.

38. Ibid.

39. Commissioners to the President, 5 June 1891, SED 14, 52d Congress, 1st Session, serial 2852: 6–7.

40. Ibid., 8.

41. Smith, *The Caddos, the Wichitas, and the United States, 1846–1901*, 149–50; SD 191, 56th Congress, 2d Session, serial 4042: 1–2.

42. Jerome to Noble, 16 May 1891, NAR 48, LR 1891: 3913.

43. Norman *Transcript*, 20 June 1891, 1.

44. These names have been spelled a variety of ways. To minimize confusion, I have chosen to use those that appear in the journal.

45. KJ, 12.

46. KJ, 18.

47. KJ, 23.

48. KJ, 25.

49. KJ, 28.

50. KJ, 34.

51. KJ, 37.

52. KJ, 49.

53. KJ, 57.

54. Commissioners to the President, 22 June 1891, NAR 48, LR 1891: 4805.

55. A. M. Gibson, *The Kickapoos*, 294.

56. HED 72, 52d Congress, 1st Session, serial 2593: 8.

57. Ibid., 6–7.

58. Commissioners to the President, 19 October 1891, NAR 48, LR 1991: 7957.

59. AR of Secretary of the Interior for 1893, serial 3209, xxi.

60. HED 72, 52d Congress, 1st Session, serial 2593: 9.

61. Kickapoos to Noble, 10 September 1891, NAR 48, LR 1891: 6949.

62. HR 1662, 52d Congress, 1st Session, serial 3048.

63. Morgan to Noble, 30 November 1891, NAR 48, LR 1891: 38418.

64. *Twelfth Annual Report of the Indian Rights Association*, 43.

65. Painter, *Cheyennes and Arapahoes Revisited*, 48–49.

66. Ibid.

67. Berthrong, *The Cheyenne and Arapaho Ordeal,* 166.

68. Gibson, *The Kickapoos,* 315.

69. Saginaw *Evening News,* 26 December 1891, 3.

70. For background on the Tonkawas, see Thomas Frank Schilz, *People of the Cross Timbers: A History of the Tonkawa Indians.*

71. Commissioners to the President, 21 October 1891, SED 13, 52d Congress, 1st Session, serial 2892: 4.

72. Jerome to Noble, 21 October 1891, NAR 48, LR 1891: 7931.

73. Tonkawas to Noble, 31 October 1891, NAR 48, LR 1891: 9317.

74. *Congressional Record,* (April 14, 1892), vol. 23, pt. 4, 3727.

CHAPTER **7**   *A Cherokee Agreement at Last*

1. Commissioners to Mayes, 11 November 1891, in CNP, R3, folder 174.

2. HR 3768, 51st Congress, 2d Session, serial 2888: 3.

3. Ibid., 4–5.

4. Ibid., 5.

5. Ibid., 17.

6. Ibid., 21.

7. Ibid., 22–25.

8. Ibid., 27.

9. Ibid.

10. Norman *Transcript,* 11 July 1891, 1.

11. AR of Secretary Noble for 1891, serial 2933: iii.

12. AR of CIA for 1891, 46.

13. Morgan to Noble, 26 January 1892, SED 63, 52d Congress, 1st Session, serial 2900: 26–27.

14. *Cherokee Advocate,* 4 March 1891, 2.

15. Ibid., 23 September 1891, 2.

16. HR 3768, 51st Congress, 2d Session, serial 2888: 3.

17. Brown, "Robert Latham Owen," 66.

18. *Cherokee Advocate,* 27 July 1892, 2.

19. Ibid., 21 October 1891, 2.

20. Ibid.

21. Brown, "Robert Latham Owen," 66.

22. *Cherokee Advocate,* 4 November 1891, 1.

23. Ibid., 5 December 1888, 2.

24. Commissioners to Mayes, 11 November 1891, CNP, R3, folder 174.

25. CJ, 2.

26. CJ, 22.

27. Ibid.

28. For a thorough discussion of Watts, see Sober, *The Intruders.*

29. CJ, 23.

30. CJ, 31.

31. CJ, 36.

32. CJ, 50.

33. Cherokees to Cherokee Commission, 27 November 1891, SED 56, 52d Congress, 1st Session, serial 2900: 14–16.

34. *Cherokee Advocate*, 18 November 1891, 2.

35. Sayre to the President, 27 November 1891, Harrison Papers, R76.

36. Ibid.

37. CJ, 61.

38. Ibid.

39. CJ, 66.

40. Ibid.

41. CJ, 67.

42. CJ. 73.

43. CJ. 73.

44. CJ, 86.

45. CJ. 87.

46. CJ, 96.

47. CJ, 107.

48. CJ, 120.

49. Jerome to Noble, 5 December 1891, NAR 48, LR 1991: 2688.

50. CJ, 137.

51. CJ, 146.

52. CJ, 149.

53. CJ, 162.

54. CJ, 169.

55. CJ, 172.

56. CJ, 181.

57. CJ, 196.

58. CJ, 198.

59. CJ, 199.

60. CJ, 205.

61. Commissioners to the President, 9 January 1892, SED 56, 52d Congress, 1st Session, serial 2900: 11.

62. Ibid., 13.

63. Ibid., 14.

64. Noble to the President, 5 March 1892, SED 56, 52d Congress, 1st Session, serial 2900: 1–4.

65. *Cherokee Advocate*, 16 March 1892, 2.

66. Ibid., 10 February 1892, 2.

67. HR 1631, 52d Congress, 1st Session, serial 3046: 3.

68. Ibid., 1.

69. SR 1079, 52d Congress, 1st Session, serial 2915: 5.

70. Ibid., 7.

71. Ibid., 8.

72. *Congressional Record*, (23 January 1893), vol. 24, pt. 3, 792.

73. *Congressional Record*, (2 March 1893), vol. 4, pt. 3, 2384.

74. Ibid., 2596.

75. Secretary of the Treasury and Secretary of the Interior to Chief Mayes, 22 March 1893, NAM M606, R78.

76. Secretary of the Treasury and Secretary of the Interior to Chief Mayes, 22 March 1893, NAM M606, R78.

77. Roy Gittinger, *The Formation of the State of Oklahoma*, 201, n. 58.

78. Ibid., 11 March 1893, 2.

79. Sober, *The Intruders*, 110.

80. Ibid., 112.

81. *Cherokee Nation* v. *United States*, Docket 173, vol. 9: 234–35.

82. Ibid., 206–207.

83. Ibid., 197–98.

84. *United States Indian Claims Commission Final Report*, 31.

85. ICC, *Cherokee Nation* v. *United States*, Docket 173, vol. 9: 173.

86. Ibid., 175.

87. Chadwick Smith and Faye Teague, *The Response of the Cherokee Nation to the Cherokee Outlet Centennial Celebration*.

CHAPTER **8**   *A Frustrating Eleven Weeks with the Poncas*

1. Saginaw *Evening News*, 26 December 1892, 3.

2. Sayre to the President, 12 January 1892, Harrison Papers, R79.

3. Harrison to Sayre, 14 January 1892, Harrison Papers, R79.

4. SED 30, 46th Congress, 3rd Session, serial 1941: 18.

5. *U.S. Statutes at Large* 23: 422.

6. PJ, 6.

7. PJ, 12.

8. AR of Agent D. J. M. Wood, in AR of CIA for 1891, 355.

9. PJ, 22.

10. PJ, 26.

11. PJ, 32.

12. PJ, 91.

13. PJ, 81. Hairy Bear sometimes appeared in the journals as Harry Bear.

14. PJ, 42.

15. PJ, 53.

16. PJ, 80.

17. AR of Stanley L. Patrick, in AR of the Secretary of the Interior for 1892, serial 3088: 403–404.

18. PJ, 55.

19. *Proceedings of Fourth Annual Lake Mohonk Conference*, 33.

20. PJ, 71–72.

21. PJ, 36.

22. Noble to Jerome, 28 March 1892, NAM M606, R75.

23. PJ, 104.

24. PJ, 128.

25. PJ, 119.

26. PJ, 204.

27. PJ, 142.

28. Jerome to Noble, 4 April 1892, NAR 48 LR 1892: 2933.

29. PJ, 136.

30. PJ, 162.

31. PJ, 163.

32. PJ, 172.

33. Ibid.

34. Ibid.

35. PJ, 206

36. PJ, 223.

37. PJ, 224.

38. PJ, 225.

39. PJ, 227.

40. PJ, 240.

41. PJ, 241.

42. PJ, 170.

43. PJ, 244.

44. PJ, 293.

45. PJ, 301.

46. PJ, 309.

47. PJ, 314.

48. PJ, 315. Hinmin also appears as Hinman in the journals.

49. Ibid.

50. Jerome to Noble, 11 May 1892, NAR 48, LR 1892.

51. PJ, 319.

52. PJ, 322.

53. PJ, 325.

54. PJ, 328–29.

55. PJ, 329.

56. PJ, 332.

57. AR of Agent D. J. M. Wood, in AR of CIA for 1892, 393.

1. Noble to Jerome, 19 May 1892, NAR 48, Box 45.

2. Noble to CIA, 5 September 1891, NAM, M606, R73.

3. Noble to Secretary of War, 21 September 1892; Noble to CIA, 21 September 1892, both in NAM, M606, R77.

4. AR of Agent George D. Day, in AR of CIA for 1892, 586.

5. As is so often the situation, multiple spellings of reservation names were common. Howeah also appears elsewhere as Howca, How–eah, Ho–wee–ah, and Hoe–we–oh. Other spellings of Quanah Parker include Que–nah, Qui–nat, Quinah, Queana, Quaneah, and Quanna.

6. KCAJ, 4.

7. KCAJ, 5–6.

8. KCAJ, 8.

9. KCAJ, 10.

10. Ibid.

11. The treatment of Quanah and the reservation setting is largely based on William T. Hagan, *Quanah Parker* and *United States—Comanche Relations*.

12. KCAJ, 10.

13. KCAJ, 11.

14. Ibid.

15. KCAJ, 12.

16. KCAJ, 18.

17. KCAJ, 19.

18. KCAJ, 21.

19. Eschiti also appears as Isa–tai, E–sa–tite, Eshi–ti, Esa–tate, and Ishita. It has also been translated as Rear End of a Wolf and Wolf Excrement.

20. KCAJ, 21.

21. KCAJ, 24.

22. KCAJ, 25–26.

23. KCAJ, 29.

24. KCAJ, 32.

25. KCAJ, 33–34.

26. Koh–ty and White Wolf to the CIA, NAR 48, LR 1889: 1003.

27. KCAJ, 37.

28. Hill to Noble, 12 September 1892, NAR 48, LR 1892: 7277.

29. KCAJ, 39.

30. KCAJ, 42.

31. Wilbur Sturtevant Nye, *Carbine and Lance*, 261.

32. KCAJ, 45.

33. KCAJ, 46.

34. KCAJ, 50.

35. KCAJ, 56.

36. KCAJ, 57.

37. KCAJ, 61.

38. KCAJ, 62.

39. KCAJ, 65.

40. KCAJ, 66.

41. KCAJ, 70.

42. KCAJ, 73.

43. KCAJ, 74.

44. KCAJ, 76.

45. KCAJ, 77.

46. KCAJ, 78.

47. KCAJ, 82.

48. KCAJ, 89.

49. KCAJ, 90.

50. KCAJ, 92.

51. Jerome to Noble, 7 October 1892, NAR 48, LR 1892: 7722.

52. Noble to Jerome, 12 October 1892, NAM, M606, R77.

53. KCAJ, 94.

54. KCAJ, 97.

55. KCAJ, 100.

56. KCAJ, 101.

57. KCAJ, 102.

58. KCAJ, 104.

59. KCAJ, 109.

60. Ibid.

61. KCAJ, 110.

62. Thomas C. Battey, *The Life and Adventures of a Quaker among the Indians*, 149.

63. KCAJ, 112.

64. Ibid.

65. KCAJ, 113.

66. Given to the CIA, 9 September 1890, NAR 75, LR 1890: 28577.

67. KCAJ, 115.

68. KCAJ, 116.

69. KCAJ, 118.

70. KCAJ, 119.

71. KCAJ, 122.

72. Kappler, *Indian Treaties*, 979.

73. KCAJ, 125.

74. KCAJ, 126.

75. KCAJ, 27.

76. KCAJ, 129.

77. KCAJ, 130.

78. KCAJ, 131.

79. KCAJ, 138.

80. KCAJ, 139.

81. KCAJ, 140.

82. Commissioners to the President, 22 October 1892, in SED 17, 52d Congress, 2d Session, serial 3055: 9.

83. Ibid.

84. Hagan, *United States—Comanche Relations*, 251.

85. Ibid., 213.

86. Mooney to Herbert Welsh, 17 October 1893, Indian Rights Association Papers, R10.

87. S. M. Brosius to Matthew Sniffen, 9 March 1900, Ibid., R15.

88. ICC, Docket 32, vol.4: 109.

89. William T. Hagan, *Theodore Roosevelt and Six Friends of the Indian*, 184.

90. Hagan, *United States—Comanche Relations*, 285.

91. ICC, Docket 32, vol. 1: 526.

92. ICC, Docket 32, vol. 5: 315.

93. ICC, Docket 259A, vol. 34: 263.

CHAPTER **10** *A Pawnee Agreement*

1. For background on the Pawnees, see Martha Royce Blaine, *Pawnee Passage: 1870–1875* and *Some Things Are Not Forgotten: A Pawnee Family Remembers*.

2. *U.S. Statutes at Large* 19: 28.

3. Ibid.

4. AR of Agent D. J. M. Wood, in AR of CIA for 1892, 396.

5. In the journal he appears as "Wicks."

6. PAJ, 2.

7. PAJ, 4.

8. PAJ, 6.

9. PAJ, 15.

10. Ibid.

11. PAJ, 19.

12. PAJ, 20.

13. PAJ, 21.

14. PAJ, 22.

15. PAJ, 23–24.

16. PAJ, 26–27.

17. PAJ, 31.

18. PAJ, 34.

19. PAJ, 36.

20. PAJ, 38.

21. Ibid.

22. Commissioners to the President, 25 November 1892, in SED 16, 52d Congress, 2d Session, serial 3055: 5.

23. PAJ, 39.

24. PAJ, 45.

25. *U.S. Statutes at Large* 24: 389.

26. PAJ, 46.

27. PAJ, 47.

28. PAJ, 48.

29. PAJ, 51.

30. Ibid.

31. PAJ, 54.

32. PAJ, 63.

33. PAJ, 68.

34. PAJ, 70.

35. PAJ, 84.

36. PAJ, 95.

37. PAJ, p.96.

38. Ibid.

39. PAJ, 102.

40. PAJ, 131.

41. PAJ, 132.

42. PAJ, 133.

43. PAJ, 139.

44. Ibid.

45. PAJ, 140.

46. PAJ, 143–44.

47. PAJ, 145.

48. PAJ, 147.

49. PAJ, 148.

50. PAJ, 149.

51. PAJ, 150.

52. PAJ, 151.

53. Ibid.

54. Commissioners to the President, 25 November 1892, in SED 16, 52d Congress, 2d Session, serial 3055: 5.

55. Ibid.

CHAPTER 11 *Running Out the Clock with the Poncas, Osages, Choctaws, and Chickasaws*

1. Jerome to Noble, 14 November 1892, NAR 48, LR 1892: 8706.

2. Noble to Jerome, 17 November 1892, NAM, M606, R77; Morgan to Noble, 19 November 1892, NAR 48, LR 1892: 9032; Noble to Morgan, 5 December 1892, NAM, M606, R77.

3. PJ, 8.

4. PJ, 15.

5. PJ, 17.

6. PJ, 24.

7. Ibid.

8. PJ, 30.

9. Ibid.

10. Vinita *Indian Chieftain,* 15 December 1892, 2

11. *Cherokee Advocate,* 7 December 1892, 2.

12. Dewey W. Grantham, *Hoke Smith and the Politics of the New South,* 59–60.

13. Smith to Jerome, 21 March 1893, NAM, M606, R78.

14. PJ, 6.

15. PJ, 7.

16. PJ, 11.

17. PJ, 16.

18. PJ, 24.

19. PJ, 29.

20. PJ, 31.

21. PJ, 46.

22. PJ. 49.

23. PJ, 52.

24. PJ, 89.

25. PJ, 102.

26. PJ, 223.

27. PJ, 116.

28. PJ, 141.

29. PJ, 180.

30. PJ, 169.

31. PJ, 226.

32. PJ, 140.

33. PJ, 217(b).

34. PJ, 218.

35. PJ, 136–37.

36. PJ, 232.

37. PJ, 234.

38. PJ, 237.

39. AR of Agent D. J. M. Ward, in AR of CIA for 1893, 257.

40. Commissioners to the President, 21 August 1893, NAR 48, LR 1893: 7801.

41. AR of Superintendent H. M. Noble, in AR of CIA for 1905, 317.

42. AR of Agent J. Jensen, in AR of CIA for 1903, 317.

43. AR of Agent A. B. Freeman, in AR of CIA for 1894, 241.

44. Commissioners to the President, 21 August 1893, NAR 48, LR 1893: 7801.

45. Ibid.

46. Ibid.

47. Ibid.

48. CIA D. M. Browning to Secretary Hoke Smith, 9 February 1894, NAR 48, LR 1894: 852.

Epilogue

1. Commissioners to the President, 25 November 1892, in SED 16, 52d Congress, 2d Session, serial 3055: 7.

2. *United States Indian Claims Commission Final Report*, 15.

Bibliography

Manuscripts and Newspapers

Indiana Historical Society Library, Indianapolis
 Wabash Times

Indiana State Archives, Indianapolis
 Warren G. Sayre biographical information

Michigan Historical Center, Lansing
 Saginaw *Evening News*

Oklahoma Historical Society, Oklahoma City
 Vinita *Indian Chieftain*
 Cherokee Advocate

United States Government, National Archives and Records Center, Washington, D.C.
 Record Group 48
 Letters Received of the Indian Division, Office of the Secretary of the Interior
 Letter Books of the Indian Division, Office of the Secretary of the Interior

 Record Group 75
 Letters Received by the Office of Indian Affairs
 Letter Books of the Office of Indian Affairs
 Cherokee Commission Journals, in Irregularly Shaped Papers, Entry 310

University of Arkansas, Fayetteville
 Alfred M. Wilson biographical information

University of Oklahoma, Bizzell Library, Norman
Norman *Transcript*
Washington *Post*

Western History Collections of the University of Oklahoma, Norman
Cherokee Nation Papers
Joel Bryan Mayes Papers
Decisions of the Indian Claims Commission. New York: Clearwater Publishing Co.,
1973. Microfiche.
Expert Testimony Before the Indian Claims Commission. New York: Clearwater
Publishing Co., 1973–1975. Microfiche.

Wisconsin Historical Society, Madison
Lucius Fairchild Papers

Books, Articles, Dissertations, and Theses

American State Papers: Indian Affairs. 2 vols. Washington, D.C.: Gales and Seaton, 1832–34.

Battey, Thomas C. *The Life and Adventures of a Quaker among the Indians.* Norman: University of Oklahoma Press, 1968.

Berthrong, Donald J. *The Cheyenne and Arapaho Ordeal.* Norman: University of Oklahoma Press, 1976.

Blaine, Martha Royce. *The Ioway Indians.* Norman: University of Oklahoma Press, 1979.

_____. *Pawnee Passage: 1870–1875.* Norman: University of Oklahoma Press, 1990.

_____. *Some Things Are Not Forgotten: A Pawnee Family Remembers.* Lincoln: University of Nebraska Press, 1997.

Brown, Kenny Lee. "Robert Latham Owen, Jr." Ph.D. diss., Oklahoma State University, 1985.

Burton, Jeffrey. *Indian Territory and the United States, 1866–1906.* Norman: University of Oklahoma Press, 1995.

Carter, Kent. *The Dawes Commission and the Allotment of the Five Civilized Tribes, 1892–1914.* Orem, Utah: Ancestry.com Incorporated, 1999.

Champagne, Duane. *Social Order and Political Change.* Palo Alto: Stanford University Press, 1992.

Chapman, Berlin B. "The Cherokee Commission at Kickapoo Village." *The Chronicles of Oklahoma,* 17 (March 1939): 62–74.

_____. "The Cherokee Commission, 1889–1893." *The Chronicles of Education* 42 (June 1946): 177–90.

_____. "Chief Joel B. Mayes of the Cherokee Nation." *The Chronicles of Oklahoma* 44 (Autumn 1966), 325–27.

_____. "The Day in Court for the Kiowa, Comanche and Apache Tribes." *Great Plains Journal* 2 (Fall 1962): 1–22.

_____. "Dissolution of the Iowa Reservation." *The Chronicles of Oklahoma* 14 (December 1936): 467–77.

_____. "Dissolution of the Wichita Reservation." *The Chronicles of Oklahoma* 22 (Summer 1944): 192–209; (Autumn 1944): 300–14.

_____. "The Final Report of the Cherokee Commission." *The Chronicles of Oklahoma* 19 (December 1941): 356–67.

_____. "How the Cherokees Acquired and Disposed of the Outlet." Part 3, *The Chronicles of Oklahoma* 15 (September 1937): 291–321; Part 5, (June 1938): 135–62.

_____. "The Opening of the Cherokee Outlet: An Archival Study." *The Chronicles of Oklahoma* 40 (Summer 1962): 158–81; (Autumn 1962): 253–85.

_____. "Secret 'Instructions and Suggestions' to the Cherokee Commission," *The Chronicles of Oklahoma* 26 (Winter 1948–49): 449–58.

Corwin, Hugh D. *The Kiowa Indians.* [Lawton, Oklahoma], 1958.

Deloria, Vine, Jr., and Raymond J. DeMallie. *Documents of American Indian Diplomacy.* 2 vols. Norman: University of Oklahoma Press, 1999.

Foreman, Grant. *The Last Trek of the Indians.* Chicago: University of Chicago Press, 1946.

Fowler, Loretta. *Arapahoe Politics, 1851–1978.* Lincoln: University of Nebraska Press, 1982.

Gibson, A. M. *The Kickapoos.* Norman: University of Oklahoma Press, 1963.

Gittinger, Roy. *The Formation of the State of Oklahoma 1803–1906.* Norman: University of Oklahoma Press, 1939.

Grantham, Dewey W. *Hoke Smith and the Politics of the New South.* Baton Rouge: Louisiana State University Press, 1958.

Hagan, William T. *The Indian Rights Association.* Tucson: University of Arizona Press, 1985.

_____. *Quanah Parker, Comanche Chief.* Norman: University of Oklahoma Press, 1993.

_____. *The Sac and Fox Indians.* Norman: University of Oklahoma Press, 1958.

_____. *United States–Comanche Relations.* Norman: University of Oklahoma Press, 1990.

Harrison, Benjamin. *Benjamin Harrison Papers.* Washington, D.C.: Library of Congress, 1964. Microfilm.

Hoig, Stanley W. *The Cherokees and Their Chiefs.* Fayetteville: University of Arkansas Press, 1998.

Horr, David Agee. *Kiowa-Comanche Indians: Transcript of Hearings of the Kiowa, Comanche, and Apache Tribes of Indians v. The United States of America.* 2 vols. New York: Garland Publishing , 1974.

Hoxie, Frederick E. *A Final Promise.* Lincoln: University of Nebraska Press, 1984.

Kappler, Charles J. *Indian Treaties 1778–1883.* New York: Interland Publishing Co., 1972.

Kavanagh, Thomas W. *Comanche Political History*. Lincoln: University of Nebraska Press, 1996.

McLoughlin, William G. *After the Trail of Tears*. Chapel Hill: University of North Carolina Press, 1993.

Mayhall, Mildred P. *The Kiowas*. Norman: University of Oklahoma Press, 1962.

Meredith, Howard. *Dancing on Common Ground*. Lawrence: University Press of Kansas, 1995.

Miner, H. Craig. *The Corporation and the Indian*. Norman: University of Oklahoma Press, 1989.

Nye, Wilbur Sturtevant. *Bad Medicine and Good*. Norman: University of Oklahoma Press, 1962.

_____. *Carbine and Lance*. Norman: University of Oklahoma Press, 1937.

_____. *Plains Indian Raiders*. Norman: University of Oklahoma Press, 1968.

Painter, C. C. *Cheyennes and Arapahoes Revisited and a Statement of Their Agreement and Contract with Attorneys*. Philadelphia: Indian Rights Association, 1893.

Pierce, Earl Boyd, and Rennard Strickland. *The Cherokee People*. Phoenix: Indian Tribal Series, 1973.

Prucha, Francis Paul. *American Indian Treaties*. Berkeley: University of California Press, 1994.

_____. *The Great Father*. 2 vols. Lincoln: University of Nebraska Press, 1984.

Rand, Jacki Thompson. "The Cherokees and Pawnees Meet the Jerome Commission." Master's thesis, University of Oklahoma, 1993.

Richardson, James D. *Messages and Papers of the Presidents*. Vol. 12. New York: Bureau of National Literature, 1897.

Rosenthal, H. D. *Their Day in Court*. New York: Garland Publishing, 1990.

Ross, Sam. *The Empty Sleeve: A Biography of Lucius Fairchild*. Madison: The State Historical Society of Wisconsin, 1964.

Savage, William W., Jr. *The Cherokee Strip Live Stock Association*. Columbia: University of Missouri Press, 1973.

_____. "Leasing the Cherokee Outlet: An Analysis of Indian Reaction, 1884–1885." *The Chronicles of Oklahoma* 46 (Autumn 1968): 285–92.

Schilz, Thomas Frank. *People of the Cross Timbers: A History of the Tonkawa Indians*. Ann Arbor: University Microfilms International, 1990.

Sievers, Harry J. *Benjamin Harrison*. 3 vols. Indianapolis: Bobbs–Merrill Co., 1968.

Smith, Chadwick, and Faye Teague. *The Response of the Cherokee Nation to the Cherokee Outlet Centennial Celebration: A Legal and Historical Analysis*. Edited by Rennard Strickland. [Cherokee Nation, 1993].

Smith, F. Todd. *The Caddos, the Wichitas, and the United States, 1846–1901*. College Station: Texas A&M University Press, 1996.

Sober, Nancy Hope. *The Intruders: The Illegal Residents of the Cherokee Nation, 1866–1907*. Ponca City: Cherokee Books, 1991.

Trenholm, Virginia Cole. *The Arapahoes, Our People*. Norman: University of Oklahoma Press, 1970.

United States Indian Claims Commission Final Report. Washington, D.C.: U.S. Government Printing Office, 1979.

Wardell, Morris L. *A Political History of the Cherokee Nation.* Norman: University of Oklahoma Press, 1938.

Wilson, Terry P. *The Underground Reservation.* Lincoln: University of Nebraska Press, 1985.

Woodward, Grace Steele. *The Cherokees.* Norman: University of Oklahoma Press, 1963.

Wright, Muriel H. *A Guide to the Indian Tribes of Oklahoma.* Norman: University of Oklahoma Press, 1951.

Zimmerman, Charles Leroy. *White Eagle: Chief of the Poncas.* Harrisburg, Penna.: Telegraph Press, 1941.

Index

of, 40; Indians' opposition to sale of, 23, 25, 38; opening of, 10, 162, 163, 166, 219; Pawnees' relocation to, 208; Poncas' relocation to, 168–69; salt marshes, 89, 95; title to, 12–14, 26, 28, 32–33, 89, 90, 94, 145–47, 149, 156, 157, 159–60. *See also* Cattle leases; Financial negotiations and agreements

Cherokees, 8; Cherokee Commission and, 20–21, 25–28, 33–38, 85–98, 144, 149–60, 165, 166, 221, 236, 240; in Civil War, 7; congressional ratification of agreement, 160–63; factional disputes of, 7; House Committee on Territories, report of, 144–47; Indian Claims Commission's decision, 165; land tenure issue among, 163–64; and Osages, 232; Poncas' meeting with, 222; removal of, 6; and Springer Bill, 10–13, 15–17; Washington negotiations, delegates to, 97. *See also* Cherokee Nation

Cherokee Strip, Kansas, 8

Cherokee Strip Livestock Association, 9, 11, 12, 26, 32

Chewathlanie, 195

Cheyennes, 6, 36, 124, 125, 128, 174, 191; cattle grazing leases, 62; Cherokee Commission and, 61, 64–83, 155; government programs, reaction to, 62–63; population, 61; rations drawn by, 71, 72, 73, 75, 78, 82; tribal attorneys, 66–67, 69, 75, 77, 79–83

Cheyennes and Arapahos Revisited and a Statement of Their Contract with Attorneys (Painter), 82–83

Chicago, Rock Island and Pacific Railroad, 205

Chickasaws, 6, 7, 71, 123, 128, 197; Cherokee Commission and, 220, 223, 233, 235; compensation for ceded land, 83–84, 133; Supreme Court ruling against, 205

Children, Indian: and allotments, 44, 45, 46, 48, 52, 172, 206, 224, 225, 231, 239; education of, 47, 71, 159, 230

Chilocco Indian school, 47

Choctaw Nation v. United States, 50

Choctaws, 6, 7, 71, 123, 128, 197; Cherokee Commission and, 220, 223, 233, 235; compensation for ceded land, 83–84, 133; Supreme Court ruling against, 205

Citizen Band Potawatomis, 55; Cherokee Commission and, 28, 32, 55–58, 60, 128,

155, 173; Indian Claims Commission decision, 57; Jerome's opinion of, 76; Supreme Court decision, 58

Citizenship, American, 161

Citizenship, in Cherokee Nation, 95, 164

Civil War, Indian tribes' participation in, 6, 7, 86–87; Tonkawas, 141; Wichitas, 124

Clark, Edward L., 203

Clarke, Ben, 82

Clarke, Helen P., 209, 216

Cleveland, Grover, 62, 229, 233

Cloud Chief, 66, 67, 69, 70, 72–74, 77, 79

Columbus, Christopher, Caddo Jake's reference to, 126, 127

Comancheros, 182

Comanches, 6, 36, 124, 125, 182–83; Cherokee Commission and, 181–205; Indian Claims Commission's award to, 206–207; population (1892), 183

Congress, U.S.: and Cherokee agreement, 160–63, 166; Cherokee Commission, appropriations for, 76, 123, 153, 220, 223; Cherokee Commission, creation of, 17; Cherokees' lobbying of, 11; Dawes Commission, 164; and intruders in Cherokee Nation, 164; and Kickapoo agreement, 138–39, 140; and Kiowa, Copmanche, and Apache agreement, 204, 205, 206; and opening of Indian lands, 10–17; and Pawnee agreement, 219; Poncas, appropriations for, 178; and Poncas' victory over Cherokee Commission, 231; Removal Act, 6; and Tonkawa agreement, 142; tribal relations, authority over, 205; and Wichita agreement, 132, 133

Contract workers, in Cherokee Nation, 22

Coons, Harry, 209, 216, 219

Council Fire, 34

Court of Claims: Cherokees' wish for access to, 96; Iowa case, 49; Sac and Fox case, 54; Wichita case, 133

Courts, federal, tribal access to, 92, 95, 96, 152, 154, 155

Courts, tribal, 93, 152, 165

Crawford, Samuel J., 67, 77, 82

Creeks, 6–10, 23; government payments to, for land, 71, 93, 128; Pawnee Reservation bought from, 208

Cullom, Shelby M., 13

Curly Chief, 210, 212, 213, 215, 217, 218

Cut Nose, 67, 69

Holman, William S., 162
Horse Chief, 222
House Committee on Appropriations, 162
House Committee on Indian Affairs, 28, 57, 138, 139
House Committee on Territories, 10, 12–13, 39; Boudinot's presentation to, 160; Cherokees, report on (1891), 144–47
House of Representatives, U.S., 16; ratification of Cherokee agreement, 160–63; Springer Bill, 13
Houston, Sam, 126
Howeah, 183, 187
Howling Wolf, 69, 77
Humanitarianism: and allotment policy, 5–6; Indian Rights Association, 10

Immigration, acceleration of, 173
Indian Affairs, Office of: Cherokee Commission's instructions from, 154, 157; Iowas, agreement with, 49
Indian Chieftain: on Jerome, 85
Indian Claims Commission, 50, 237, 240; Cherokee agreement, decision on, 165; and Cheyennes' and Arapahos' suit, 83; and Kiowa, Comanche, and Apache suit, 206–207; and Pawnees' award, 219; and Potawatomi suit, 57; and Sac and Fox claims, 54
Indian Commissioners, Board of, 42–43, 91, 178
Indian Offenses, Court of, 198
Indian police forces, 62, 63
Indian Rights Association, 10, 80, 82, 139, 204, 205, 206
Indian Service appropriation bill, 16, 17
Indian Territory, 6–10, 13
Ingalls, J. J., 41
Interior Department, U.S., 20; and Cherokee negotiations, 97; intruders in Cherokee Nation, legalization of, 161; and leasing issue, 9, 13. *See also* Noble, John W.; Smith, Hoke
Intruders: on Cherokee land, 22, 92, 93, 95, 96, 150, 151, 152, 155, 161–65; on Ponca land, 171; on Sac and Fox land, 53
Iowas, 128, 155, 238; Cherokee Commission and, 28–32, 44–50, 59; Court of Claims decision, 49; opening of lands of, 146; Supreme Court opinions on agreements with, 50

Iseeo, 191, 197–98

Jerome, David H., 42–43, 140, 167, 233, 235–37; and Cherokees, 85, 87–94, 96–98, 149–59; and Cheyennes and Arapahos, 64–66, 68–75, 77–81; and Choctaws and Chickasaws, 220; and Iowas, 44–48, 50; and Kaws, 233; and Kickapoos, 58–59, 133–37; and Kiowas, Comanches, and Apaches, 183–86, 188–203; on Mayes, 157; Noble and, 76, 181; and Osages, 232; and Pawnees, 209–19; and Poncas, 169–80, 221–30; and Potawatomis, 56; and Sac and Fox, 51–54; on Senate investigation of Cherokee Commission, 89; and Shawnees, 56; and Tonkawas, 142, 143; and tribal attorneys, 76–77, 80; and Wichitas, 125–32
Jerome Commission. *See* Cherokee Commission
Jones, Horace P., 203
Jones, James K., 18, 233
Joseph, Chief, 43, 177
Joshua Given, 200, 203, 204, 209

Kansas, 6, 8
Kansas City Times, 27
Kaws, 8; Cherokee Commission and, 141, 232–33, 235
Keokuk, Moses, 30, 51, 53, 76
Keshokame, 134, 137, 138, 139
Kewaitsidde, 126
Kichais, 123
Kickapoos, 31. *See also* Mexican Kickapoos
Kickapoos, The (Gibson), 140
King, C. L., 43
King, Harry, 222, 226, 228
Kiowas, 6, 36, 124, 182–83; Cherokee Commission and, 181–205; Indian Claims Commission's award to, 206–207; population (1892), 183
Kitkahahkis, 208, 210
Knife Chief, 214, 217
Knox, Henry, 5
Komalty, 193, 194, 201

LaFlesche, Frank, 170, 174, 175, 221
Lake Mohonk conferences, 10, 27, 173, 218
Lakota Indians, 43
Land titles. *See* Titles, land

Owen, Robert L., 24, 40–41, 148, 223

Painter, Charles, 80–83, 139–40
Pa-pa-shekit, 139
Parker, Isaac Charles, 14, 18, 93, 96, 149
Parker, Quanah. *See* Quanah Parker
Parthee, 134, 135, 136
Pasture rent, in Cherokee Outlet. *See* Cattle
   leases
Pawnees, 8, 141, 163; Cherokee Commis-
   sion and, 208–19; opening of lands of,
   219
Peel, Samuel W., 18, 160
Peffer, William Alfred, 146, 162
Peters, Sergeant, 216
Pike, Luther H., 129–32, 133
Pitahawiratas, 208, 210
Plains Indians, 36, 61, 182, 239. *See also spe-
   cific tribes*
*Plan for Saving the Cherokee People Millions
   of Dollars, A* (Owen), 148
Plumb, Preston B., 10
Police, Indian. *See* Indian police forces
Polygamy, 183, 185
Pomeroy, S. C., 6–7
Ponca Agency reservations, 141–43
Poncas, 8, 168–69; Cherokee Commission
   and, 141, 169–80, 221–31; land base, ero-
   sion of, 231; victory over Cherokee Com-
   mission, 230–31, 235
Poor Buffalo, 192
Potawatomis, 55. *See also* Citizen Band
   Potawatomis
Primeaux, Peter, 172–73, 175

Quahada Comanches, 182, 183, 184, 187, 192
Quanah Parker, 184–90, 192–96, 204, 205,
   214–15, 239
Quapaw Reservation, 168
Quapaws, 123

Railroad companies, 87, 90, 94, 155, 205
Randlett, James F., 205
Rations, 182, 237; for Arapahos and
   Cheyennes, 71–73, 75, 78, 82, 191; for Kick-
   apoos, 136; for Kiowas, Comanches, and
   Apaches, 183, 186; for Wichitas, 126, 127,
   132
Rector, Elias, 124
Red Cloud, 43
Red River War (1874–75), 62, 182, 187

Red Wolf, 70
Religion: Messiah movement and Ghost
   Dance, 63, 65, 69, 74, 75, 191, 198, 211; pey-
   ote-based, 183
Removal Act, 6
Removals and relocations, 6–7, 91, 239; of
   Iowas, 29; of Kickapoos, 31; of Osages,
   231–32; of Pawnees, 208; of Ponca Agency
   tribes, 141; of Poncas, 168; of
   Potawatomis, 55; of Sac and Fox, 30
Reservations, 6; of Cheyennes and Arapa-
   hos, 61, 63–64, 65, 67; Ponca Agency, 141;
   of Potawatomis, 55, 56; of Wichitas, 123,
   124, 131, 132
Reynolds, M. J., 67, 77, 81, 82
Robertson, Alice M., 27, 38, 39, 43
Rogers, Clement V., 164
Roosevelt, Theodore, 206
Ross, William P., 86, 87, 88, 91–97, 165
Rowe, David, 97, 98, 147
Row of Lodges, 67, 70
Rushing in Battle, 221, 222, 224–25

Sac and Fox: Cherokee Commission and,
   28, 30–32, 51–54, 59, 155; Indian Claims
   Commission and Court of Claims decisions, 54; Jerome's view of, 76; opening of
   lands of, 146
St. Louis Globe-Democrat, 11, 21, 27, 28; on
   Senate investigation of Cherokee Commission, 88–89
Salt marshes, on Cherokee Outlet, 89, 95
Sayre, Warren G., 34, 35, 42, 140, 233, 235–37,
   240; and Cherokees, 35–40, 85, 87, 88, 90,
   92–95, 97, 98, 150, 153–58, 221; and Cheyennes and Arapahos, 65–68, 71, 72, 74, 77,
   78, 81; and Iowas, 44, 46–48; and Kickapoos, 134–36, 138; and Kiowas, Comanches, and Apaches, 184, 188–89, 191, 195,
   201; Noble's meetings with, 76, 223; Oklahoma judgeship, interest in, 167–68; and
   Pawnees, 216–18; and Poncas, 170, 171,
   174, 175, 177, 180, 224, 226–30; and Sac and
   Fox Indians, 52–54; and Shawnees and
   Potawatomis, 58; and tribal attorneys, 76,
   80; and Wichitas, 125, 126, 127–29, 131, 132
Scales, J. A., 149, 158
Scott, H. L., 191, 197, 203, 204
Scraper, Arch, 86
Seger, John H., 82
Seminoles, 6–10, 71, 128